Whillans's Tax Tables

Sixty-sixth edition

Edited by Gina Antczak FCA CTA
Robert Wareham BSc (Econ) FCA
and
Sheila Parrington LLB

LexisNexis™ UK

Members of the LexisNexis Group worldwide

United Kingdom	LexisNexis UK, a Division of Reed Elsevier (UK) Ltd, Halsbury House, 35 Chancery Lane, LONDON, WC2A 1EL, and 4 Hill Street, EDINBURGH EH2 3JZ
Argentina	LexisNexis Argentina, BUENOS AIRES
Australia	LexisNexis Butterworths, CHATSWOOD, New South Wales
Austria	LexisNexis Verlag ARD Orac GmbH & Co KG, VIENNA
Canada	LexisNexis Butterworths, MARKHAM, Ontario
Chile	LexisNexis Chile Ltda, SANTIAGO DE CHILE
Czech Republic	Nakladatelství Orac sro, PRAGUE
France	Editions du Juris-Classeur SA, PARIS
Germany	LexisNexis Deutschland GmbH, FRANKFURT and MUNSTER
Hong Kong	LexisNexis Butterworths, HONG KONG
Hungary	HVG-Orac, BUDAPEST
India	LexisNexis Butterworths, NEW DELHI
Ireland	Butterworths (Ireland) Ltd, DUBLIN
Italy	Giuffrè Editore, MILAN
Malaysia	Malayan Law Journal Sdn Bhd, KUALA LUMPUR
New Zealand	LexisNexis Butterworths, WELLINGTON
Poland	Wydawnictwo Prawnicze LexisNexis, WARSAW
Singapore	LexisNexis Butterworths, SINGAPORE
South Africa	LexisNexis Butterworths SA, DURBAN
Switzerland	Stämpfli Verlag AG, BERNE
USA	LexisNexis, DAYTON, Ohio

A CIP Catalogue record for this book is available from the British Library.

ISBN 0 406 96707-5

Typeset by Wyvern 21 Ltd, Bristol, BS4 3EH
Printed and bound in Great Britain by Antony Rowe Ltd, Chippenham, Wiltshire

Visit LexisNexis UK at www.lexisnexis.co.uk

Overseas

Average rates of exchange

Average for year ending	29.12.00	30.3.01	31.12.01	28.3.02	31.12.02	31.3.03
Algeria (Dinar)	112·7047	111·9071	110·1959	111·0258	119·1138	122·9761
Argentina (Peso)	1·5153	1·4787	1·4399	1·7986	4·7816	5·3381
Australia ($A)	2·6092	2·661	2·7864	2·7864	2·8049	2·7925
Austria (Schilling)	22·5939	22·4336	22·134	1/4/01–27/2/02 22·2856		
(Euro)				1/1/02–28/3/02 1·6264	1·5906	1·5573
Bahrain (Dinar)	0·5716	0·5578	0·5433	0·5403	0·5671	0·5836
Bangladesh (Taka)	79·0938	78·2862	80·4604	81·1787	86·7838	89·656
Barbados (BD$)	3·0195	2·9467	2·8675	2·8524	3·0091	3·0957
Belgium (Franc)	66·2402	65·7704	64·8897	1/4/01–27/2/02 65·3356		
(Euro)				1/1/02–28/3/02 1·6264	1·5906	1·5573
Bolivia (Boliviano)	9·3162	9·2479	9·5259	9·6567	10·8081	11·3623
Botswana (Pula)	7·7717	7·8691	8·5971	8·9924	9·4098	9·1141
Brazil (Real)	2·7724	2·8004	3·3991	3·5119	4·4345	4·9817
Brunei ($)	2·6169	2·5729	2·5864	2·5979	2·691	2·7364
Burma (Kyat)	9·7314	9·647	9·6176	9·6342	9·8609	9·9464
Burundi (Franc)	1,087·1708	1,106·252	1,184·7758	1,214·928	1,427·9542	1,541·758
Canada (Can$)	2·2505	2·2238	2·23	2·2412	2·3585	2·3955
Cayman Islands (CI$)	1·2442	1·2207	1·1805	1·1752	1·2372	1·272
Chile (Peso)	816·8918	821·4341	916·7394	945·912	1,039·465	1,095·468
China (Renminbi Yuan)	12·5381	12·2233	11·9157	11·8539	12·4779	12·8385
Colombia (Peso)	3,174·5532	3,216·9658	3,316·9487	3,307·4299	3,790·01	4,153·78
Congo Dem Rep (Zaire) (Congolese Franc)	6·8223	6·6577	1/1/01–12/10/01 6·4914 19/10/01–31/12/01 458·7516	1/4/01–12/10/01 6·4617 19/10/01–28/3/02 466·494	525·7336	571·9449
Costa Rica (Colon)	466·4669	462·2145	474·1405	481·1747	544·9313	574·9884
Cuba (Peso)	30·9054	30·107	30·231	30·0972	31·6836	32·5763
Cyprus (£)	0·9448	0·9372	0·9294	0·9347	0·9139	0·8945
Czech Republic (Koruna)	58·5144	57·5581	54·7895	53·8133	48·8242	47·7581
Denmark (Krone)	12·2386	12·1593	11·9873	12·0585	11·8184	11·5705
Ecuador (Sucre)	37,859·2583	27,843·72	1·4396	1·4322	1·5077	1·5513
Egypt (£)	5·358	5·393	5·8423	6·0799	6·9638	7·4503
El Salvador (Colon)	13·2329	12·8998	12·5911	12·5362	13·197	13·5688
Ethiopia (Birr)	12·2714	12·0439	12·0068	11·9931	12·6417	12·9708
European Union (Euro)	1·6237	1·6114	1·6085	1·6202	1·5906	1·5573
Fiji (F$)	3·2249	3·2331	3·282	3·2756	3·2671	3·2512
Finland (Markka)	9·788	9·7153	9·5635	1/4/01–27/2/02 9·6301		
(Euro)				1/1/02–28/3/02 1·6264	1·5906	1·5573
France (Franc)	10·7706	10·6942	10·5516	1/4/01–27/2/02 10·6241		
(Euro)				1/1/02–28/3/02 1·6264	1·5906	1·5573
French Cty/Africa (CFA franc)	1,079·9175	1,069·841	1,058·6883	1,065·729	1,042·0842	1,017·883
French Pacific Is (CFP franc)	197·1027	195·4233	181·2759	182·5448	189·3468	184·3393
Gambia (Dalasi)	19·848	20·6167	23·4964	24·2786	30·1816	33·5087
Germany (Deutsche Mark)	3·2114	3·1886	3·1461	1/4/01–27/2/02 3·1677		
(Euro)				1/1/02–28/3/02 1·6264	1·5906	1·5573
Ghana (Cedi)	8,362·358	9,498·54	10,522·25	10,566·23	12,006·85	12,669·67
Greece (Drachma)	553·1315	552·1486	548·0827	1/4/01–27/2/02 551·8999		
(Euro)				1/1/02–28/3/02 1·6264	1·5906	1·5573

Average rates of exchange — continued

Average for year ending	**29.12.00**	**30.3.01**	**31.12.01**	**28.3.02**	**31.12.02**	**31.3.03**
Grenada/Wind. Isles (EC$)	4·0935	3·9947	3·8906	3·8596	4·0515	4·1764
Guyana (G$)	280·418	274·0524	260·0487	258·6602	270·7951	278·0578
Honduras (Lempira)	22·456	22·0814	22·288	22·4965	24·7993	25·8732
Hong Kong (HK$)	11·8145	11·5332	11·2318	11·1682	11·7178	12·4969
Hungary (Forint)	428·9736	428·6946	412·8118	406·5053	385·0885	376·5623
Iceland (Krona)	119·2531	121·3855	140·5823	145·2241	137·0658	132·2964
India (Rupee)	68·0779	67·5606	67·9907	68·3407	73·0477	74·8503
Indonesia (Rupiah)	12,687·52	13,292	14,800·2838	14,876·8079	13,992·992	13,916·933
Iran (Rial)	2,629·251	2,587·011	2,520·331	2,507·895	5,888·04	8,472·51
Iraq (Dinar)	0·4931	0·4615	0·4473	0·4444	0·4679	0·4814
Ireland (Rep. of) (Punt)	1·2932	1·284	1·2669	1/4/01–27/2/02 1·2753		
(Euro)				1/1/02–28/3/02 1·6264	1·5906	1·5773
Israel (Shekel)	6·1811	6·0609	6·0676	6·2059	7·1293	7·4159
Italy (Lira)	3,179·27	3,156·72	3,114·6298	1/4/01–27/2/02 3,136·0334		
(Euro)				1/1/02–28/3/02 1·6264	1·5906	1·5773
Jamaica (J$)	64·0371	64·0382	65·8707	66·2455	72·6379	76·6837
Japan (Yen)	163·378	163·482	174·8889	179·0169	187·8315	188·3036
Jordan (Dinar)	1·0771	1·0512	1·0234	1·0174	1·0651	1·0964
Kenya (Shilling)	113·3867	114·6715	113·2002	112·628	118·4879	121·3613
Korea South (Won)	1,723·1075	1,742·825	1,866·9225	1,869·044	1,875·2217	1,884·351
Kuwait (Dinar)	0·4825	0·4716	0·4418	0·4397	0·4569	0·4672
Laos (New Kip)	11,545·9667	11,216·97	10,989·6667	10,941·25	11,466·425	11,789·48
Lebanon (£)	2,289·722	2,237·333	2,180·197	2,169·318	2,274·688	2,339·06
Libya (Dinar)	0·7533	0·7621	0·8506	1·1028	1·8923	1·9259
Luxembourg (Franc)	66·2364	65·7666	64·89	1/4/01–27/2/02 65·336		
(Euro)				1/1/02–28/3/02 1·6264	1·5906	1·5773
Malawi (Kwacha)	89·3763	99·8568	104·1	100·0558	115·074	125·355
Malaysia (Ringgit)	5·7611	5·6221	5·4754	5·4464	5·7167	5·882
Malta (Lira)	0·6542	0·6529	0·6483	0·6498	0·6505	0·6451
Mauritius (Rupee)	39·6999	39·6706	41·8852	42·4821	45·0819	45·412
Mexico (Peso)	14·349	14·1202	13·4825	13·1936	14·5782	15·6552
Morocco (Dirham)	16·1161	15·8934	16·3617	16·6136	16·5284	16·3463
Nepal (Rupee)	107·5093	106·9198	108·2814	108·8094	116·3692	119·1846
Netherlands (Guilder)	3·6184	3·589	3·5408	1/4/01–27/2/02 3·5689		
(Euro)				1/1/02–28/3/02 1·6264	1·5906	1·5773
N'nd Antilles (Guilder)	2·69	2·6223	2·5625	2·5511	2·6856	2·7612
New Zealand (NZ$)	3·3285	3·3641	3·4283	3·4237	3·2393	3·1306
Nicaragua (Gold Cordoba)	18·7369	18·4729	19·2644	19·5256	21·5082	22·4138
Nigeria (Naira)	158·8476	160·0406	165·943	165·6166	184·0362	194·3859
Norway (Krone)	13·323	13·2635	12·8993	12·833	11·954	11·6072
Oman (Rial Omani)	0·5837	0·5697	0·561	0·5579	0·5792	0·596
Pakistan (Rupee)	81·5945	82·5336	88·9265	88·6041	89·5939	91·3941
Papua New Guinea (Kina)	4·2012	4·19	4·856	4·9971	5·9099	6·095
Paraguay (Guarani)	5,289·0655	5,250·9205	5,922·722	6,318·8118	8,691·2127	9,756·686
Peru (New Sol)	5·2868	5·1815	5·0538	5·0044	5·2931	5·4531
Philippines (Peso)	66·9936	68·5464	73·3236	73·7096	77·7051	81·0754
Poland (Zloty)	6·6123	6·4235	5·8764	5·8728	6·1322	6·2282
Portugal (Escudo)	329·1632	326·8482	322·4898	1/4/01–27/2/02 324·7059		
(Euro)				1/1/02–28/3/02 1·6264	1·5906	1·5773

Average for year ending	**29.12.00**	**30.3.01**	**31.12.01**	**28.3.02**	**31.12.02**	**31.3.03**
Qatar (Riyal)	5·5195	5·3865	5·245	5·2156	5·4756	5·6355
Romania (Leu)	33,138·1833	35,363·23	42,159·75	43,855·99	49,889·0667	51,638·82
Russia (Rouble–Market)	42·7404	41·6317	42·1512	42·763	47·4183	49·0329
Rwanda (R Franc)	539·3179	538·3299	611·8478	635·8418	708·029	748·4881
Saudi Arabia (Riyal)	5·6864	5·5492	5·4034	5·3738	5·641	5·805
Seychelles (Rupee)	8·6478	8·8073	8·4104	8·0777	8·4761	8·7149
Sierra Leone (Leone)	3,024·77	2,938·786	2,786·703	2,878·362	3,094·516	3,173·768
Singapore (S$)	2·6127	2·57	2·5816	2·5972	2·6899	2·7354
Solomon Islands (SI$)	7·7079	7·5651	7·7128	7·9864	10·4913	11·3636
Somalia (Schilling)	3,966·2592	3,868·396	3,770·09	3,753·399	3,952·9042	4,064·276
South Africa (Rand)	10·4972	10·8197	12·4064	13·661	15·7465	14·9793
Spain/Balearic Islands (Peseta)	273·1989	271·2611	267·6439	1/4/01–27/2/02 269·4832		
(Euro)				1/1/02–28/3/02 1·6264	1·5906 1·5906	1·5773 1·5573
Sri Lanka (Rupee)	116·3355	118·2743	128·922	131·0694	143·9681	149·2486
Sudan (Dinar)	390·8893	382·0302	372·417	370·7689	390·3116	401·9422
Surinam (Guilder)	1,288·1075	1,319·532	1/1/01–31/8/01 1,409·0588 1/9/01–31/12/01 3,150·1375	1/4/01–31/8/01 1,400·426 1/9/01–28/3/02 3,131·016	3,286·7917	3,467·533
Swaziland (Lilangeli)	10·5756	10·868	12·583	13·773	15·5637	14·788
Sweden (Krona)	13·869	13·9687	14·8847	15·0502	14·5697	14·2735
Switzerland (Franc)	2·5572	2·5092	2·4295	2·4224	2·3336	2·2819
Syria (Pound)	78·9066	80·1564	74·5315	73·5174	74·7231	75·5653
Taiwan (New T$)	56·5057	46·844	48·6974	49·3319	51·9757	53·3776
Tanzania (Schilling)	1,211·789	1,190·039	1,263·71	1,303·673	1,452·96	1,522·58
Thailand (Baht)	60·8115	61·4603	64·1079	63·9513	64·6788	66·2242
Tonga Islands (Pa 'Anga)	2·6282	2·6823	2·8083	2·7917	2·7637	2·7496
Trinidad and Tobago (TT$)	9·4465	9·2274	8·8631	8·779	9·1895	9·4752
Tunisia (Dinar)	2·0742	2·067	2·0695	2·0914	2·1331	2·1332
Turkey (Lira)	945,505·394	1,014,631·97	1,778,556·77	1,966,915·2	2,287,542·21	2,464,005·116
Uganda (New Shilling)	2,490·5547	2,525·946	2,530·906	2,509·444	2,704·318	2,840·852
United Arab Emirates (Dirham)	5·5062	5·3736	5·2927	5·2638	5·5247	5·6854
Uruguay (Peso Uruguayo)	18·3314	18·2361	19·1927	19·8333	32·3184	38·3931
USA (US$)	1·5163	1·4793	1·4401	1·432	1·5023	1·5466
Venezuela (Bolivar)	1,030·271	1,022·147	1,043·522	1,091·276	1,758·525	2,108·819
Vietnam (Dong)	21,471·7083	21,115·76	21,329·6083	21,434·79	23,038·5083	23,813·17
Yemen (Rial)	244·0709	237·9881	240·0541	243·6008	262·9526	272·0802
Zambia (Kwacha)	4,935·725	5,178·623	5,204·957	5,383·712	6,729·64	7,137·79
Zimbabwe (Dollar)	67·1213	71·8766	79·653	79·3536	83·4043	187·0132

Note

The Inland Revenue average rates of exchange for the years ended 31.12.03 and 31.3.04 will be published in the 2004–05 Finance Act (sixty-eighth) edition of Whillans's Tax Tables. If these rates are required before the publication of that edition, they can be obtained (normally available from June) from the IR website (www.inlandrevenue.gov.uk/exrate/index.htm), from the Inland Revenue, Business Tax on 020 7438 4278 or from the editors at LexisNexis UK on 020 8686 9141.

Rates of exchange on year-end dates

	29.12.00	30.3.01	31.12.01	28.3.02	31.12.02	31.3.03
Australia ($A)	2·6884	2·9117	2·8432	2·6682	2·859	2·6157
Austria (Schilling)	21·894	22·1294	22·4919	27/2/02 22·5599		
(Euro)				28/3/02 1·6323	1·5342	1·4486
Belgium (Franc)	64·1847	64·8747	65·9375	27/2/02 66·1368		
(Euro)				28/3/02 1·6323	1·5342	1·4486
Canada (Can$)	2·2437	2·2386	2·3232	2·2719	2·5433	2·3251
Denmark (Krone)	11·8756	12·0122	12·1532	12·1341	11·3954	10·7573
European Union (Euro)	1·5911	1·6082	1·6346	1·6323	1·5342	1·4486
France (Franc)	10·4369	10·5491	10·7219	27/2/02 10·7544		
(Euro)				28/3/02 1·6323	1·5342	1·4486
Germany (Deutsche Mark)	3·112	3·1454	3·1969	27/2/02 3·2066		
(Euro)				28/3/02 1·6323	1·5342	1·4486
Hong Kong (HK$)	11·6515	11·0878	11·349	11·1069	12·5546	12·3282
Irish Republic (Punt)	1·2531	1·2666	1·2873	27/2/02 1·2912		
(Euro)				28/3/02 1·6323	1·5342	1·4486
Italy (Lira)	3,080·79	3,113·91	3,164·92	27/2/02 3,174·49		
(Euro)				28/3/02 1·6323	1·5342	1·4486
Japan (Yen)	170·592	178·161	190·745	188·73	191·047	187·433
Luxembourg (Franc)	64·1847	64·8747	65·9375	27/2/02 66·1368		
(Euro)				28/3/02 1·6323	1·5342	1·4486
Netherlands (Guilder)	3·5064	3·544	3·6021	27/2/02 3·613		
(Euro)				28/3/02 1·6323	1·5342	1·4486
Norway (Krone)	13·1731	12·95	13·0539	12·5763	11·153	11·4703
Portugal (Escudo)	318·986	322·416	327·697	27/2/02 328·688		
(Euro)				28/3/02 1·6323	1·5342	1·4486
South Africa (Rand)	11·3081	11·3875	17·4575	16·1838	13·8138	12·4413
Spain/Balearic Islands (Peseta)	264·736	267·582	271·966	27/2/02 272·788		
(Euro)				28/3/02 1·6323	1·5342	1·4486
Sweden (Krona)	14·0948	14·6707	15·2667	14·7501	14·0276	13·4023
Switzerland (Franc)	2·4207	2·4538	2·4164	2·3949	2·226	2·1362
USA (US$)	1·4938	1·4217	1·4554	1·424	1·6099	1·5807

Note

The Inland Revenue rates of exchange on 31.12.03 and 31.3.04 will be published in the 2004–05 Finance Act (sixty-eighth) edition of Whillans's Tax Tables. If these rates are required before the publication of that edition, they can be obtained (normally available from June) from the IR website (www.inlandrevenue.gov.uk/exrate/index.htm), from the Inland Revenue, Business Tax on 020 7438 4278 or from the editors at LexisNexis UK on 020 8686 9141.

Double taxation agreements (including protocols and regulations)

Taxes on income and capital gains

Agreements terminated or superseded within the last six years are printed in italic. Amending protocols and exchanges of notes are printed in square brackets. Entry into force after 5.4.70 is indicated in the third column.

Country	SI/SR & O	Entry into force
Antigua & Barbuda	1947/2865	
	[1968/1096]	
Argentina	1997/1777	1.8.97
Armenia†	(*1986/224*	*30.1.86*)
Australia§§	1968/305	3.10.95
	[1980/707]	21.5.80
	(talks 2001)	
Austria*	1970/1947	17.12.70
	[1979/117]	6.2.79
	[1994/768]	1.12.94
Azerbaijan	1995/762	3.10.95
Bangladesh	1980/708	8.7.80
Barbados	1970/952	26.6.70
	[1973/2096]	12.12.73
Belarus‡	1986/224	30.1.86
	1995/2706	
Belgium*§§	1987/2053	21.10.89
Belize	1947/2866	
	[1968/573]	
	[1973/2097]	12.12.73
Bolivia	1995/2707	23.10.95
Bosnia Herzegovina‡	1981/1815	16.9.82
Botswana§§	1978/183	9.2.78
	(talks 1998)	
Brazil	(talks 1997)	
Brunei	1950/1977	
	[1968/306]	
	[1973/2098]	12.12.73
Bulgaria	1987/2054	28.12.87
Canada	1980/709	17.12.80
	[1980/1528]	18.12.80
	[1985/1996]	23.12.85
	1980/780 (dividend)	*1.7.80*
	[1987/2071]	*1.1.88*
	1996/1782	*30.7.96*
	(amending protocol signed)	
Chile	(text agreed)	
China◇	1984/1826	23.12.84
	[1996/3164]	4.3.97
Croatia¶§§	1981/1815	16.9.82
	(talks 2001)	
Cyprus	1975/425	18.3.75
	[1980/1529]	15.12.80
Czech Republic§	1991/2876	20.12.91
Denmark	1980/1960	17.12.80
	[1991/2877]	19.12.91
	[1996/3165]	20.6.97
Ecuador	(text agreed)	
Egypt	1980/1091	23.8.80
Estonia	1994/3207	19.12.94
European Economic Community	(Convention and Directives 90/434/EEC, 90/435/EEC, 90/436/EEC: see TA 1988 s 815B)	23.7.90
Falkland Islands	*1984/363*	*27.6.84*
	[1992/3206]	*30.12.92*
	1997/2985	18.12.97
Fiji*	1976/1342	17.8.76
Finland	1970/153	
	[1980/710]	25.4.81
	[1985/1997]	20.2.87
	[1991/2878]	23.12.91
	[1996/3166]	8.8.97
France*§§	1968/1869	
	[1973/1328]	6.8.73
	[1987/466]	7.4.87
	[1987/2055]	23.12.87
Gambia	1980/1963	5.7.82
Georgia†§§	(*1986/224*	*30.1.86*)
	(talks 2001)	
Germany*§§	1967/25	
	[1971/874]	1.6.71
Ghana	1993/1800	10.8.94
Greece*	1954/142	
Grenada	1949/361	
	[1968/1867]	
Guernsey	1952/1215	
	[1994/3209]	3.1.95
Guyana	1992/3207	18.12.92
Hungary	1978/1056	27.8.78
Iceland	1991/2879	19.12.91
India	1993/1801	25.10.93
Indonesia	1994/769	14.4.94
	(talks 2000)	
Iran	(talks 2003)	
Irish Republic*	1976/2151	23.12.76
	[1976/2152]	23.12.76
	[1995/764]	21.9.95
	[1998/3151]	23.12.98
Isle of Man	1955/1205	
	[1991/2880]	19.12.91
	[1994/3208]	3.1.95
Israel	1963/616	
	[1971/391]	25.3.71
Italy§§	1990/2590	31.12.90
Ivory Coast	1987/169	10.2.87
Jamaica	1973/1329	31.12.73
Japan	1970/1948	25.12.70
	[1980/1530]	31.10.80
Jersey	1952/1216	
	[1994/3210]	3.1.95
Jordan	2001/3924	24.3.02
Kazakhstan	1994/3211	15.7.96
	[1998/2567]	2.11.98
Kenya*	1977/1299	18.10.77
Kiribati	1950/750	
	[1968/309]	
	[1974/1271]	25.7.74
Korea	*1978/786*	*31.5.78*
	1996/3168	30.12.96
Kuwait	1999/2036	1.7.2000
Kyrgyzstan†	(*1986/224*	*30.1.86*)
Latvia	1996/3167	30.12.96
Lesotho	*1949/2197*	
	[1968/1868]	
	1997/2986	23.12.97
Lithuania†	(*1986/224*	*30.1.86*)
	2001/3925	28.11.02
	[2002/2847]	28.11.02
Luxembourg*§§	1968/1100	
	[1980/567]	21.5.80
	[1984/364]	19.3.84
Macedonia¶	1981/1815	16.9.82
Malawi	1956/619	
	[1964/1401]	
	[1968/1101]	
	[1979/302]	14.3.79

Double taxation agreements — continued

Country	SI/SR & O	Entry into force
Malaysia	*1973/1330*	*13.9.73*
	[1987/2056]	*26.1.88*
	1997/2987	8.7.98
Malta	1995/763	27.3.95
Mauritius*	1981/1121	19.10.81
	[1987/467]	26.10.87
	[amending protocol signed]	
Mexico	1994/3212	15.12.94
Moldova†	(*1986/224*	*30.1.86*)
Mongolia	1996/2598	4.12.96
Montserrat	1947/2869	
	[1968/576]	
Morocco	1991/2881	29.11.90
Myanmar*	1952/751	
Namibia*§§	1962/2352	
	[1962/2788]	
	[1967/1489]	
	[1967/1490]	
	(agreement initialled)	
Netherlands*§§	*1967/1063 (dividend)*	
	1980/1961	6.4.81
	[1990/2152]	20.12.90
	(talks 2001)	
New Zealand§§	1984/365	16.3.84
Nigeria	1987/2057	27.12.87
Norway*	*1985/1998*	*20.12.85*
	2000/3247	21.12.2000
Oman◇◇	1998/2568	9.11.98
Pakistan	1987/2058	8.12.87
Papua New Guinea	1991/2882	20.12.91
Philippines	1978/184	9.2.78
Poland§§	1978/282	25.2.78
Portugal*	1969/599	
Qatar§§	(talks 2001)	
Romania	1977/57	17.1.77
Russian Federation	1994/3213	18.4.97
St Christopher and Nevis	1947/2872	
Serbia and Montenegro¶§§	1981/1815	16.9.82
Sierra Leone	1947/2873	
	[1968/1104]	
Singapore	*1967/483*	
	[1978/787]	*4.8.78*
	1997/2988	19.12.97
Slovakia§	1991/2876	20.12.91
Slovenia¶§§	1981/1815	16.9.82
Solomon Islands	1950/748	
	[1968/574]	
	[1974/1270]	25.7.74
South Africa*	*1969/864*	
	2002/3138	17.12.02
Spain	1976/1919	25.11.76
	[1995/765]	26.5.95
Sri Lanka	1980/713	21.5.80
Sudan	1977/1719	25.10.77
Swaziland*	1969/380	
Sweden	1984/366	26.3.84
	(talks 1998)	
Switzerland*	1978/1408	7.10.78
	[1982/714]	18.5.82
	[1994/3215]	19.12.94
Taiwan§§	2002/3137	23.12.02
Tajikistan‡	1986/224	30.1.86
Thailand§§	1981/1546	20.11.81
Trinidad and Tobago	1983/1903	22.12.83
Tunisia	1984/133	8.2.84
Turkey	1988/932	26.10.88
Turkmenistan‡	1986/224	30.1.86
Uganda	1993/1802	21.12.93
Ukraine	1993/1803	11.8.93
United Arab Emirates	(text agreed)	
USA	*1946/1331 (dividend)*	
	[1955/499]	
	[1961/985]	
	[1980/779]	*22.5.80*
	1980/568	*25.4.80*
	[1994/1418] (dividend)	*16.6.94*
	[1996/1781] (dividend)	*30.7.96*
	2002/2848	31.3.03
Uzbekistan	1994/770	10.6.94
Venezuela	1996/2599	31.12.96
Vietnam	1994/3216	15.12.94
Zambia*	1972/1721	29.3.73
	[1981/1816]	14.1.83
Zimbabwe	1982/1842	11.2.83

* Individuals resident in these countries are entitled to personal reliefs, similar to the relief under TA 1988 s 278, under the provisions of double taxation treaties between these countries and the UK. Non-resident nationals of all EEA countries are entitled to personal allowances as from 6 April 1996: see FA 1996 s 145.

† SP 4/01: these countries do not consider themselves bound by the Convention with the former USSR, which the UK has applied as described in SP 3/92. In consequence, the UK will not apply the terms of the Convention to profits arising *after* 31 March 2002 (corporation tax) and to income and gains arising *after* 5 April 2002 (income tax and corporation tax).

‡ SP 4/01: these countries and the UK will continue to operate the Convention with the former USSR in respect of their residents.

¶ SP 6/93: the treaty with former Yugoslavia is treated as remaining in force between the UK and, respectively, Croatia and Slovenia, until bilateral agreements are signed. The UK also applies that treaty to Bosnia Herzegovina, Macedonia and 'rump' Yugoslavia (i.e. Serbia and Montenegro). Macedonia applies the treaty *vis à vis* the UK, but the Inland Revenue is not aware of the position taken by Bosnia Herzegovina or Serbia and Montenegro. Discussions are to be held about a comprehensive double taxation convention between the UK and Croatia and between the UK and Serbia and Montenegro (IR Press Release 7 March 2003).

§ SP 5/93: the treaty with the former Czechoslovakia is treated as remaining in force between the UK and, respectively, the Czech Republic and Slovakia.

§§ Completion of work on new or updated treaties, protocols or negotiations with these countries, and with Bahrain, Hong Kong SAR and Saudia Arabia, are seen as a priority (IR Press Release of 16 June 2003).

◇The 1984 Agreement does not apply to the Hong Kong Special Administrative Region.

◇◇Certain provisions relating to profits, income and gains from ships and aircraft operated in international traffic take effect from 1 January 1979 (Article 29(2)).

Shipping and air transport profits

Country	SI or SR & O	Country	SI or SR & O
Algeria (air)	1984/362	Jordan	1979/300
Armenia (USSR air)*	1974/1269	Kuwait (air)**	1984/1825
Bahrain (air)	(text agreed)	Kyrgyzstan (USSR air)*	1974/1269
Belarus (USSR air)*	1974/1269	Lebanon	1964/278
Brazil	1968/572	Moldova (USSR air)*	1974/1269
Cameroon (air)	1982/1841	Qatar (air)	(text agreed)
China (air)	1981/1119	*Russia (USSR air)**	*1974/1269*
Congo Democratic Republic	1977/1298	Saudi Arabia (air)	1994/767
Ethiopia (air)	1977/1297	Tajikistan (USSR air)*	1974/1269
Georgia (USSR air)*	1974/1269	Turkmenistan (USSR air)*	1974/1269
Hong Kong (air)	1998/2566	United Arab Emirates (air)	(text agreed)
(shipping)	2000/3248	*USSR (air)**	*1974/1269*
Iran (air)	1960/2419		

* The Revenue has confirmed that this Arrangement will be treated in the same way as the Convention covering income and capital gains SI 1986/224. See notes † and ‡ on p 8.

** Superseded by the comprehensive Agreement (SI 1999/2036, Art. 30) which entered into force on 1 July 2000, p 7 above.

Estates, inheritances and gifts

France*	1963/1319	South Africa	1979/576
India*	1956/998	Sweden	1981/840
Ireland	1978/1107		1989/986
Italy*	1968/304	Switzerland	1994/3214
Netherlands	1980/706	USA	1979/1454
	[1996/730]		(talks 2000)
Pakistan*	1957/1522		

* Agreements pre-date UK inheritance tax/capital transfer tax.

Income arising abroad — Schedule D assessment

	Case IV	Case V		
	Securities	Professions, trades, etc	Pensions	Possessions
NON-RESIDENTS	Exempt	Exempt	Exempt	Exempt
RESIDENTS				
1) **Foreign domicile**	Remittance	Remittance	Remittance	Remittance
2) **UK domicile**				
(a) Non Commonwealth citizen[1]	Arising	Arising	90%[3] arising	Arising
(b) Commonwealth citizen[2]				
(i) ordinarily resident	Arising	Arising	90%[3] arising	Arising
(ii) not ordinarily resident	Remittance	Remittance	Remittance	Remittance

[1] But not citizen of the Republic of Ireland.
[2] Or citizen of the Republic of Ireland.
[3] Pensions paid by the governments of the Federal Republic of Germany or of Austria to victims of Nazi persecution are exempt.

It was announced in the Budget Speech on 17 April 2002 that the Government is reviewing the residence and domicile rules as they affect the tax liabilities of individuals (2002) SWTI 521.

Employment income liability of non-resident employees see p 78.

Tax-free (FOTRA) securities

Under FA 1996 s 154 interest on certain securities ('FOTRA securities') issued by the Treasury is exempt from tax where the beneficial owner is not ordinarily resident in the UK. Except in the case of 3½% War Loan 1952 or after, the exemption does not apply where the securities are held for the purposes of a trade or business carried on in the UK. From 6 April 1998, FOTRA status has been extended to all government stock on the terms of FA 1996 s 154 (FA 1998 s 161).

General

Certificates of tax deposit

The Series 7 Prospectus came into operation on 1 October 1993.

From 1 October 1993, certificates are not available for purchase for use against corporation tax liabilities, although certificates purchased before that date can be used before 1 October 1999 and set against all liabilities listed in the schedule to the Series 6 Prospectus.

Certificates are available to individuals, trustees, companies or other persons or bodies for the payment of any taxes or other liabilities listed in the schedule to the Prospectus. Minimum first deposit £2,000; subsequent deposits not less than £500.

Interest is paid without deduction of tax and is assessed under Schedule D Case III. It will only be paid for the first 6 years of a deposit. Under the Series 7 Prospectus a deposit bears interest for the first year at the rate in force at the time of the deposit and for each subsequent year at the rate in force on the anniversary of the deposit. No bonus or interest supplement is payable.

Series 7

Deposits of £100,000 or over: rate varies according to number of months held for in relevant year:

A = under £100,000
B = £100,000 or over

From	*Amount*	*Held for (mths in yr)*	*Pay't of tax %*	*Cashed %*
Series 7 (1.10.93)				
7.5.97	A	no limit	2.75	1.5
	B	under 1	2.75	1.5
		1-under 3	5.5	2.75
		3-under 6	5.25	2.75
		6-under 9	5.5	2.75
		9-12	5.25	2.75
9.6.97	A	no limit	3	1.5
	B	under 1	3	1.5
		1–12	5.5	2.75
11.7.97	A	no limit	3.25	1.75
	B	under 1	3.25	1.75
		1-under 3	6	3
		3-under 9	5.75	3
		9–12	6	3
8.8.97	A	no limit	4.5	2.25
	B	under 1	4.5	2.25
		1-under 9	6	3
		9–12	5.75	3
7.11.97	A	no limit	4	2
	B	under 1	4	2
		1-under 6	6.5	3.25
		6–12	6.25	3.25
5.6.98	A	no limit	4	2
	B	under 1	4	2
		1-under 3	6.5	3.25
		3-under 9	6.25	3.25
		9–12	6	3
9.10.98	A	no limit	3.75	2
	B	under 1	3.75	2
		1-under 3	6.25	3.25
		3-under 6	5.75	3
		6-under 9	5.5	2.75
		9–12	5.25	2.75
6.11.98	A	no limit	3.25	1.75
	B	under 1	3.25	1.75
		1-under 3	5.75	3
		3-under 6	5.25	2.75
		6-under 9	5	2.5
		9–12	4.75	2.5
11.12.98	A	no limit	3.25	1.75
	B	under 1	3	1.5
		1-under 3	5.25	2.75
		3-under 6	4.75	2.5
		6-under 9	4.5	2.25
		9–12	4.25	2.25
8.1.99	A	no limit	2.5	1.25
	B	under 1	2.5	1.25
		1-under 3	5	2.5
		3-under 6	4.5	2.25
		6–12	4	2
5.2.99	A	no limit	1.75	1
	B	under 1	1.75	1
		1-under 3	4.5	2.25
		3-under 6	4	2
		6–12	3.75	2
9.4.99	A	no limit	1.75	1
	B	under 1	1.75	1
		1-under 3	4.25	2.25
		3-under 6	4	2
		6–12	3.75	2
11.6.99	A	no limit	1.5	0.75
	B	under 1	1.5	0.75
		1–12	4	2
9.9.99	A	no limit	1.75	1
	B	under 1	1.75	1
		1–12	4.5	2.25
4.11.99	A	no limit	2	1
	B	under 1	2	1
		1-under 3	5	2.5
		3-under 12	4.75	2.5
14.1.00	A	no limit	2.25	1.25
	B	under 1	2.25	1.25
		1-under 9	5	2.5
		9–12	5.25	2.75
11.2.00	A	no limit	2.5	1.25
	B	under 1	2.5	1.25
		1-under 3	5.25	2.75
		3-under 6	5	2.5
		6–12	5.25	2.75
9.2.01	A	no limit	2.25	1.25
	B	under 1	2.25	1.25
		1-under 3	4.75	2.5
		3-under 9	4.25	2.25
		9–12	4	2
6.4.01	A	no limit	2	1
	B	under 1	2	1
		1-under 3	4.25	2.25
		3-under 6	4	2
		6-under 9	3.75	2
		9–12	3.5	1.75
11.5.01	A	no limit	2	1
	B	under 1	2	1
		1-under 6	4	2
		6–12	3.75	2
3.8.01	A	no limit	1.5	0.75
	B	under 1	1.5	0.75
		1-under 3	4	2
		3–12	3.75	1.875
19.9.01	A	no limit	1.25	0.75
	B	under 1	1.25	0.75
		1-under 3	3.5	1.75
		3-under 9	3.25	1.75
		9–12	3	1.5
5.10.01	A	no limit	1	0.5
	B	under 1	1	0.5
		1-under 3	3.25	1.75
		3–12	3	1.5
9.11.01	A	no limit	0.5	0.25
	B	under 1	0.5	0.25
		1-under 3	2.75	1.5
		3-under 6	2.5	1.25
		6–12	2.25	1.25
7.2.03	A	no limit	0.25	0
	B	under 1	0.25	0
		1-under 3	2.75	1.25
		3-under 9	2.25	1
		9–12	2	1
11.7.03	A	no limit	0	0
	B	under 1	0	0
		1-under 3	2.50	1.25
		3-under 6	2.25	1
		6–12	2	1

Due dates of tax

Capital gains tax

From 1996–97:
(TMA 1970 s 59B. There are no provisions for payment on account for capital gains tax.)
Normally 31 January following end of year of assessment.
(See also *Extended due dates* under **Income tax**, below.)

Corporation tax

Generally (accounting periods ending after 30 September 1993: pay and file and self assessment)
(TMA 1970 s 59D, substituted by FA 1998 Sch 19 para 29 for accounting periods ending after 30 June 1999.)
9 months and 1 day after end of accounting period.

Instalments for larger companies (TMA 1970 s 59E, SI 1998/3175)
(Large: profits exceeding upper relevant maximum amount in force at end of accounting period, subject to certain restrictions: reg 3.)
1st instalment: 6 months and 13 days from start of accounting period (or date of final instalment if earlier);
(2nd instalment: 3 months after 1st instalment, if length of accounting period allows);
(3rd instalment: 3 months after 2nd instalment, if length of accounting period allows);
Final instalment: 3 months and 14 days from end of accounting period.

Transitional provisions (reg 4) percentage of total liability payable by instalments for accounting periods ending:
after 30 June 1999 but before 1 July 2000: 60%
after 30 June 2000 but before 1 July 2001: 72%
after 30 June 2001 but before 1 July 2002: 88%
(balance due and payable in accordance with *Generally* above).

Advance corporation tax (abolished from 6 April 1999) (FA 1993 ss 31, 32, Sch 3)
Tax in respect of franked payments to be included in a return is due 14 days after a return period ends. Return periods end on 31 March, 30 June, 30 September, 31 December and at the end of each accounting period, when not one of the above.

Close companies: tax on loans to participators
Loans etc made in accounting periods ending after 30 March 1996: 9 months and 1 day after the end of the accounting period. Previously 14 days after the end of the accounting period in which the loan was made. To be included in instalment payments for large companies in respect of accounting periods ending after 30 June 1999 (TMA 1970 s 59E(11), see above).

Income tax

From 1997–98:
(1) *Payment on account* (TMA 1970 s 59A)
A payment on account is required where a taxpayer was assessed to income tax in respect of the immediately preceding year in an amount exceeding the amount of tax deducted at source in respect of that year (subject to a de minimis limit, see below). This excess is known as the 'relevant amount'.
The payment on account is made in 2 equal instalments due on:
(a) 31 January during the year of assessment, and
(b) 31 July in the following year of assessment.
No payments on account are required where:
(a) the aggregate of the relevant amount (see above) and the Class 4 NIC liability for the preceding year is less than £500; or
(b) more than 80% of the taxpayer's income tax and Class 4 NIC liability for the immediately preceding year was met by tax deducted at source.

From 1996–97:
(2) *Payment of income tax* (TMA 1970 s 59B, Sch 3ZA)
Balance of income tax due for a year of assessment (after deducting payments on account, tax deducted at source and credits in respect of dividends, etc) is due on:
31 January following end of year of assessment (TMA 1970 s 59B(4)).

Extended due dates:
(*a*) If a taxpayer has given notice of liability within 6 months of the end of the year of assessment (as required by TMA 1970 s 7), but a notice to make a return is not given until after 31 October following the end of the year of assessment, the final payment is not due until 3 months after the notice is given (TMA 1970 s 59B(3)).
(*b*) If tax is payable as a result of a taxpayer's notice of amendment, a Revenue notice of correction or a Revenue notice of closure following enquiry, in each case given less than 30 days before the due date (or the extended due date at (*a*) above), the additional tax is payable on or before the day following the end of a 30-day period beginning on the day on which the notice is given (TMA 1970 s 59B(5), Sch 3ZA as amended/inserted by FA 2001, Sch 29 paras 14–16).
(*c*) If an assessment other than a self-assessment is made, tax payable under the assessment is due on the day following the end of a 30-day period beginning on the day on which notice of the assessment is given (TMA 1970 s 59B(6)).
The extensions under (b) and (c) do *not* alter the due date *for interest purposes* (see p 12).

Interest on overdue tax see p 12.
Repayment supplement see p 15.
Remission of tax see p 14.

Inheritance tax

Chargeable transfers other than on death, made between:

6 April and 30 September	– 30 April in next year.
1 October and 5 April	– 6 months after end of month in which chargeable transfer is made.

Chargeable events following conditional exemption for heritage etc property and charge on disposal of trees or underwood before the second death
– 6 months after end of month in which chargeable event occurs.

Transfers on death
Earlier of *(a)* 6 months after end of month in which death occurs, and
(b) delivery of account by personal representatives.

Tax or extra tax becoming payable on death:
(1) chargeable transfers and potentially exempt transfers within 7 years of death, or
(2) gifts in excess of £100,000 made to political parties before 15 March 1988 and within 1 year of death: due 6 months after end of month in which death takes place.

Interest on overdue tax

Interest on overdue income tax and capital gains tax

(NB: These rules apply with respect to liabilities for 1996–97 and subsequent years and to liabilities for 1995–96 and earlier years assessed after 5 April 1998. However, for partnerships with trades, etc set up and commenced before 6 April 1994, the previous rules continued to apply for the year 1996–97.)

For payments on account (under TMA 1970 s 59A(2)), tax not postponed pending an appeal (under TMA 1970 s 55) and balancing payments (under TMA 1970 s 59B), interest runs from the due date to the date of payment, on the amount outstanding. For the due date, see p 11. In respect of payments on account, interest is charged on the difference between the amount that ought to have been paid and the amount actually paid.

For tax resulting from amendments/corrections to returns and from discovery assessments (under TMA 1970 s 29), interest normally runs from the annual filing date for the relevant tax year.

Where a claim made under TMA 1970 s 59A(3) or (4) to reduce payments on account proves to be excessive, an underpayment may arise. In such a case, interest is charged on the difference between the amount actually paid and the amount that ought to have been paid if the claim had been made correctly.

Surcharge on unpaid income tax and capital gains tax (TMA 1970 s 59C, amended by FA 1995 s 109)

Applies from 1996-97, and for assessments for 1995–96 or an earlier year of assessment made after 5 April 1998 (FA 1995 s 109(2)). (Tax taken into account in determining certain other penalties (under TMA 1970 ss 7, 93(5), 95 and 95A) is ignored for the purposes of calculating the surcharge.)

28 days: Where income tax or capital gains tax becomes payable and all or part of it remains unpaid the day following 28 days after the due date, the taxpayer is liable to a surcharge of 5% of the unpaid tax.

6 months: The taxpayer is liable to a further surcharge of 5% on any of the tax remaining unpaid 6 months and 1 day from the due date.

Interest is payable on surcharge from the expiry of 30 days beginning on the day on which the surcharge is imposed until the date of payment. It is charged at the rate applying to overdue income tax and capital gains tax (see p 13).

Corporation tax (accounting periods ending after 30 September 1993)

Interest runs from the due date (see p 11) to the date of payment: TMA 1970 s 87A (wording amended by FA 1994 Sch 19 para 24 and SI 1998/3175 reg 7 for accounting periods ending after 30 June 1999) and ss 59D (substituted from the same date) and 59E (inserted from the same date).

For instalment payments by large companies for accounting periods ending after 30 June 1999, a special rate of interest runs from the due date to the earlier of the date of payment and nine months after the end of the accounting period (after which the normal rate applies): SI 1989/1297 regs 32A and 32B (inserted by SI 1998/3176 reg 6).

Inheritance tax

Interest runs from the due date (see above) to the date of payment.

PAYE and national insurance

Employer's tax and Class 1 national insurance payable under PAYE	19 April following deduction year to date of payment
Class 1A national insurance	19 July following year in which contributions due to date of payment
PAYE settlement agreement and Class 1B national insurance	19 October following year to which agreement relates to date of payment
Class 4 national insurance	See under income tax on p 11

Stamp duties see page 91.

Prescribed rate

	Rate	*Period*
Income tax, capital gains tax, Class 1, 1A, 4 and (from 6 April 1999) **1B national insurance contributions and** (from 1 October 1999) **stamp duty and stamp duty reserve tax:** (SI 1999/2538; SI 1999/2536)	5.5%	from 6 August 2003
	6.5%	6 November 2001–5 August 2003
	7.5%	6 May 2001–5 November 2001
	8.5%	6 February 2000–5 May 2001
	7.5%	6 March 1999–5 February 2000
	8.5%	6 January 1999–5 March 1999
	9.5%	6 August 1997–5 January 1999
	8.5%	31 January 1997–5 August 1997
	6.25%	6 February 1996–30 January 1997
	7%	6 March 1995–5 February 1996
Corporation tax self assessment: (accounting periods ending after 30 June 1999) (a) Instalment payments (except where tax still unpaid nine months after end of accounting period)	4.5%	from 21 July 2003
	4.75%	17 February 2003–20 July 2003
	5%	19 November 2001–16 February 2003
	5.5%	15 October 2001–18 November 2001
	5.75%	1 October 2001–14 October 2001
	6%	13 August 2001–30 September 2001
	6.25%	21 May 2001–12 August 2001
	6.5%	16 April 2001–20 May 2001
	6.75%	19 February 2001–15 April 2001
	7%	20 April 2000–18 February 2001
	8%	21 February 2000–19 April 2000
	7.75%	24 January 2000–20 February 2000
	7.5%	15 November 1999–23 January 2000
	7.25%	20 September 1999–14 November 1999
	7%	21 June 1999–19 September 1999
	7.25%	19 April 1999–20 June 1999
	7.5%	15 February 1999–18 April 1999
	8%	18 January 1999–14 February 1999
	8.25%	7 January 1999–17 January 1999
(b) Payments other than instalment payments (or for instalment payments still unpaid nine months after end of accounting period)	5.5%	from 6 August 2003
	6.5%	6 November 2001–5 August 2003
	7.5%	6 May 2001–5 November 2001
	8.5%	6 February 2000–5 May 2001
	7.5%	6 March 1999–5 February 2000
Corporation tax pay and file: (accounting periods ending after 30 September 1993)	4.25%	from 6 August 2003
	5%	6 November 2001–5 August 2003
	6%	6 May 2001–5 November 2001
	6.75%	6 February 2000–5 May 2001
	5.75%	6 March 1999–5 February 2000
	6.5%	6 January 1999–5 March 1999
	7.5%	6 August 1997–5 January 1999
	6.25%	6 February 1996–5 August 1997
	7%	6 March 1995–5 February 1996
	6·25%	6 October 1994–5 March 1995
	5·5%	6 January 1994–5 October 1994
	6·25%	1 October 1993–5 January 1994
Corporation tax: (accounting periods ending before 1 October 1993)	4.25%	from 6 August 2003
	5%	6 November 2001–5 August 2003
	5.75%	6 May 2001–5 November 2001
	6.5%	6 March 2001–5 May 2001
	—	31 January 1997–5 March 2001
	6.25%	6 February 1996–30 January 1997
	7%	6 March 1995–5 February 1996
	6.25%	6 October 1994–5 March 1995
	5.5%	6 January 1994–5 October 1994
	6·25%	6 March 1993–5 January 1994
Income tax on company payments (due on or after 14 October 1999)	5.5%	from 6 August 2003
	6.5%	6 November 2001–5 August 2003
	7.5%	6 May 2001–5 November 2001
	8.5%	6 February 2000–5 May 2001
	7.5%	14 October 1999–5 February 2000
Income tax on company payments (due before 14 October 1999), **advance corporation tax, development land tax, petroleum revenue tax** (including **advance petroleum revenue tax**) and **stamp duty reserve tax** (before 13 October 1999)	4.25%	from 6 August 2003
	5%	6 November 2001–5 August 2003
	5.75%	6 May 2001–5 November 2001
	6.5%	6 February 2000–5 May 2001
	5.75%	6 March 1999–5 February 2000
	6.5%	6 January 1999–5 March 1999
	7.25%	6 August 1997–5 January 1999
	6.25%	6 February 1996–5 August 1997
	7%	6 March 1995–5 February 1996

Prescribed rate – continued

	Rate	*Period*
Inheritance tax and **capital transfer tax:** The rates for periods before 16 December 1986 applied *unless* the transfer was one of those mentioned below	2%	from 6 August 2003
	3%	6 November 2001–5 August 2003
	4%	6 May 2001–5 November 2001
	5%	6 February 2000–5 May 2001
	4%	6 March 1999–5 February 2000
	5%	6 October 1994–5 March 1999
	4%	6 January 1994–5 October 1994
	5%	6 December 1992–5 January 1994
	6%	6 November 1992–5 December 1992
	8%	6 July 1991–5 November 1992
	9%	6 May 1991–5 July 1991
	10%	6 March 1991–5 May 1991
	11%	6 July 1989–5 March 1991
	9%	6 October 1988–5 July 1989
	8%	6 August 1988–5 October 1988
	6%	6 June 1987–5 August 1988
	8%	16 December 1986–5 June 1987
	11%	1 May 1985–15 December 1986
	8%	1 December 1982–30 April 1985
	12%	1 January 1980–30 November 1982
	9%	before 1 January 1980

Inheritance tax: chargeable transfers on death or potentially exempt transfers **Capital transfer tax:** chargeable transfers on death *only*	9%	1 May 1985–15 December 1986
	6%	1 December 1982–30 April 1985
	9%	1 January 1980–30 November 1982
	6%	before 1 January 1980

Remission of tax

By concession, arrears of tax may be waived if they result from the Revenue's failure to make proper and timely use of information supplied by the taxpayer or, where it affects the taxpayer's coding, by his or her employer. From 26 April 1994 the concession also applies to information supplied by the DSS affecting the taxpayer's entitlement to a retirement or widow's pension (see Concession A19). The concession only applies where the taxpayer could reasonably have believed that his or her affairs were in order and (unless the circumstances are exceptional) where the taxpayer is notified of the arrears more than 12 months after the end of the tax year in which the Revenue received the information indicating that more tax was due.

Repayment supplement

Income tax, capital gains tax, Class 1, 1A, 4 and (from 6 April 1999) **1B national insurance contributions and** (from 1 October 1999) **stamp duty and stamp duty reserve tax**

Calculated as simple interest on the amount of tax repaid. The supplement is tax free. (From 31 January 1997 the rate is determined under SI 1989/1297 as amended by SI 1996/3187, see below.)

See pages 16 and 17 for rates applicable to corporation tax and page 91 with respect to stamp duties.

Period to which supplement relates	*Rate*
from 6 August 2003	1·75%
6 November 2001–5 August 2003	2·5%
6 May 2001–5 November 2001	3·5%
6 February 2000–5 May 2001	4%
6 March 1999–5 February 2000	3%
6 January 1999–5 March 1999	4%
6 August 1997–5 January 1999	4·75%
6 February 1997–5 August 1997	4%
6 February 1996–5 February 1997	6·25%
6 March 1995–5 February 1996	7%
6 October 1994–5 March 1995	6·25%
6 January 1994–5 October 1994	5·5%
6 March 1993–5 January 1994	6·25%
6 December 1992–5 March 1993	7%
6 November 1992–5 December 1992	7·75%
6 October 1991–5 November 1992	9·25%
6 July 1991–5 October 1991	10%
6 May 1991–5 July 1991	10·75%
6 March 1991–5 May 1991	11·5%
6 November 1990–5 March 1991	12·25%
6 November 1989–5 November 1990	13%
6 July 1989–5 November 1989	12·25%
6 January 1989–5 July 1989	11·5%
6 October 1988–5 January 1989	10·75%
6 August 1988–5 October 1988	9·75%
6 May 1988–5 August 1988	7·75%
6 December 1987–5 May 1988	8·25%
6 September 1987–5 December 1987	9%
6 June 1987–5 September 1987	8·25%
6 April 1987–5 June 1987	9%

Income tax (TA 1988 s 824; FA 1997 s 92)

From 1996–97 (1997–98 for partnerships whose trade, profession or business commenced before 6 April 1994) repayment supplement applies to:

(*a*) amounts paid on account of income tax
(*b*) income tax paid by or on behalf of an individual
(*c*) surcharges on late payments of tax
(*d*) penalties incurred by an individual under any provision of TMA 1970

but excluding amounts paid in excess of the maximum the taxpayer is required to pay.

Except for tax deducted at source, the repayment supplement runs *from* the date on which the tax, penalty or surcharge was paid *to* the date on which the order for repayment is issued. For tax deducted at source, repayment supplement runs from 31 January after the end of the tax year for which the tax was deducted.

Capital gains tax (TCGA 1992 s 283; FA 1997 s 92)

From 1996–97 repayment supplement runs *from* the date on which the tax was paid *to* the date on which the order for repayment is issued.

Companies: interest on tax overpaid

Accounting periods ending after 30 September 1993 and before 1 July 1999

Repayments of corporation tax, repayments of ACT in respect of foreign income dividends, repayments of income tax in respect of payments received, and payments of tax credits in respect of franked investment income received, made after the material date. Advance corporation tax is abolished from 6 April 1999 (FA 1998 ss 31, 32, SI 1999/358).

Calculated *from* the material date *to* the date the repayment order is issued.

For corporation tax, the material date is the later of

(a) the date on which the tax was paid and

(b) the date on which the tax became, or would have become, due and payable – generally, nine months and one day after the end of the accounting period.

For ACT, the material date is the date on which corporation tax for the accounting period in which the distribution was made became, or would have become, due and payable – generally, 9 months and 1 day after the end of the accounting period.

For repayments of income tax in respect of payments received and payments of tax credits in respect of franked investment income received, the material date is the date on which corporation tax for the accounting period in which the payments or the franked investment income were received became, or would have become, due and payable. Again, this is generally 9 months and 1 day after the end of the accounting period.

This rule is qualified in instances where there is a carry-back of surplus ACT or a carry-back of trading losses for more than 12 months.

Surplus ACT (s 826(7) repealed for accounting periods beginning on or after 6 April 1999 by FA 1998 Sch 3) Where there is in any accounting period ('the later period') an amount of surplus ACT and a claim is made under TA 1988 s 239(3) to carry this surplus ACT back to an earlier accounting period ('the earlier period'), then interest on any repayment of corporation tax for the earlier period (or of income tax on a payment received in the earlier period) resulting from the claim under s 239(3) begins to run only after the date on which the corporation tax for the *later* period (the period in which the surplus ACT arose) became due and payable.

This rule is in itself subject to modification where the surplus ACT arises because of a trading loss carried back (see below).

A similar rule (s 826(7C)) applies to the carry-back of a non-trading deficit on a company's loan relationships as applies to the carry-back of surplus ACT.

Trading losses carried back for more than 12 months (s 826(7A), (7B))
Where a claim is made under TA 1988 s 393A(1) to set off a loss incurred in a later period against the profits of an earlier period not falling within the 12 months immediately preceding the later period, and

(a) a repayment of corporation tax in respect of that earlier period or a repayment of income tax in respect of a payment received in the earlier period; or

(b) following a claim under TA 1988 s 242 to include surplus franked investment income in profits available for set-off, a payment of the whole or part of the tax credit comprised in franked investment income of the earlier period,

is made, interest in respect of that part of the repayment due to the claim under TA 1988 s 393A(1) or TA 1988 s 242 (so far as it relates to the claim under s 393A(1)) begins to run only after the date on which the corporation tax in respect of the later period (the lossmaking period) became, or would have become, due and payable.

Carry-back of trading loss giving rise to carry-back of surplus ACT (s 826(7AA) repealed for accounting periods beginning on or after 6 April 1999 by FA 1998 Sch 3). Where –

(a) a trading loss carried back under s 393A(1) from a later period ('the lossmaking period') gives rise to an amount of surplus ACT, and that surplus ACT is then carried back under s 239(3) to a still-earlier period and

(b) as a result a repayment of corporation tax for the still-earlier period (or of income tax on a payment received in the still-earlier period) falls to be made

then interest on those repayments begins to run only after the date on which the corporation tax for the *lossmaking period* became due and payable.

A similar rule (s 826(7CA)) applies to the carry-back of surplus ACT following the carry-back of a non-trading deficit on a company's loan relationships.

Rates	
from 6 August 2003	1.25%
6 November 2001–5 August 2003	2%
6 May 2001–5 November 2001	2.75%
6 February 2000–5 May 2001	3.5%
6 March 1999–5 February 2000	2.75%
6 January 1999–5 March 1999	3.25%
6 August 1997–5 January 1999	4%
6 February 1996–5 August 1997	3.25%

Accounting periods ending after 30 June 1999

SI 1989/1297 regs 3BA and 3BB (inserted by SI 1998/3176 reg 8)

For instalment payments by large companies and early payments by other companies, a special rate of interest runs from the date the excess arises (but not earlier than the due date of the first instalment) to the earlier of the date the repayment order is issued and 9 months after the end of the accounting period after which the normal rate of interest applies.

Rates on overpaid instalment payments and on corporation tax paid early (but not due by instalments):	
from 21 July 2003	3.25%
17 February 2003–20 July 2003	3.5%
19 November 2001–16 February 2003	3.75%
15 October 2001–18 November 2001	4.25%
1 October 2001–14 October 2001	4.5%
13 August 2001–30 September 2001	4.75%
21 May 2001–12 August 2001	5%
16 April 2001–20 May 2001	5.25%
19 February 2000–15 April 2001	5.5%
21 February 2000–18 February 2001	5.75%
24 January 2000–20 February 2000	5.5%
15 November 1999–23 January 2000	5.25%
20 September 1999–14 November 1999	5%
21 June 1999–19 September 1999	4.75%
19 April 1999–20 June 1999	5%
15 February 1999–18 April 1999	5.25%
18 January 1999–14 February 1999	5.75%
7 January 1999–17 January 1999	6%

Rates on overpaid corporation tax in respect of periods after normal due date (SI 1989/1297 reg 3BB):

from 6 August 2003	2%
6 November 2001–5 August 2003	3%
6 May 2001–5 November 2001	4%
6 February 2000–5 May 2001	5%
6 March 1999–5 February 2000	4%

Penalties

A) Personal tax returns: offences by taxpayers

Offence	*Penalty*
Failure to give notice of chargeability to income or capital gains tax within 6 months from end of year of assessment (TMA 1970 s 7).	Amount not exceeding tax assessed (either self-assessed under TMA 1970 s 9 or under a TMA 1970 s 29 'discovery' assessment) for that year and not paid before 1 February following that year.
Failure to comply with notice requiring return for income tax or capital gains tax (TMA 1970 s 93).	(a) Initial penalty of £100; and (b) upon direction by Commissioners, further penalty not exceeding £60 for each day on which failure continues after notification of direction; (c) if failure continues after six months following filing date, and no application for a direction under (b) has been made, a further penalty of £100. (d) In addition, if failure continues after first anniversary of filing date, and there would have been a liability to tax shown in the return, a penalty not exceeding the liability that would have been shown in the return. (e) If the taxpayer can prove that the liability to tax shown in the return would not have exceeded a particular amount, the sum of penalties under (a) and (c) above are not to exceed that amount.
Failure to comply with notice requiring partnership return (TMA 1970 s 93A).	(a) Initial penalty on each 'relevant partner' of £100; and (b) upon direction by Commissioners, further penalty on each relevant partner not exceeding £60 for each day on which failure continues after notification to representative partner of direction; (c) if failure continues after six months following filing date, and no application for a direction under (b) has been made, a further penalty on each relevant partner of £100. NB: A 'relevant partner' is any person who was a partner at any time during the period for which the return is required.
Fraudulently or negligently delivering incorrect return or accounts or making an incorrect statement in connection with a claim for an allowance, deduction or relief (TMA 1970 s 95).	Penalty not exceeding the difference between the amount payable under the return etc and the amount which would have been payable if the return etc had been correct.
Fraudulently or negligently delivering incorrect partnership return or accounts or making an incorrect statement or declaration in connection with such a return (TMA 1970 s 95A).	Penalty on each relevant partner not exceeding the difference between the amount payable by him or her under the return, etc and the amount that would have been payable by him or her if the return, etc had been correct. For the meaning of 'relevant partner', see under TMA 1970 s 93A above.
(From 31.1.01) Failure to register as self-employed (and liable to Class 2 NIC) within three months after the month in which self-employment begins (SI 2001/1004 reg 87).	£100.

B) Corporation tax returns under pay and file and corporation tax self assessment

Offence	*Penalty*
Pay and file (accounting periods ending before 1 July 1999)	
Failure to give notice of chargeability to corporation tax within 12 months after end of accounting period (TMA 1970 s 10).	Penalty not exceeding amount of tax unpaid 12 months after end of accounting period (after set-off of income tax credits).
Failure to comply with notice requiring return for corporation tax (TMA 1970 s 94).	(a) If return is delivered within 3 months of due date – £100 (£500 in respect of default for third consecutive period); (b) if return is delivered more than 3 months after due date – £200 (£1,000 in respect of default for third consecutive period); and (c) if return is delivered between 18 months and 2 years after end of return period – an additional penalty of 10% of tax unpaid at end of 18-month period; (d) if return is delivered more than 2 years after end of return period – an additional penalty of 20% of tax unpaid at end of 18-month period.
Fraudulently or negligently delivering incorrect return or accounts or making an incorrect statement in connection with a claim for an allowance, deduction or relief (TMA 1970 s 96).	Penalty not exceeding the difference between the amount payable under the return etc and the amount which would have been payable if the return etc had been correct.

Offence	*Penalty*
Self assessment (accounting periods ending on or after 1 July 1999)	*(For the restriction of penalties where multiple tax-related penalties are payable in respect of the same accounting period see FA 1998 Sch 18 para 90)*
Failure to give notice of chargeability to corporation tax within 12 months after end of accounting period (FA 1998 Sch 18 para 2).	Penalty not exceeding amount of tax payable for that accounting period remaining unpaid 12 months after end of accounting period (taking no account of relief deferred under TA 1988 s 419(4A)).
Failure to deliver a company tax return by the filing date (FA 1998 Sch 18 paras 17, 18).	*Flat-rate penalties* (Unless FA 1998 Sch 18 para 19 (excuse for late delivery of returns) applies) (a) If return is delivered within 3 months of the filing date: £100 (£500 for third successive failure); (b) in any other case: £200 (£1,000 for third successive failure); (the increased penalties under (a) and (b) apply with modifications where the first or second period ends before 1 July 1999 (para 17(4)). *Tax-related penalties* (c) If return is delivered between 18 months (or the filing date, if later) and 2 years after the end of the return period: an additional penalty of 10% of the unpaid tax; (d) if return delivered more than 2 years after the end of the return period: an additional penalty of 20% of the unpaid tax. (In determining the amount of unpaid tax no account is taken of relief deferred under TA 1970 s 419(4A)).
Fraudulently or negligently delivering a company tax return which is incorrect (FA 1998 Sch 18 para 20).	An amount not exceeding the amount of tax understated (taking no account of relief deferred under TA 1988 s 419(4A)).
On discovering that a company tax return delivered by it (neither fraudulently nor negligently) is incorrect, a company does not remedy the error without reasonable delay (FA 1998 Sch 18 para 20).	An amount not exceeding the amount of tax understated (taking no account of relief deferred under TA 1988 s 419(4A)).
Fraudulently or negligently making an incorrect return, statement or declaration in connection with a claim for any tax allowance, deduction or relief, or submitting any incorrect accounts in connection with the ascertainment of the company's tax liability (FA 1998 Sch 18 para 89).	Penalty not exceeding the amount of tax understated (excluding relief deferred under TA 1988 s 419(4A)).

C) PAYE returns

Offence	*Penalty*
Failure to submit return P9D or P11D (benefits in kind) by due date (6 June following tax year 1995–96; 6 July following subsequent tax years) (TMA 1970 s 98(1)).	(a) An initial penalty not exceeding £300; and (b) a continuing penalty not exceeding £60 for each day on which the failure continues after imposition of the initial penalty.
Fraudulently or negligently submitting incorrect return P9D or P11D (TMA 1970 s 98(2)).	Penalty not exceeding £3,000.
Failure to submit returns P14 (individual end of year summary), P35 (annual return), P38 or P38A (supplementary returns for employees not on P35) by due date (19 May following tax year) (TMA 1970 s 98A).	(a) First 12 months: penalty of £100 for each 50 employees (or part thereof) for each month the failure continues; (b) failures exceeding 12 months: a penalty not exceeding the amount of PAYE or NIC due and unpaid after 19 April following year of assessment. (For late 1995–96 returns, the Revenue will normally limit the amount of the penalty to the total of the tax and NIC that should be reported on the return or to £100, whichever is greater: Revenue Press Release dated 14 June 1996.)
Fraudulently or negligently submitting incorrect form P14, P35, P38 or P38A (TMA 1970 s 98A).	Penalty not exceeding the difference between the amount payable under the return and the amount which would have been payable if the return had been correct.
Failure to submit returns P11D(b) (Class 1A NIC returns) by due date (19 July following tax year, extended for 2000/01 only to 19 September 2001) (SI 2001/1004 reg 81).	(a) First 12 months: penalty of £100 for each 50 employees (or part thereof) for each month the failure continues (but total penalty not to exceed total Class 1A NIC due); (b) failures exceeding 12 months: a penalty not exceeding the amount of Class 1A NIC due and unpaid after 19 July following year of assessment.

D) Inheritance tax returns and information

Offence	*Penalty*
Failure to deliver an account under IHTA 1984, s 216 or 217. (IHTA 1984 s 245; FA 1999 s 108)	(a) An initial penalty not exceeding £100; (b) further penalty not exceeding £60 (where penalty determined by court or Special Commissioners) for each day on which the failure continues after imposition of initial penalty; and (c) if failure continues after six months following the date on which the account is due, and proceedings have not commenced, a further penalty not exceeding £100.
Failure to make a return under IHTA 1984, s 218 or failure to comply with a notice under s 219.	(a) An initial penalty not exceeding £300; and (b) further penalty not exceeding £60 (where penalty determined by court or Special Commissioners) for each day on which the failure continues after imposition of initial penalty.
Failure to comply with a notice under IHTA 1984, s 219A(1) or (4). (IHTA 1984 s 245A; FA 1999 s 108)	(a) An initial penalty not exceeding £50; and (b) further penalty not exceeding £30 (where penalty determined by court or Special Commissioners) for each day on which the failure continues after imposition of initial penalty.
The taxpayer fraudulently or negligently delivering, furnishing or producing incorrect accounts, information or documents. (IHTA 1984 s 247(1); FA 1999 s 108)	(a) In the case of fraud, a penalty not exceeding the aggregate of £3,000 and the difference between the amount payable according to the information furnished and the amount that would have been payable if the accounts etc had been correct; and (b) in the case of negligence, a penalty not exceeding the aggregate of £1,500 and the difference between the amount payable according to the information furnished and the amount that would have been payable if the accounts etc had been correct.
A person other than the taxpayer fraudulently or negligently delivering, furnishing or producing incorrect accounts, information or documents. (IHTA 1984 s 247(3); FA 1999 s 108)	(a) In the case of fraud, a penalty not exceeding £3,000; and (b) in the case of negligence, a penalty not exceeding £1,500.
Any person assisting in or inducing the delivery, furnishing or production of any account, information or document knowing it to be incorrect. (IHTA 1984 s 247(4); FA 1999 s 108)	A penalty not exceeding £3,000.

E) Special returns of information

Offence	*Penalty*
Failure to comply with a notice to deliver a return or other document, furnish particulars or make anything available for inspection under any of the provisions listed in column 1 of the table in TMA 1970 s 98. (FA 1999 s 89 extends this to corporation tax payment by instalments.)	(a) An initial penalty not exceeding £300 (£3,000 for failure to comply with TA 1988 s 765A(2)(a) or (b)); and (b) a continuing penalty not exceeding £60 (£600 for failure to comply with TA 1988 s 765A(2)(a) or (b)) for each day on which the failure continues after imposition of the initial penalty.
Failure to comply with requirement to furnish information, give certificates or produce documents or records under any of the provisions listed in column 2 of the table in TMA 1970 s 98. (FA 1999 s 86 extends this to advance pricing agreements.)	(a) An initial penalty not exceeding £300; and (b) a continuing penalty not exceeding £60 for each day on which the failure continues after imposition of the initial penalty.
Fraudulently or negligently delivering any incorrect document, information etc required under any of the provisions listed in column 1 or 2 of the table in TMA 1970 s 98.	Penalty not exceeding £3,000.
(Accounting periods ending after 30 June 1999.) Failure of a company to produce documents, etc., for the purposes of an enquiry (FA 1998 Sch 18 para 29).	(a) £50; (b) If failure continues after imposition of penalty under (a), an additional penalty for each day the failure continues, not exceeding: (i) £30 if determined by the Revenue under TMA 1970 s 100; and (ii) £150 if determined by the Commissioners under TMA 1970 s 100C.
Fraudulently or negligently making a false or misleading statement in the preparation of, or application to enter into, any advance pricing agreement (FA 1999 s 86).	Penalty not exceeding £10,000.

F) Other offences by taxpayers, agents etc

Offence	*Penalty*
Failure to retain records as required by TMA 1970 s 12B(1) (TMA 1970 s 12B(5)).	Penalty not exceeding £3,000.
Falsification of documents (TMA 1970 s 20BB).	On summary conviction, a fine not exceeding the statutory maximum (£5,000); on conviction on indictment, imprisonment for a term not exceeding 2 years or a fine or both.
Failure to produce documents required under TMA 1970 s 19A (power to enquire into self-assessment return, etc) (TMA 1970 s 97AA).	(a) Initial penalty of £50; and (b) further penalty not exceeding £30 (where penalty determined by officer of Board) or £150 (where penalty determined by Commissioners) for each day on which failure continues after imposition of initial penalty.
Offences in connection with the supply of information regarding European Economic Interest Groupings—	
(i) failure to supply information	An initial penalty not exceeding £300 per member of the Grouping at the time of failure and after direction by the Commissioners a continuing penalty not exceeding £60 per member of the Grouping at the end of the day for each day on which the failure continues after notification of the direction.
(ii) fraudulent or negligent delivery of an incorrect return, accounts or statement. (TMA 1970 s 98B).	Not exceeding £3,000 for each member of the Grouping at the time of delivery.
Assisting in the delivery of incorrect returns, accounts or information (TMA 1970 s 99).	Not exceeding £3,000.
Fraudulently or negligently giving a certificate of non-liability to income tax for the purposes of receiving interest gross on a bank or building society account, or failing to comply with an undertaking given in such a certificate (TMA 1970 s 99A).	Not exceeding £3,000.
Refusal to allow a deduction of income tax authorised by the Taxes Acts (TMA 1970 s 106).	£50.
Obstruction of officer of the Board in inspection of property to ascertain its market value (TMA 1970 s 111).	Not exceeding level 1 on the standard scale.
Issue by a company of a certificate of approval for enterprise investment scheme relief fraudulently or negligently or without the authority of the inspector (TA 1988 s 306(6)).	Not exceeding £3,000.
False statement to obtain relief for payments to secure a retirement annuity, a purchased life annuity or under a personal pension scheme (TA 1988 ss 619(7), 653, 658(5)).	Not exceeding £3,000.
Creation or transfer of shares or debentures in a non-resident subsidiary company without the consent of HM Treasury (TA 1988 s 766).	On conviction on indictment— (a) imprisonment for not more than 2 years or a fine, or both; or (b) in the case of a UK company, a fine not exceeding the greater of— (i) £10,000; or (ii) three times the tax payable by the company attributable to income and gains arising in the previous 36 months.
Failure by a Lloyd's syndicate's managing agent to comply with notice requiring return of syndicate's profit or loss (FA 1993 Sch 19 para 2(3), (4)).	£60 for each 50 members of syndicate (or part thereof) for each day the failure continues.
Delivery by a Lloyd's syndicate's managing agent fraudulently or negligently of an incorrect return of syndicate profits (FA 1993 Sch 19 para 2(5)).	Not exceeding £3,000 for each member of the syndicate.

F) Other offences by taxpayers, agents etc — continued

Offence	*Penalty*
Obstructing, molesting or hindering an officer or other person employed in relation to inland revenue in the execution of his or her duty (Inland Revenue Regulation Act 1890 s 11).	Level 3 on the standard scale.
(Accounting periods ending after 30 June 1999). Deliberately or recklessly failing to pay corporation tax due in respect of total liability of company for accounting period, or fraudulently or negligently making claim for repayment (TMA 1970 s 59E(4); SI 1998/3175 reg 13).	Penalty not exceeding twice amount of interest charged under SI 1998/3175 reg 7.
(Accounting periods ending after 30 June 1999) Failure of a company to keep and preserve records (other than those only required for claims, etc, or dividend vouchers and certificates of income tax deducted where other evidence is available) (FA 1998 Sch 18 para 23).	Penalty not exceeding £3,000.

G) Standard scale penalties under Criminal Justice Act[1]

Level	*Amount*	
	1.5.84–30.9.92 £	From 1.10.92 £
1	50	200
2	100	500
3	400	1,000
4	1,000	2,500
5 (statutory maximum)	2,000	5,000

[1] Criminal Justice Act 1982 s 37.

Mitigation of penalties

The Board has discretion to mitigate or entirely remit any penalty or to stay or compound any penalty proceedings (TMA 1970 s 102).

Interest on penalties

From 1996–97 penalties under TMA 1970 Parts II (ss 7–12B), IV (ss 28A–43B), VA (ss 59A–59D) and X (ss 93–107) carry interest at the prescribed rate (see p 14): TMA 1970 s 103A. Surcharges on unpaid income tax and capital gains tax carry interest under TMA 1970 s 59C (with effect from 9 March 1998, by virtue of SI 1998/310). As regards corporation tax, the provisions apply for accounting periods ending on or after 1 July 1999.

Stamp duties see p 91.

VAT see p 94.

Time limits for claims and elections

Whenever possible, a claim or election must be made on the tax return or by an amendment to the return (TMA 1970 s 42 and FA 1998 Sch 18 paras 9, 10, 67 and 79). Exceptions to this general rule are dealt with in TMA 1970 Sch 1A.

Except where another period is expressly prescribed, a claim for relief in respect of income tax and capital gains tax must be made within five years from the 31 January following the year of assessment to which it relates (TMA 1970 s 43(1) as amended). The time limit for claims by companies remains at six years from the end of the accounting period to which it relates (TMA 1970 s 43(1) (b) and, for accounting periods ending after 1 July 1999, FA 1998 Sch 18 para 55).

The tables below set out the main exceptions to the general limits.

Income tax only

Claim	*Time limit*
Farming and market gardening: Averaging relief to be available to a person carrying on a trade of farming or market gardening (TA 1988 s 96(8)).	1 year after 31 January next following end of second year which enters into the averaging calculation.
Post-cessation receipts: Post-cessation receipts to be charged as if received on the date of discontinuance or change of basis of computation (TA 1988 s 108).	1 year after 31 January following end of year of assessment in which sum received.
Post-cessation expenditure: Unrelieved qualifying post-cessation expenditure to be set against income (TA 1988 s 109A(1)).	1 year after 31 January following year of assessment in which payment made.
Loan benefits: Election by employee for alternative method to be applied in calculating the cash equivalent of the benefit obtained from a loan (ITEPA 2003 s 183).	1 year after 31 January next following year of assessment.
Election for treatment of all beneficial loans to a director by a close company, as a single loan (ITEPA 2003 s 187).	92 days after the end of the year of assessment.
Returns: Inspector to be required to issue a return to a person with PAYE income (ITEPA 2003 s 711).	5 years after 31 October next following year of assessment.
Jointly held property: Income from jointly owned property to be assessed on husband and wife in unequal shares (TA 1988 s 282B(2)).	60 days after date of declaration.
Enterprise investment scheme: Relief to be given for the enterprise investment scheme (TA 1988 s 306(1) as amended).	Not earlier than 4 months after the company commences its qualifying activity and no later than fifth anniversary of 31 January next following year of assessment in which shares issued.
Trading losses: Loss sustained in a trade, profession or vocation to be set against other income of the year or the last preceding year. Extended to certain pre-trading expenditure by TA 1988 s 401 (TA 1988 s 380(1) as substituted).	1 year after 31 January next following year of assessment in which loss arose.
Losses of new trade etc: Loss sustained in the first 4 years of a new trade, profession or vocation to be offset against other income arising in the 3 years immediately preceding the year of loss. Extended to certain pre-trading expenditure by TA 1988 s 401 (TA 1988 s 381(1)).	1 year after 31 January next following year of assessment in which loss sustained.
Schedule A losses: Claim for relief against total income (TA 1988 s 379A(3)).	1 year after 31 January next following year of assessment.
Copyright, assignment: *Certain sums received by an author in respect of the assignment of a copyright to be assessed as if received over a period of up to 3 years (repealed for payments receivable after 5 April 2001, see now TA 1988 Sch 4A below) (TA 1988 s 534(1), (5) as amended).*	*1 year after 31 January next following the latest year of assessment in which payment receivable.*
Copyright, assignment after 10 years: *Spreading claim made under TA 1988 s 535(1) in respect of sums received by author more than 10 years after first publication of the work to be recalculated on the death of the author or the discontinuance of his or her profession (repealed for payments receivable after 5 April 2001, see now TA 1988 Sch 4A below) (TA 1988 s 535(8A)).*	*1 year after 31 January next following year of assessment in which payment receivable.*
Design rights, assignment: *Sums received by a designer for the assignment of rights in a design to be assessed as if received over a period of up to 3 years (repealed for payments receivable after 5 April 2001, see now TA 1988 Sch 4A below) (TA 1988 s 537A(5), (5A) as amended).*	*1 year after 31 January next following the latest year of assessment in which payment receivable.*
Loss on disposal of unlisted shares: Loss on disposal by an individual of shares in a qualifying trading company to be offset against other income of the year of loss or the last preceding year (TA 1988 s 574(1) as substituted).	1 year after 31 January next following year of assessment in which loss incurred.

Claim	*Time limit*
Retirement annuity premiums: Relief to be given in respect of a qualifying premium paid under a retirement annuity contract entered into before 1 July 1988 and treated as paid in the immediately preceding year of assessment (or the year before that if no net relevant earnings in the immediately preceding year) (TA 1988 s 619(4) as amended).	31 January next following year of assessment in which premium paid.
Retirement annuity premiums, carry-forward of unused relief: Unused relief to be available against a qualifying premium paid under a retirement annuity contract entered into before 1 July 1988 where an assessment becomes final and conclusive more than 6 years after the year to which it relates (TA 1988 s 625(3)).	6 months after the date when the assessment becomes final.
Personal pension schemes, carry-back of relief: *Relief to be given in respect of a contribution paid under approved personal pension arrangements for the immediately preceding year of assessment (or the year before that if no net relevant earnings in the immediately preceding year) (repealed for contributions paid after 5 April 2001) (TA 1988 s 641(1), (4) as amended).*	*31 January next following year of assessment in which contributions paid.*
Personal pension schemes, contributions: Contributions paid before 1 February to be treated in whole or part as paid in preceding year of assessment (TA 1988 s 641A)	On or before date of payment of contribution.
Personal pension schemes, carry-forward of relief: *Unused relief to be available for relief against a contribution paid under approved personal pension arrangements where an assessment to tax for a year of assessment becomes final and conclusive more than 6 years after the end of that year (repealed from 2001–02) (TA 1988 s 642(4)).*	*6 months after the date when the assessment for the year in question becomes final and conclusive.*
Maintenance funds for historic buildings: Income arising to trustees of maintenance funds for historic buildings not to be treated as the income of the settlor (TA 1988 s 691(2), (4) as amended).	1 year from 31 January next following year of assessment to which it relates.
Completion of administration: Income of a beneficiary to be adjusted for past years on completion of the administration of a deceased's estate (TA 1988 s 700(1), (3) as amended).	3 years after 31 January next following year of assessment in which the administration is completed.
Creative artists, relief for fluctuation profits: Relevant profits of an individual in two consecutive years to be averaged (TA 1988 Sch 4A).	1 year after 31 January next following later tax year to which it relates (or in which adjustment for other reason is made).
Deduction of trading losses: Unrelieved trading losses to be set against capital gains (FA 1991 s 72, TA 1988 s 380(1)).	12 months from 31 January next following year of assessment in which loss sustained.
Rent a room relief: Relief not to be applied to an individual for a year of assessment (F(No 2)A 1992 Sch 10 para 10).	1 year after 31 January next following year of assessment or such later date as Board may allow.
Rent a room relief: Relief to be applied where the total of all relevant sums for a year exceed the individual's limit (F(No 2)A 1992 Sch 10 paras 11, 12).	1 year after 31 January next following year of assessment or such later date as Board may allow.
Enterprise Management Incentives: Notification of grant of options in shares under the Enterprise Management Incentives scheme to Inland Revenue (ITEPA 2003 Sch 5 para 44).	92 days from grant of option where option granted after 11 May 2001 (previously 30 days).
Gift aid: Election to treat donations to charity under gift aid made after 5 April 2003 as made in the previous year of assessment (FA 2002 s 98).	On or before the date on which the donor delivers his tax return for the previous year of assessment and not later than 31 January next following the end of that year.
Foster care receipts: Election to tax on the alternative method of calculating profits (FA 2003 s 176, Sch 36).	1 year after 31 January next following year of assessment (or such later date as the Board may allow).
Cash basis withdrawal for barristers and advocates: Election for increased adjustment under the transitional spreading provisions (FA 2002 Sch 22 para 12).	31 January following the tax year in question.

Corporation tax only

Claim	*Time limit*
Carry back of surplus ACT: *Surplus ACT paid to be carried back for offset against corporation tax liabilities for accounting periods beginning within six years prior to the period of payment (TA 1988 s 239(3)) (repealed for accounting periods beginning after 5 April 1999).*	*2 years.*
Trading losses: Loss sustained by a company in a trade in an accounting period to be offset against— (a) profits of that accounting period; (b) profits of the preceding year. Extended to certain pre-trading expenditure by TA 1988 s 401 (TA 1988 s 393A(1) (2A)(10)).	2 years or such further period as Board may allow.
Group relief: Group relief to be given for accounting periods ending after 30 September 1993 and before 1 July 1999. The surrendering company must consent to the claim (TA 1988 s 412, Sch 17A para 2).	2 years after the end of the surrendering company's accounting period or the date on which the relevant assessment becomes final, whichever is later.
Group relief: Group relief to be given for accounting periods ending after 30 June 1999. The surrendering company must consent to the claim (FA 1998 Sch 18 paras 66 to 77).	The last of: (a) 1 year from the filing date of the claimant company's return for the accounting period for which the claim is made; (b) 30 days after the end of an enquiry into the return; (c) if the Revenue amend the return after an enquiry, 30 days after issue of notice of amendment; (d) if an appeal is made against the amendment, 30 days after the determination of the appeal; (or such later time as the Revenue may allow).
Relief for investment companies: Loss on disposal by an investment company of shares in a qualifying trading company to be offset against other income of the period of loss or preceding accounting period (TA 1988 s 573(2)).	2 years.
Non-trading deficit on loan relationship: Claim for non-trading deficits on loan relationships (including non-trading debits on derivative contracts) in a company in an accounting period ending after 30 September 2002 to be:	
(a) offset against profits of the same period or carried back (FA 1996 s 83, Sch 8 paras 1, 3);	2 years after the end of the accounting period in which deficit arose (or such later time as the Revenue may allow).
(b) treated as a non-trading deficit of subsequent accounting period to be carried forward to succeeding accounting periods (FA 1996 s 83, Sch 8 para 4).	2 years after the end of that subsequent accounting period.
Non-trading deficit on loan relationship: *Relief for non-trading deficits on loan relationships in a company in an accounting period ending after 31 March 1996 but before 1 October 2002 to be claimed by:* *(a) offset against profits of the same period;* *(b) group relief;* *(c) offset against post 31 March 1996 profits of earlier accounting periods (as for trading losses above); or* *(d) offset against non-trading profits for the next accounting period, and so on.* *(FA 1996 s 83, Sch 8)*	*2 years or such further period as Board may allow.*
Corporate Venturing Scheme: Relief to be given for losses on disposal of shares against income under Corporate Venturing Scheme (FA 2000 Sch 15 para 68).	2 years from end of accounting period in which loss is incurred.
Qualifying land remediation expenditure: Election for such expenditure of a capital nature to be allowed as a deduction from trade or Schedule A business profits (FA 2001 Sch 22 para 1(8)).	2 years after end of accounting period in which expenditure made.
Intangible assets: Election to replace accounts depreciation with fixed writing down allowance of 4% (FA 2002 Sch 29 para 10).	2 years after the end of the accounting period in which the asset was created or acquired.
Election to exclude from intangible assets provisions certain expenditure on computer software (FA 2002 Sch 29 para 83).	2 years after the end of the accounting period in which the expenditure was incurred.
Controlled foreign companies: Claims for losses in pre-direction accounting periods to be taken into account in computing chargeable profits (TA 1988 Sch 24 para 9).	20 months after the end of the accounting period.
Research and development: Claim for tax credit to be made, amended or withdrawn in the company tax return (or amended return) (FA 1998 Sch 18 para 83E).	1 year from the filing date for the return or such later time as the Board may allow.

Income tax and corporation tax

Claim	*Time limit*
Gifts to educational establishments: Relief for gifts of plant and machinery to educational establishments (TA 1988 s 84(3), (3A)).	1 year after 31 January next following year of assessment in the basis period of which the gift was made (income tax); 2 years after end of accounting period in which the gift was made (corporation tax).
Herd basis: Herd basis to apply (TA 1988 s 97, Sch 5 para 2 as amended).	1 year after 31 January next following first year of assessment for which profits computed by reference to period in which herd was kept (income tax); 1 year after 31 January next following year of assessment in which fell the end of the first period of account in which herd was kept (partnerships); 2 years after end of first accounting period in which herd was kept (corporation tax).
Valuation of work in progress: Work in progress at date of discontinuance of profession or vocation to be valued at actual cost (TA 1988 s 101(2), (2A)).	1 year after 31 January next following year of assessment in which discontinuance occurred (income tax); 2 years after end of accounting period in which discontinuance occurred (corporation tax).
Furnished holiday lettings: Averaging treatment to be applied in determining the number of days on which holiday accommodation is let (TA 1988 s 504(6), (6A)).	1 year after 31 January next following year of assessment in which accommodation let (income tax); 2 years after end of accounting period in which accommodation let (corporation tax).
Patents (UK residents): UK resident in receipt of a capital sum from the sale of patent rights to be charged to tax for period of receipt (TA 1988 s 524(2), (2A)).	1 year after 31 January next following year of assessment in which sum received (income tax); 2 years after end of accounting period in which sum received (corporation tax).
Patents (non-residents): Non-resident in receipt of a capital sum on the sale of non-UK patent rights to be charged to tax as if the sum was received over a period of 6 years (TA 1988 s 524(4) as amended).	1 year after 31 January next following year of assessment in which sum is paid.
Know-how: Consideration for know-how sold together with a trade or part of a trade not to be treated as a payment for goodwill. Time limit runs from the date of the disposal. Both purchaser and vendor must elect (TA 1988 s 531(3)).	2 years from date of disposal.
Unremittable overseas income: Unremittable overseas income to be excluded from assessment (TA 1988 s 584(2), (6) (as substituted)).	1 year after 31 January next following year of assessment in which income arises (income tax); 2 years after end of accounting period in which income arises (corporation tax).
Appropriations to and from trading stock: Election for market value to be adjusted in certain cases where a chargeable gain or allowable loss would otherwise arise (TCGA 1992 s 161(3A)).	1 year after 31 January next following year of assessment in which assets are appropriated (income tax); 2 years after end of accounting period in which assets are appropriated (corporation tax—for accounting periods ending on or after 1 July 1999, otherwise 6 years after the end of the accounting period in question).
Directors' remuneration: Adjustment of employer's Schedule D calculation for emoluments paid subsequently, but within 9 months of the end of the employer's period of account (FA 1989 s 43(5); ITEPA 2003 Sch 6 para 157).	2 years from end of period of account.

Capital allowances

Claim	*Time limit*
Income tax claims: Claim for income tax capital allowances made in taxing the trade (CAA 2001 s 3(2), (3)(*a*)).	Claim to be made in return.
Disapply change in law made by CAA 2001: Election for a change in the law effected by CAA 2001 not to have effect for a period of account ending on 6 April 2001 or straddling that date and ending in 2001–02 (CAA 2001 s 577(1), Sch 3 para 8).	1 year after 31 January next following tax year in which relevant chargeable period ends (income tax). 2 years after end of relevant chargeable period (corporation tax).

Claim	*Time limit*
Corporation tax claims (accounting periods ending after 30 June 1999): Claims, amended claims and withdrawals of claims in respect of corporation tax capital allowances for accounting periods ending after 30 June 1999 (CAA 2001 s 3(2), (3)(*b*), FA 1998 Sch 18 para 82).	The last of: (a) 1 year after the filing date of the claimant company's return for the accounting period for which the claim is made; (b) 30 days after the end of an enquiry into the return; (c) if the Revenue amend the return after an enquiry, 30 days after issue of notice of amendment; (d) if an appeal is made against the amendment, 30 days after the determination of the appeal; (or such later time as the Revenue may allow).
Corporation tax claims (accounting periods ending before 1 July 1999): *Claims, amended claims and withdrawals of claims in respect of corporation tax capital allowances for accounting periods ending after 30 September 1993 and before 1 July 1999 (CAA 1990 s 145A, Sch A1 paras 2, 3). (New provisions apply for self-assessment by companies for accounting periods ending after 30 June 1999, see below.)*	*The latest of —* *(a) 2 years after the end of the accounting period;* *(b) the date on which the company's corporation tax assessment for the period becomes final; and* *(c) the date on which the determination of the company's losses or the amount available for group relief for the accounting period becomes final.*
Films: Expenditure on production or acquisition of films etc to be reallocated (F(No 2)A 1992 s 40B(6)).	1 year after 31 January next following year of assessment in which relevant period ends (income tax); 2 years after end of relevant period (corporation tax).[1]
Plant and machinery: Writing down allowance to be available where first year allowance not claimed (CAA 1990 s 25(3) as amended, (3A)). *The requirement for an election to pool expenditure is abolished for periods ending on or after 6 April 2001 (income tax) and 1 April 2001 (corporation tax).*	1 year after 31 January next following year of assessment in which ends chargeable period related to incurring of expenditure (income tax);[1] 2 years after end of chargeable period related to incurring of expenditure (corporation tax).
Short life assets: Plant or machinery to be treated as a short life asset (CAA 2001 s 85(2)).	1 year after 31 January next following year of assessment in which chargeable period in which qualifying expenditure occurred ends (income tax);[1] 2 years after end of chargeable period (corporation tax).
Short life asset transferred to connected person: Transfer of short life asset to a connected person to be treated as taking place at tax written down value (CAA 2001 s 89(6)).	2 years after end of chargeable period in which disposal occurred.
Ships: Single ship pool treatment not to apply to the whole or part of the expenditure (CAA 2001 s 129(2)).	1 year after 31 January next following year of assessment in which chargeable period ends (income tax);[1] 2 years after end of chargeable period (corporation tax).
Ships: Part or all of a first year allowance in respect of expenditure on a ship to be postponed to a later period (CAA 2001 s 130(4)).	1 year after 31 January next following year of assessment in which period of account ends (income tax);[1] 2 years after end of accounting period for which allowance made (corporation tax).
Oilfields: Oilfield abandonment expenditure to be deductible in relation to a ring fence trade (CAA 2001 s 164(2)).	2 years after end of chargeable period related to incurring of expenditure.
Equipment lessors: Plant or machinery which becomes a fixture and is subject to an equipment lease to be treated as belonging to equipment lessor. Election to be made by both lessor and lessee but not permitted if they are connected persons (CAA 2001 s 177(5)).	1 year after 31 January next following year of assessment in which chargeable period ends (income tax);[1] 2 years after end of chargeable period (corporation tax).
Lessee to be treated as owner of fixture: Plant or machinery which has become a fixture on land which is subsequently let to be treated as belonging to lessee. Election to be made by both lessor and lessee but not permitted if they are connected persons (CAA 2001 s 183(2)).	2 years after date on which lease takes effect.

Capital allowances — continued

Claim	*Time limit*
Excess corporation tax allowances: Excess of corporation tax capital allowances given by discharge or repayment of tax over the relevant class of income to be set against the profits of that period and the immediately preceding period (CAA 2001 s 260(6)).	2 years after the end of the accounting period for which allowances claimed.
Connected persons: Succession to a trade between connected persons to be ignored in computing capital allowances (CAA 2001 s 266).	2 years after the date of the succession.
Industrial buildings: Grant of a long lease of a building to be treated as a sale of the relevant interest by the lessor. Both lessor and lessee must elect (CAA 2001 ss 290, 291).	2 years after the date when the lease takes effect.
Agricultural buildings: Cessation of use, demolition or destruction of agricultural buildings or acquisition of relevant interest in capital expenditure on agricultural land and buildings to be treated as a balancing event (CAA 2001 ss 381, 382).	1 year after 31 January next following year of assessment in which chargeable period ends (income tax);[1] 2 years after end of chargeable period (corporation tax).
Connected persons: Disposal and acquisition of property between persons one of which controls the other or which are under common control to be treated as made at the lower of open market value and tax written down value (CAA 2001 s 570(5)).	2 years after the date of the disposal.

[1] For the purposes of income tax, applies from 1997–98 in respect of trades etc set up and commenced before 6 April 1994 and from 1996–97 for trades etc commenced after 5 April 1994: see FA 1996 s 135(3), Sch 21.

Capital gains

Claim	*Time limit*
Assets of negligible value: Loss to be allowed where the value of an asset has become negligible (TCGA 1992 s 24(2)).	Year for which loss to be allowed, or up to 2 years after the end of that year if the value is still negligible when claim made.
Assets held on 31 March 1982: Events occurring prior to 31 March 1982 to be ignored in computing gains arising after 5 April 1988 (TCGA 1992 s 35 (5), (6) as amended).	1 year after 31 January next following year of assessment in which disposal made (capital gains tax) or 2 years after end of accounting period in which disposal made (corporation tax).
Variation or disclaimer: Variation or disclaimer of the terms of a will or intestacy, made within two years of the death, to be treated as effected by the deceased (TCGA 1992 s 62(6), (7)).	6 months after instrument of variation or disclaimer effected or such longer time as the Board may allow.
Same-day acquisition of shares: Election to treat certain shares acquired after 5 April 2002 under employee share options as acquired separately from other shares under same-day rules (TCGA 1992 ss 105A, 105B).	1 year after 31 January following year of assessment in which disposal is made.
Pre-April 1982 share pools: Quoted ordinary (and participating preference) shares and units in certain unit trusts held (or deemed to have been held) at 6 April 1965 to be pooled at their 6 April 1965 values for disposals after 5 April 1985 (31 March 1985 for companies) or 19 March 1968, as the case may be (TCGA 1992 s 109(4), (5), Sch 2 paras 4(2), (11) as amended, 5).	1 year after 31 January next following year of assessment in which first relevant disposal made (capital gains tax); 2 years after end of accounting period in which first relevant disposal made (corporation tax); or such further time as the Board may allow.
Incorporation relief: Election to disapply incorporation relief under TCGA 1992 s 162 on a transfer of a business after 5 April 2002 (TCGA 1992 s 162A).	2 years after 31 January following year of assessment in which transfer takes place (reduced by 1 year where transferor disposes of all shares received in exchange by the end of the tax year following that in which transfer takes place).
Subsidiary company ceasing to be UK resident: Postponement of charge on deemed disposal of assets where a subsidiary company ceases to be resident in the UK (TCGA 1992 s 187(1)).	2 years after date of ceasing to be resident in UK.
Main residence: Determination of main residence for principal private residence exemption (TCGA 1992 s 222(5)(a)).	2 years from the beginning of the period for which a determination is required, ie the date of acquisition of a second or further residence, but provided that an initial notice has been given within the time limit it may subsequently be varied and the notice of variation may have effect for up to 2 years prior to the date on which it is made.

Claim	*Time limit*
Employee share ownership trusts: Rollover relief on disposal of shares to trustees of qualifying employee share ownership trust (TCGA 1992 s 229(1)).	2 years after date of acquisition of replacement assets.
Relief for loans to trades: Losses on certain loans to traders to be allowed as capital losses (TCGA 1992 s 253(3)).	The loss is treated as accruing on the date that the claim is made, or at an earlier date, which is: (a) no more than 2 years before the beginning of the year of assessment in which the claim is made (capital gains tax) or (b) no earlier than the first day of the earliest accounting period ending no more than 2 years before the date of the claim.
Relief for loans to traders (payments by guarantor): Losses arising from payments by guarantor of certain irrecoverable loans to traders to be allowed as capital losses at time of claim or 'earlier time' (TCGA 1992 s 253(4), (4A); FA 1996 s 135(2)).	5 years after 31 January next following year of assessment in which payment made (capital gains tax); 6 years after end of accounting period in which the payment was made (corporation tax accounting periods ending after 30 June 1999).
Deferred unascertainable consideration: Election for relevant loss to be treated as accruing in earlier year subject to certain conditions (TGCA 1992 ss 279A–279D; FA 2003 s 162).	1 year after 31 January next following the year of loss.
Tax paid by instalments: Tax to be paid by instalments where the consideration is payable over a period (TCGA 1992 s 280 as amended).	Date of payment of tax.
Election for valuation at 6 April 1965: Gain on a disposal of an asset held at 6 April 1965 to be computed as if the asset had been acquired on that date. An election once made is irrevocable (TCGA 1992 Sch 2 para 17).	1 year after 31 January next following year of assessment in which disposal made (capital gains tax); 2 years after end of accounting period in which disposal made (corporation tax); or such further time as the Board may by notice allow.
Assets held on 31 March 1982: Halving of postponed charges, or held over or rolled over gains, on disposals of assets acquired after 31 March 1982 (but before 6 April 1988) from a person who acquired (or is deemed to have acquired) them before 31 March 1982 (TCGA 1992 Sch 4 para 9).	1 year after 31 January next following year of assessment in which disposal (or other event) occurred (capital gains tax); 2 years after the end of the accounting period in which the disposal (or other event) occurred, or such longer time as the Board may allow (corporation tax).
Retirement relief: Retirement relief generally. (TCGA 1992 Sch 6 as amended paras 2, 5, 12,16). (Phased out from 6 April 1999 and not available for disposals after 5 April 2003 (FA 1998 s 140).)	1 year after 31 January next following year of assessment.
Relief for trading losses: Election to base the calculation for relief for trading losses incurred in 2002–03 and 2003–04 against capital gains using pre-tapered gains (FA 2002 s 48).	1 year after 31 January following year of assessment in which loss is incurred.

Inheritance tax

Claim	*Time limit*
Maintenance funds for historic buildings: Transfer of property to a maintenance fund for historic buildings etc to be exempt (IHTA 1984 s 27 as amended).	2 years after the date of the transfer or such longer period as the Board may allow (transfers of value made after 16 March 1998).
Conditionally exempt transfers of qualifying heritage assets: Transfer of property of national, scientific, historic or artistic etc interest designated as such by the Treasury to be conditionally exempt (IHTA 1984 ss 30, 31 as amended).	2 years after the date of the transfer of value or death or such longer period as the Board may allow (transfers of value or death after 16 March 1998).
Conditional exemption for heritage property leaving discretionary trusts: Qualifying heritage assets leaving discretionary trusts to be conditionally exempt (IHTA 1984 s 78 as amended).	2 years after the date of transfer or other event or such longer period as the Board may allow (transfers of property made and other events occurring after 16 March 1998).
Woodlands: Tax in respect of trees or underwood forming part of the value of a person's estate immediately before death to be deferred (IHTA 1984 ss 125, 126).	2 years after death or such longer period as the Board may allow.
Variations of dispositions on death: Variations or disclaimers of dispositions taking effect on death to be treated as if effected by the deceased (IHTA 1984 s 142).	6 months after the date of the instrument.

Exchanges

Recognised stock exchanges

The following is a list of countries with exchanges which have been designated as recognised stock exchanges under TA 1988 s 841. Unless otherwise specified, any stock exchange (or options exchange) in a country listed below is a recognised stock exchange for the purposes of TA 1988 s 841, provided it is recognised under the law of the country concerned relating to stock exchanges.

The Revenue's interpretation of the phrase 'listed on a recognised stock exchange' and similar phrases is set out in its policy statement published on 27 November 2002.

Country	*Date of recognition*
Australia	
Australian Stock Exchange and its stock exchange subsidiaries	22 September 1988
Austria[3]	22 October 1970
Belgium[3]	22 October 1970
Brazil	
Rio De Janeiro Stock Exchange	17 August 1995
São Paulo Stock Exchange	11 December 1995
Canada	
Any stock exchange prescribed for the purposes of the Canadian Income Tax Act	22 October 1970
China	
Hong Kong – Any stock exchange recognised under Section 2A(1) of the Hong Kong Companies Ordinance	26 February 1971
Denmark	
Copenhagen Stock Exchange	22 October 1970
Finland	
Helsinki Stock Exchange	22 October 1970
France[3]	22 October 1970
Germany[3]	5 August 1971
Greece	
Athens Stock Exchange	14 June 1993
Guernsey[3]	10 December 2002
Irish Republic[3]	22 October 1970
Italy[3]	3 May 1972
Japan[3]	22 October 1970
Korea	10 October 1994
Luxembourg[3]	21 February 1972
Malaysia	
Kuala Lumpur Stock Exchange	10 October 1994
Mexico	10 October 1994
Netherlands[3]	22 October 1970
New Zealand	22 September 1988
Norway[3]	22 October 1970
Portugal[3]	21 February 1972
Singapore	30 June 1977
South Africa	
Johannesburg Stock Exchange	22 October 1970
Spain[3]	5 August 1971
Sri Lanka	
Colombo Stock Exchange	21 February 1972
Sweden	
Stockholm Stock Exchange	16 July 1985
Switzerland	
Swiss Stock Exchange	12 May 1997
Thailand	10 October 1994
United Kingdom	6 April 1965
United States	
Any stock exchange registered with the Securities and Exchange Commission as a national securities exchange[1]	22 October 1970
Nasdaq Stock Market[2]	10 March 1992

[1] The term 'national securities exchange' does not include any local exchanges registered with the Securities and Exchange Commission.

[2] As maintained through the facilities of the National Association of Securities Dealers Inc and its subsidiaries.

[3] Any stock exchange which is a stock exchange within the meaning of the law of the country concerned relating to stock exchanges.

Recognised futures exchanges

The following is a list of exchanges which have been designated as recognised futures exchanges under TCGA 1992 s 288(6). By concession, those exchanges were recognised futures exchanges for the tax year of recognition onwards.

Country	*Tax year of recognition*
Australia	
Sydney Futures Exchange	1988–89
Canada	
Montreal Exchange	1987–88
China	
Hong Kong Futures Exchange	1987–88
Sweden	
OM Stockholm	1991–92
United Kingdom	
International Petroleum Exchange of London	1985–86
London Gold Market	1985–86
London International Financial Futures and Options Exchange (LIFFE)	1991–92
London Metal Exchange	1985–86
London Silver Market	1985–86
OMLX	1991–92
United States	
Chicago Board of Trade	1987–88
Chicago Mercantile Exchange	1986–87
Commodity Exchange (COMEX)	1988–89
Mid America Commodity Exchange	1987–88
New York Board of Trade[1]	—[1]
New York Mercantile Exchange	1986–87
Philadelphia Board of Trade	1986–87

[1] Formed by the merger of Citrus Associate of New York Cotton Exchange (1988–89), Coffee, Sugar and Cocoa Exchange, New York (1987–88) and New York Cotton Exchange (1988–89).

Applications for clearances and approvals

Clearance application	*Address*
Transfer of long term insurance business (TCGA 1992 s 211, TA 1988 s 444A)	Both parties UK-resident: Robert Peel, Revenue Policy, Business Tax, Room 5W2, 5th Floor, 22 Kingsway, London WC2B 6NR At least one party not UK-resident: Richard Thomas, Revenue Policy, Business Tax, Room 5W2, 5th Floor, 22 Kingsway, London WC2B 6NR
Demergers (TA 1988 s 215); Company purchase of own shares (TA 1988 s 225); Transactions in securities (TA 1988 s 707); Share exchanges (TCGA 1992 ss 138, 139, 140B, 140D); and Intangible fixed assets (FA 2002 Sch 29 para 88)	Revenue Policy, Business Tax, 5th Floor, 22 Kingsway, London WC2B 6NR (Market sensitive applications to Ray McCann; non-market sensitive applications to Mohini Sawhney — see note below)[1]
Company migration (FA 1988 s 130)	Mark Ritchie, Revenue Policy, International, Business Tax Group (Company Migrations), Victory House, 30–34 Kingsway, London WC2B 6ES
Advance pricing agreements (FA 1999 ss 85–87)	Ian Wood, Revenue Policy, International, Business Tax Group (APAs), Victory House, 30–34 Kingsway, London WC2B 6ES For APAs involving oil taxation: Janice Cross, Revenue Policy, International, Oil Taxation Office (APAs), Melbourne House, Aldwych, London WC2B 4LL.
Controlled foreign companies (TA 1988 ss 747–756, Schs 24–26)	Stephen Hewitt, Revenue Policy, International, Business Tax Group (CFC Clearances), Victory House, 30–34 Kingsway, London WC2B 6ES
Corporate Venturing Schemes (FA 2000 Sch 15)	Small Company Enterprise Centre, TIDO, Ty Glas, Llanishen, Cardiff CF14 5ZG

Approval application	*Address*
Pensions (TA 1988 ss 590, 591)	Inland Revenue, Pension Schemes Office, Yorke House, PO Box 62, Castle Meadow Road, Nottingham NG2 1BG
Employee share schemes (TA 1988 Sch 9)	Kevin Meehan, Revenue Policy, Capital and Savings, Employee Share Schemes, Second Floor, New Wing, Somerset House, London WC2R 1LB
Qualifying life assurance policies (TA 1988 Sch 15)	Claire Ritchie, Revenue Policy, Business Tax (Insurance), Room 5W4, 5th Floor, 22 Kingsway, London WC2B 6NR
Professional bodies (relief for subscriptions) (TA 1988 s 201)	Inland Revenue, Personal Taxation Division, Sapphire House, 550 Streetsbrook Road, Solihull, West Midlands B91 1QU (Note, the approved list of professional bodies and learned societies can be found on the Inland Revenue website.)

Application for treasury consent	*Address*
Transactions in shares or debentures (TA 1988 ss 765, 765A)	Mark Ritchie, Revenue Policy, International, Business Tax Group (Treasury Consent), Victory House, 30–34 Kingsway, London WC2B 6ES

Confirmation or pre-transaction advice	*Address*
Funding issues (TA 1988 ss 209, 703)	Dave Smith, Revenue Policy, International Business Tax Group (Advice on funding), Victory House, 30–34 Kingsway, London WC2B 6ES
Transactions in land (TA 1988 ss 35, 776)	Applications for clearance should be sent to the Inspector of Taxes who deals with the returns

[1] Where clearance is sought under any one or more of TA 1988 ss 215, 225, 707; TCGA 1992 ss 138, 139, 140B, 140D; or FA 2002 Sch 29 para 88, clearance applications may be sent in a single letter to the above London address for clearances under those sections. The letter should make clear what clearance is required. Email applications can be sent to reconstructions@gtnet.gov.uk and fax applications to 020 7438 4409. For market sensitive information, call Ray McCann on 020 7438 6585 before sending an email or fax. A reply by email should be requested if required.

Inland Revenue explanatory pamphlets

Tax Bulletin: published six times a year. Available on annual subscription or at the Revenue internet site (below): contact Mr Bryan Kearney, Room G7, New Wing, Somerset House, London WC2R 1LB (020 7438 6373).

Copies of the pamphlets listed below are obtainable from Inland Revenue Enquiry Centres, Tax Offices and Inland Revenue National Insurance Contributions offices with the exception of:

Inheritance tax: IRCT: (England and Wales) Ferrers House, PO Box 38, Castle Meadow Road, Nottingham NG2 1BB (0845 302 0900); (Scotland) Meldrum House, 15 Drumsheugh Gardens, Edinburgh EH3 7UG (0845 302 0900); (Northern Ireland) Dorchester House, 52–58 Great Victoria Street, Belfast BT2 7QL (0845 302 0900); (Stationery Orderline 0845 234 1000).

Pension Schemes: IR76, IR12 and IR12 Supplement available only from the Revenue website from 30 November 2003.

Charities: COP4, COP5 available from IR Charities, Repayments, St. John's House, Merton Road, Bootle, Merseyside L69 9BB (0151 472 6293/4); IR2004 available from IR Charities, Meldrum House, 15 Drumsheugh Gardens, Edinburgh EH5 3LU (0131 777 4040).

Digest of DT agreements is available from Inland Revenue International, Centre for Non-Residents, Fitz Roy House, PO Box 46, Nottingham NG2 1BD (0845 070 0040).

Employee share schemes: IR98, IR102 available from the Inland Revenue Visitor's Information Centre, Ground Floor, South West Wing, Bush House, Strand, London WC2B 4RD.

Shares Valuation: SV1 available as for Inheritance tax above.

Stamp duty: series available from local stamp offices, by phoning 0845 603 0135, or from (England and Wales) Birmingham Stamp Office, 5th Floor, Norfolk House, Smallbrook, Queensway, Birmingham B5 4LA; Bristol Stamp Office, 1st Floor, The Pithay, All Saints Street, Bristol BS1 2NY; London–Worthing Stamp Office, Room 35, East Block, Barrington Road, Worthing BN12 4SE; Manchester Stamp Office, Upper 5th Floor, Royal Exchange, Manchester M2 7EB; (Scotland) Edinburgh Stamp Office, Grayfield House, Spur X, 4 Bankhead Avenue, Edinburgh EH11 4AE; (Northern Ireland) Belfast Stamp Office, Ground Floor, Dorchester House, 52-58 Great Victoria Street, Belfast BT2 7QE.

Guide to corporation tax self-assessment (£15) available from Inland Revenue Library, Room 28, New Wing, Somerset House, Strand, London WC2R 1LB.

Special Compliance Office (COP8, COP9): Special Compliance Office, Angel Court, 199 Borough High Street, London SE1 1HZ (020 7234 3708).

Education Service Pack (The Red Box) (free): Helpline: 020 7401 4070, e-mail: requests@edcoms.co.uk. Education service pages are available at www.redbox.gov.uk.

Internet: Most publications are available on the internet at: www.inlandrevenue.gov.uk

Pamphlet	*Date*	*Supp*	*Title*
Catalogue	2002		Catalogue of leaflets and booklets
IR 1	2002		Extra-statutory concessions
IR 2	2003		Occupational pension schemes
IR 3	2003		Personal pension schemes
IR 4	2003		Bankruptcy proceedings in England and Wales
IR 5	2002		Winding-up proceedings in England and Wales
IR 6	1994		Double taxation relief for companies
IR 8	2002		Solicitor's Office Enforcement Section, winding-up petitions
IR 12	2001	(2001)	Practice notes on approval of occupational pension schemes
IR 14/15 (CIS)	2003		Construction industry scheme
IR 16	1997		Share acquisitions by directors and employees – explanatory notes
IR 20	1999		Residents and non-residents – liability to tax in the UK
IR 33	2000		Income tax and school leavers
IR 34	1996		Pay As You Earn
IR 37	2003		Appeals against tax (see also correction)
IR 40 (CIS)	2003		Construction industry scheme: conditions for getting a subcontractor's tax certificate
IR 41	2000		Income tax and jobseekers
IR 45	2001		What to do about tax when someone dies
IR 46	2000		Clubs, societies and voluntary associations
IR 56	1999		Employed or self-employed? A guide for tax and national insurance
IR 59	2003		Collection of student loans
IR 60	2002		Students and the Inland Revenue
IR 64	2000		Giving to charity by businesses
IR 65	2000		Giving to charity by individuals
IR 68	2002		Accrued income scheme. Taxing securities on transfer
IR 69	2002		Expenses payments and benefits in kind. How to save yourself work
IR 72	1995		Investigations: the examination of business accounts
IR 73	1994		Inland Revenue investigations: how settlements are negotiated
IR 76	2001		Personal pension schemes. Guidance notes
IR 78	2001		Looking to the future: tax reliefs to help you save for retirement
IR 87	1999		Letting and your home
IR 95	1996		Approved profit-sharing schemes – an outline for employees
IR 96	1996		Approved profit-sharing schemes – explanatory notes
IR 97	1996		Approved SAYE share option schemes – an outline for employees
IR 98	2002		Approved SAYE share option schemes – explanatory notes
IR 101	1996		Approved company share option plans – an outline for employees
IR 102	1996		Approved company share option plans – explanatory notes
IR 109	2002		Employer compliance reviews and negotiations
IR 110	2002		A guide for people with savings

Inland Revenue explanatory pamphlets — continued

Pamphlet	*Date*	*Supp*	*Title*
IR 115	2003		Income tax, national insurance contributions and childcare
IR 116 (CIS)	2003		Guide for subcontractors with tax certificates
IR 117 (CIS)	1999		Guide for subcontractors with Registration Cards
IR 121	2000		Income tax and pensioners
IR 122	2002		Volunteer drivers
IR 124	2002		Using your own vehicle for work
IR 125	2002		Using your own car or motor bike for work
IR 126	1995		Corporation tax pay and file: a general guide
IR 131	2002		Inland Revenue Statements of Practice
IR 134	2000		Income tax and national insurance contributions on relocation packages
IR 136	2001		Income tax and company vans
IR 137	2003		The Enterprise Investment Scheme
IR 138	1995		Living or retiring abroad? A guide to UK tax on your UK income and pension
IR 139	1995		Income from abroad? A guide to UK tax on overseas income
IR 140	2002		Non-resident landlords, their agents and tenants
IR 141	2001		Open government
IR 143	2000		Income tax and redundancy
IR 144	2002		Income tax and incapacity benefit
IR 145	2001		Low interest loans provided by employers
IR 148	2001		Are your workers employed or self-employed? A guide for tax and national insurance for contractors in the construction industry
IR 150	1999		Taxation of rents – a guide to property income
IR 152	2002		Trusts – an introduction
IR 153	1997		Tax exemption for sickness or unemployment insurance payments
IR 155	2001		PAYE settlement agreements
IR 156	1996		Our heritage. Your right to see tax exempt works of art
IR 160	2002		Inland Revenue enquiries under self-assessment
IR 166	2002		The euro
IR 167	2003		Charter for Inland Revenue taxpayers
IR 168	2002		How tax credit settlements are negotiated
IR 169	2002		Venture capital trusts (VCTs) – a brief guide
IR 170	1999		Blind person's allowance
IR 172	2001		Income tax and company cars
IR 173	1999		Tax credits: a summary for employers
IR 175	2001		Supplying services through a limited company or partnership
IR 176	2003		Tax, national insurance contributions and green travel
IR 177	2001		Share incentive plans and your entitlement to benefits
IR 178	2000		Giving shares and securities to charity
IR 179	2000		R & D tax credits
IR 180 (CIS)	2003		Construction Industry Scheme. A guide for non-residents
IR 303	1999		Help sheet for non-resident entertainers and sportspersons
IR 2000	2001		The corporate venturing scheme
IR 2001	2001		Trading by charities
IR 2002	2001		Share incentive plans. A guide for employees
IR 2003	2001		Supplying services. How to calculate the deemed payment
IR 2004	2001		Setting up a charity in Scotland
IR 2005	2001		Share Incentive Plans. Guidance for employers and advisers
IR 2006	2001		Enterprise Management Incentives. A guide
IR 2007	2001		Capital Allowances for flats over shops
IR 2008	2002		ISAs, PEPs and TESSAs
IR 2009	2001		Why pay cash?
IR 2010	2001		Electronic payment methods
IR 2011	2001		Paying PAYE electronically
IR 2012	2001		Paying Self Assessment electronically
IR 2013	2002		Record-keeping for self-assessment
480	2003		Expenses and benefits. A tax guide
490	2002		Employee travel. A tax and NICs guide for employers
FEU50	2000		A guide to paying foreign entertainers
DT Digest	2003		Digest of double taxation treaties
PSO3	2001		Occupational pension schemes – A guide for trustees of small self-administered schemes
CGT 1	2002		Capital gains tax – An introduction
CGT1/FS1	2002		Capital Gains Tax. A quick guide
IHT 2	2003		Inheritance tax on lifetime gifts
IHT 3	2001		Inheritance tax – an introduction
IHT 4	2001		Notes on informal calculations of inheritance tax
IHT 8	2002		Alterations to an inheritance following a death
IHT 11	2002		Payment of inheritance tax from national savings or British Government Stock
IHT 12	2002		When is an excepted estate grant appropriate?
IHT 13	2001		Inheritance tax and penalties
IHT 14	2003		The personal representatives' responsibilities
IHT 15	1996		How to calculate the liability
IHT 16	2002		Settled property
IHT 17	2002		Businesses, farms and woodlands
IHT 19	2003		Delivery of a reduced Inland Revenue account

Pamphlet	*Date*	*Supp*	*Title*
CIL	2002		Customer information leaflet
—	2000		Stamp duty. Information for customers
SO 1	2000		Stamp duty on buying a freehold house in England, Wales and Northern Ireland
SO 1 (Scotland)	2002		Stamp duty on buying land or buildings in Scotland
SO 2	2000		Stamp Office customer promise and service information
SO 3	2000		If things go wrong ... complaints and lost documents
SO 5	2002		Common stamp duty forms and how to complete them
SO 5 (Scotland)	1996		Common Scottish stamp duty forms and how to complete them
SO 6	1996		A short history of stamp duties
SO 7	2000		Stamp duty and leases
SO 7 (Scotland)	2002		Stamp duty and leases in Scotland
SO 8	2002		Stamp duty on agreements securing short tenancies
SO 10	2001		Stamp duty interest and penalties
SO 11	1997		Stamp duty and charities
SO 13	1998		Stamp Office Audit and Compliance Unit – code of practice SDRT inspections
SO 14	1998		SDRT enquiries. How settlements are negotiated
SO 99	2000		Changes to stamp duty from 1st October 1999
CIQRG			Quick reference guide to stamp duty rates
Collection 1			1995 Distraint
Collection 1 (Scotland)			1994 Summary Warrant
Collection 1 (N Ireland)			2000 Distraint
Collection 2			1994 Magistrates' Court proceedings
Collection 2 (Scotland)			1994 Sheriff Court proceedings
Collection 2 (N Ireland)			2000 Magistrates' Court proceedings
Collection 3			1995 County Court proceedings
Collection 3 (Scotland)			1994 Court of Session proceedings
Collection 3 (N Ireland)			2000 High Court proceedings
Collection 4 (Scotland)			2000 Sequestration and winding up
Collection 4 (N Ireland)			2000 Bankruptcy and winding up
COP 1	2003		Putting things right when we make mistakes
COP 3	2003		Reviews of employers' and contractors' records
COP 4	2002		Inspection of schemes operated by financial intermediaries
COP 5	1998		Inspection of charities' records
COP 6	1994		Collection of tax
COP 6 (Sco)	1995		Collection of tax
COP 7	1994		Collection of amounts due from employers and contractors in the construction industry
COP 7 (Sco)	1994		Collection of amounts due from employers and contractors in the construction industry
COP 8	2003		Special Compliance Office Investigations: cases other than suspected serious fraud
COP 9	2002		Special Compliance Office Investigations: cases of suspected serious fraud
COP 10	1999		Information and advice
COP 11	2002		Enquiries into tax returns by local tax offices
COP 14	2003		Enquiries into Company Tax Returns
COP 17	1999		Enquiries into applications for WFTC or DPTC
COP 19	2000		National minimum wage. Information for employers. Enquiries by the Inland Revenue
COP 20	2000		National minimum wage. Information for workers. How the Inland Revenue handles workers' complaints
COP 22	2001		Orders for the delivery of documents
COP-AT	2003		Anti-terrorism, Crime and Security Act: disclosure of information
—	1999		Code of practice on consultation
AO1	2001		How to complain about the Inland Revenue and the Valuation Office Agency
CTSA/BK3	2000		A modern system for corporation tax payments
CTSA/BK4	2000		A general guide to corporation tax self-assessment
CSS1	2002		Customer service standards
CSS/TCO	2000		Inland Revenue Tax Credit Office
CSS/TCO(NI)	2001		Inland Revenue Northern Ireland (Tax Credits)
WFTC/BK1	2003		Your guide to working families' tax credit
DPTC/BK1	2003		Your guide to disabled person's tax credit
CTC/BK1	2002		Help with the cost of childcare
CTCR/1	2000	(2002)	Children's tax credit
WFTC/FS1	2003		Factsheet – working families' tax credit
DPTC/FS1	2003		Factsheet – disabled person's tax credit
CTC/FS1	2001		Factsheet – working families' tax credit, disabled person's tax credit and childcare
WFTC/FF/FS1	2003		Factsheet – working families' tax credit: a guide for farming families
TC/FS1	2001		New help with a new child. Working families' tax credit and disabled person's tax credit
DPTC/FS2	2002		Staying in work. Help for employed and self-employed people with an illness or disability

Inland Revenue explanatory pamphlets — continued

Pamphlet	*Date*	*Supp*	*Title*
WFTC/AP	1999		Appeals against tax credit decisions
WFTC/APNI	1999		Appeals against tax credit decisions (Northern Ireland)
E6	2002		An employer's guide to tax credits
WTC1	2002		Child tax credit and working tax credit – an introduction
WTC2	2003		Child tax credit and working tax credit – a guide
WTC5	2003		Child tax credit and working tax credit: help with the costs of childcare
WTC6	2003		Child tax credit and working tax credit – other types of help you might be able to get
WTC/AP	2003		Child tax credit and working tax credit: how to appeal against a tax credit decision or award
WTC/E6	2003		Working tax credit paid with wages
SA/BK3	2002		Self-assessment – a guide to keeping records for the self-employed
SA/BK4	2003		Self-assessment – a general guide to keeping records
SA/BK6	2003		Self-assessment – penalties for late tax returns
SA/BK7	2003		Self-assessment – surcharges for late payment of tax
SA/BK8	2002		Self-assessment – your guide
SAT 1	1995		Self-assessment: the new current year basis of assessment
SAT 2	1995		Self-assessment: the legal framework
SV 1	2001		Shares Valuation Division. An introduction
NE 1	1999		First steps as a new employer
NE 3	2001		New and small employers – Support with your payroll
P/SE/1	2001		Thinking of working for yourself?
P/TXB/1	2000		Tax back – Are you paying too much tax on your savings?
CWL 2	2003		NI contributions for self-employed people. Class 2 and Class 4
CWL4	2001		Fund-raising events: exemption for charities and other qualifying bodies
CWL5	2002		The Voluntary Arrangements Service
CWG 2	2003		Employer's further guide to PAYE and NICs
—	2002		Red Box Education pack

National Insurance Contributions Leaflets see p 88.

Internal guidance booklets and manuals:

Accounts Office Interest Review Unit (AORU) Manual
Advanced Instruction Manual
Applicant Compliance Guide
Assessed Taxes
Assessment Procedures Manual
Banking Manual
Capital Allowances Manual
Capital Gains Manual
Collection Manual
Collection of Student Loans
Company Taxation Manual
Construction Industry Scheme
Corporate Finance Manual
Corporate Intangibles Research and Development (CIRD) Manual
COTAX Manual
Creditors' Voluntary Liquidation Manual
Debt Management Manual
Decision Maker's Guide (DMG)
Departmental Project Management Methodology Manual
Departmental Security Manual
Double Taxation Relief Manual
Employee Share Schemes Unit Manual
Employer Compliance Handbook
Employers Section Manual
Employment Procedures Manual
Employment Status Manual
Enforcement Manual
Enforcement Manual (Scotland)
Enquiry Manual
European Economic Interest Groupings
Finance Leasing Manual
General Examination Manual
General Insurance Manual
Independent Taxation Manual
Inheritance Tax Double Taxation Conventions and Agreements Manual
Insolvency Manual
Inspector's Manual
International Tax Handbook
Life Assurance Manual
Lloyd's Manual
Manufactured Overseas Dividends Guidance Manual
Movements Manual (PAYE)
National Audit Group Instructions
National Insurance Manual
Oil Taxation Manual
PAYE Instructions (Collection)
PAYE Settlement Agreement Handbook
Pension Schemes Office Manual
PEP and ISA Manual
Personal Contact Manual
Profit Related Pay Unit Manual
Property Income Manual
PSA Handbook
Purchasing Manual
Receivables Telephone Centre Manual
Recovery and Enforcement Process Extensions Guidance Manual
Recovery Manual
Redress Handbook
Relief Instructions
Repayment Claims Manual
Residence Guide
SE Manual
Self Assessment Manual
Share Schemes Manual
Shares Valuation Division
Shares Valuation Manual
Stamp Office Manual
Tax Credits Office Manual
Tax Credits Technical Manual
Tonnage Tax Manual
Trusts, Settlements and Estates Manual
Venture Capital Schemes Manual

Copies of the manuals are available online and on CD-rom, with an updating service, as part of a database, from LexisNexis UK, 2 Addiscombe Road, Croydon, Surrey CR9 5AF: telephone 020 8662 2000; fax 020 8662 2012. Extracts published in looseleaf format as *Simon's Direct Tax Service,* Binders 12 and 13: prices available on application to the publishers.

All internal guidance manuals are available for inspection free of charge in Inland Revenue Tax Enquiry Centres and on the Revenue internet site. The inheritance tax manuals may be inspected free of charge at certain Capital Taxes Offices.

Capital gains tax

Annual exemption

Individuals, personal representatives[1] and certain trusts[2]

Exempt amount of net gains	1998–99	1999–2000	2000–01	2001–02	2002–03	2003–04
	£6,800	£7,100	£7,200	£7,500	£7,700	£7,900

[1] Year of death and following 2 years (maximum).
[2] Trusts for mentally disabled persons and those in receipt of attendance allowance or disability living allowance. Exemption divided by number of qualifying settlements created (after 9 March 1981) by one settlor, subject to a minimum of one-tenth.

Trusts[1] generally

Exempt amount of net gains	1998–99	1999–2000	2000–01	2001–02	2002–03	2003–04
	£3,400	£3,550	£3,600	£3,750	£3,850	£3,950

[1] Exemption divided by number of qualifying settlements created (after 6 June 1978) by one settlor, subject to a minimum of one-fifth.

Chattel exemption

	Disposals exemption	*Marginal relief: Maximum chargeable gain*
1989-90 to 2002–03	£6,000	5/3 excess over £6,000

Rate of tax

2000–01 to 2003–04	**Individuals:** gains taxed as top slice of income: 10% to starting rate limit, 20% to basic rate limit, 40% above, subject to taper relief in certain cases. **Trusts, personal representatives:** 34%, subject to taper relief in certain cases
1999–2000	**Individuals:** gains taxed as top slice of income: 20% to basic rate limit, 40% above, subject to taper relief in certain cases. **Trusts, personal representatives:** 34%, subject to taper relief in certain cases.
1998–99	**Individuals:** gains taxed at income tax rates (as top slice of income[1]), subject to taper relief in certain cases. **Trusts, personal representatives:** 34%, subject to tapering in certain cases.
1997–98	**Individuals:** gains taxed at income tax rates (as top slice of income[1]) **Trusts, personal representatives:** 23% (34% for trusts charged to rate applicable to trusts)
1996–97	**Individuals:** gains taxed at income tax rates (as top slice of income[1]) **Trusts, personal representatives:** 24% (34% for trusts charged to rate applicable to trusts)

[1] Adjustment is necessary for savings income (including interest from banks and building societies, interest distributions from authorised unit trusts, interest from gilts and other securities including corporate bonds, purchased life annuities, and discounts). Adjustment is also necessary for dividends or other qualifying distributions from a UK-resident company.

Retirement relief (phased out from 6 April 1999)

Retirement relief is no longer available for disposals after 5 April 2003.

Disposals after	*Minimum age*	*100% relief on gains up to*	*50% relief on gains between*	*Maximum relief*
5 April 2002	50	£50,000	£50,000.01–£200,000	£125,000
5 April 2001	50	£100,000	£100,000.01–£400,000	£250,000
5 April 2000	50	£150,000	£150,000.01–£600,000	£375,000
5 April 1999	50	£200,000	£200,000.01–£800,000	£500,000
27 November 1995	50	£250,000	£250,000.01–£1,000,000	£625,000

(% determined by qualifying period. Relief also available where early retirement occurs for reasons of ill-health. Relief given after indexation allowance but before tapering relief.)

Indexation allowance

(TCGA 1992 ss 53–57, 109)

For gains on disposals by individuals, trustees and personal representatives, an indexation allowance is given up to April 1998 and taper relief applies thereafter on disposals made after 5 April 1998 (see below). Indexation allowance is deducted before applying taper relief. The indexation allowance is calculated by multiplying each item of allowable expenditure by:

$$\frac{RD - RI}{RI}$$

where RD = Retail prices index figure for month of disposal
RI = Retail prices index for month of expenditure (or March 1982 if later)

See pages 43–51 for indexation allowances and page 52 for RPI values.

For disposals after 31 March 1998 of assets acquired on or before that date the factors below can be used to calculate the indexation allowance available to April 1998 for acquisitions in the month shown.

	Jan	Feb	Mar	Apr	May	Jun	Jul	Aug	Sep	Oct	Nov	Dec
1982	–	–	1·047	1·006	0·992	0·987	0·986	0·985	0·987	0·977	0·967	0·971
1983	0·968	0·960	0·956	0·929	0·921	0·917	0·906	0·898	0·889	0·883	0·876	0·871
1984	0·872	0·865	0·859	0·834	0·828	0·823	0·825	0·808	0·804	0·793	0·788	0·789
1985	0·783	0·769	0·752	0·716	0·708	0·704	0·707	0·703	0·704	0·701	0·695	0·693
1986	0·689	0·683	0·681	0·665	0·662	0·663	0·667	0·662	0·654	0·652	0·638	0·632
1987	0·626	0·620	0·616	0·597	0·596	0·596	0·597	0·593	0·588	0·580	0·573	0·574
1988	0·574	0·568	0·562	0·537	0·531	0·525	0·524	0·507	0·500	0·485	0·478	0·474
1989	0·465	0·454	0·448	0·423	0·414	0·409	0·408	0·404	0·395	0·384	0·372	0·369
1990	0·361	0·353	0·339	0·300	0·288	0·283	0·282	0·269	0·258	0·248	0·251	0·252
1991	0·249	0·242	0·237	0·222	0·218	0·213	0·215	0·213	0·208	0·204	0·199	0·198
1992	0·199	0·193	0·189	0·171	0·167	0·167	0·171	0·171	0·166	0·162	0·164	0·168
1993	0·179	0·171	0·167	0·156	0·152	0·153	0·156	0·151	0·146	0·147	0·148	0·146
1994	0·151	0·144	0·141	0·128	0·124	0·124	0·129	0·124	0·121	0·120	0·119	0·114
1995	0·114	0·107	0·102	0·091	0·087	0·085	0·091	0·085	0·080	0·085	0·085	0·079
1996	0·083	0·078	0·073	0·066	0·063	0·063	0·067	0·062	0·057	0·057	0·057	0·053
1997	0·053	0·049	0·046	0·040	0·036	0·032	0·032	0·026	0·021	0·019	0·019	0·016
1998	0·019	0·014	0·011	–	–	–	–	–	–	–	–	–

For disposals after 30 November 1993, indexation allowance cannot be used to create or increase a capital loss.

Taper relief

(TCGA 1992 s 2A, Sch A1; FA 2000 ss 66, 67; FA 2002 ss 46, 47, Sch 10; FA 2003 s 160)

Taper relief is available for disposals made after 5 April 1998. The chargeable gain is reduced according to the length of time for which the asset has been held (counting from 6 April 1998). Non-business assets acquired before 17 March 1998 and business assets acquired before 17 March 1998 and disposed of before 6 April 2000 qualify for an addition of one year to the period for which they are held after 5 April 1998. There is no one-year addition for disposals of business assets after 5 April 2000.

There are specific rules to distinguish between business and non-business assets. Taper relief applies to gains after all deductions and before the annual exemption. Losses are set against pre-tapered gains in the most beneficial way possible.

Business assets			
Number of complete yrs after 5.4.98 for which asset held	*% of gain chargeable*	*Equivalent tax rates: Higher rate taxp'r*	*Equivalent tax rates: 20% rate taxp'r*
Disposals after 5 April 2002			
0	100	40	20
1	50	20	10
2 or more	25	10	5
Disposals after 5 April 2000 and before 6 April 2002			
0	100	40	20
1	87·5	35	17·5
2	75	30	15
3	50	20	10
4 or more	25	10	5
Disposals before 6 April 2000			
0	100	40	20
1	92·5	37	18·5
2	85	34	17·0
3	77·5	31	15·5

Non-business assets			
Number of complete yrs after 5.4.98 for which asset held	*% of gain chargeable*	*Equivalent tax rates: Higher rate taxp'r*	*Equivalent tax rates: 20% rate taxp'r*
0	100	40	20
1	100	40	20
2	100	40	20
3	95	38	19
4	90	36	18
5	85	34	17
6	80	32	16
7	75	30	15
8	70	28	14
9	65	26	13
10 or more	60	24	12

Leases

Depreciation table (TCGA 1992 Sch 8 para 1)

Yrs	%	Yrs	%	Yrs	%
50 (or more)	100	33	90·280	16	64·116
49	99·657	32	89·354	15	61·617
48	99·289	31	88·371	14	58·971
47	98·902	30	87·330	13	56·167
46	98·490	29	86·226	12	53·191
45	98·059	28	85·053	11	50·038
44	97·595	27	83·816	10	46.695
43	97·107	26	82·496	9	43·154
42	96·593	25	81·100	8	39·399
41	96·041	24	79·622	7	35·414
40	95·457	23	78·055	6	31·195
39	94·842	22	76·399	5	26·722
38	94·189	21	74·635	4	21·983
37	93·497	20	72·770	3	16·959
36	92·761	19	70·791	2	11·629
35	91·981	18	68·697	1	5·983
34	91·156	17	66·470	0	0

Formula: fraction of expenditure disallowed—

$$\frac{\left.\begin{array}{l}\text{Percentage for duration of lease}\\ \text{at acquisition or expenditure}\end{array}\right\} \quad \textit{minus} \quad \left\{\begin{array}{l}\text{Percentage for duration of}\\ \text{lease at disposal}\end{array}\right.}{\text{Percentage for duration of lease at acquisition or expenditure}}$$

Fractions of years:
Add one-twelfth of the difference between the percentage for the whole year and the next higher percentage for each additional month. Odd days under 14 are not counted; 14 odd days or more count as a month.

Short leases: premiums treated as rent (TA 1988 s 34, TCGA 1992 Sch 8 para 5)
Part of premium for grant of a short lease which is chargeable to income tax under Schedule A—

P – (2% x (n – 1) x P)

Where P = amount of premium
n = number of complete years which lease has to run when granted

Length of Lease (complete years)	*Amount chargeable to CGT %*	*Income tax Sch A %*	*Length of Lease (complete years)*	*Amount chargeable to CGT %*	*Income tax Sch A %*	*Length of Lease (complete years)*	*Amount chargeable to CGT %*	*Income tax Sch A %*
Over 50	100	0	34	66	34	17	32	68
50	98	2	33	64	36	16	30	70
49	96	4	32	62	38	15	28	72
48	94	6	31	60	40	14	26	74
47	92	8	30	58	42	13	24	76
46	90	10	29	56	44	12	22	78
45	88	12	28	54	46	11	20	80
44	86	14	27	52	48	10	18	82
43	84	16	26	50	50	9	16	84
42	82	18	25	48	52	8	14	86
41	80	20	24	46	54	7	12	88
40	78	22	23	44	56	6	10	90
39	76	24	22	42	58	5	8	92
38	74	26	21	40	60	4	6	94
37	72	28	20	38	62	3	4	96
36	70	30	19	36	64	2	2	98
35	68	32	18	34	66	1 or less	0	100

Gilt-edged securities exempt from tax on chargeable gains

The following securities have been specified for the purposes of TCGA 1992 Sch 9 and are exempt from capital gains tax. A similar exemption exists for qualifying corporate bonds issued after 13 March 1984. A 1-year qualifying limit applied to disposals before 2 July 1986. The gain accruing on the disposal of an option or contract to acquire or dispose of gilt-edged securities or qualifying corporate bonds after 1 July 1986 is also exempt from capital gains tax. (Securities redeemed before 1 September 2003 do not appear on this list.)

Readers should note that under the loan relationship provisions of FA 1996 Part IV Chapter II, the definition of 'qualifying corporate bond' for the purposes of corporation tax only has been extended (see TCGA 1992 ss 117, 117A, 117B).

Stocks		*Redemption dates*	*Dividend due dates*	
10%	Treasury Stock 2003	8 September 2003	8 March	8 September
6½%	Treasury Stock 2003	7 December 2003	7 June	7 December
10%	Treasury Stock 2004[R]	18 May 2004	18 May	18 November
4⅜%	Index-Linked Treasury Stock 2004	21 October 2004	21 April	21 October
9½%	Conversion Stock 2004[R]	25 October 2004	25 April	25 October
6¾%	Treasury Stock 2004	26 November 2004	26 May	26 November
5%	Treasury Loan 2004	7 June 2004	7 June	7 December
9½%	Conversion Stock 2005	18 April 2005	18 April	18 October
10½%	Exchequer Stock 2005[R]	20 September 2005	20 March	20 September
12½%	Treasury Stock 2003-05*[R]	21 November 2003/ 21 November 2005	21 May	21 November
8½%	Treasury Stock 2005	7 December 2005	7 June	7 December
2%	Index-Linked Treasury Stock 2006	19 July 2006	19 January	19 July
7¾%	Treasury Stock 2006	8 September 2006	8 March	8 September
9¾%	Conversion Stock 2006[R]	15 November 2006	15 May	15 November
7½%	Treasury Stock 2006	7 December 2006	7 June	7 December
7¼%	Treasury Stock 2007	7 June 2007	7 June	7 December
8½%	Treasury Loan 2007	16 July 2007	16 January	16 July
13½%	Treasury Stock 2004-08*[R]	26 March 2004/26 March 2008	26 March	26 September
9%	Treasury Loan 2008[R]	13 October 2008	13 April	13 October
5%	Treasury Stock 2008	7 March 2008	7 March	7 September
2½%	Index-Linked Treasury Stock 2009	20 May 2009	20 May	20 November
4%	Treasury Stock 2009	7 May 2009	7 March	7 September
8%	Treasury Stock 2009[R]	25 September 2009	25 March	25 September
5¾%	Treasury Stock 2009	7 December 2009	7 June	7 December
6¼%	Treasury Stock 2010	25 November 2010	25 May	25 November
9%	Conversion Loan 2011	12 July 2011	12 January	12 July
2½%	Index-Linked Treasury Stock 2011	23 August 2011	23 February	23 August
5%	Treasury Stock 2012	7 March 2012	7 March	7 September
9%	Treasury Stock 2012[R]	6 August 2012	6 February	6 August
5½%	Treasury Stock 2008-12*	10 September 2008/ 10 September 2012	10 March	10 September
2½%	Index-Linked Treasury Stock 2013	16 August 2013	16 February	16 August
8%	Treasury Stock 2013	27 September 2013	27 March	27 September
5%	Treasury Stock 2014	7 September 2014	7 March	7 September
7¾%	Treasury Loan 2012-15*	26 January 2012/26 January 2015	26 January	26 July
8%	Treasury Stock 2015	7 December 2015	7 June	7 December
2½%	Index-Linked Treasury Stock 2016	26 July 2016	26 January	26 July
8¾%	Treasury Stock 2017	25 August 2017	25 February	25 August
12%	Exchequer Stock 2013-17*[R]	12 December 2013/ 12 December 2017	12 June	12 December
2½%	Index-Linked Treasury Stock 2020	16 April 2020	16 April	16 October
8%	Treasury Stock 2021	7 June 2021	7 June	7 December
2½%	Index-Linked Treasury Stock 2024	17 July 2024	17 January	17 July
5%	Treasury Stock 2025	7 March 2025	7 March	7 September
6%	Treasury Stock 2028	7 December 2028	7 June	7 December
4⅛%	Index-Linked Treasury Stock 2030	22 July 2030	22 January	22 July
4¼%	Treasury Stock 2032	7 June 2032	7 June	7 December
2%	Index-Linked Treasury Stock 2035	26 January 2035	26 January	26 July
4¼%	Treasury Stock 2036	7 March 2036	7 March	7 September
4%	Consolidated Loan[R]	1 February 1957 or after	1 February	1 August
3½%	War Loan	1 December 1952 or after	1 June	1 December
3½%	Conversion Loan[R]	1 April 1961 or after	1 April	1 October
3%	Treasury Stock[R]	5 April 1966 or after	5 April	5 October
2½%	Consolidated Stock[R]	5 April 1923 or after	5 January 5 July	5 April, 5 October
2½%	Treasury Stock 1975 or after	1 April 1975 or after	1 April	1 October
2½%	Annuities[R]	5 January 1905 or after	5 January 5 July	5 April, 5 October
2¾%	Annuities[R]	5 January 1905 or after	5 January 5 July	5 April, 5 October

* Repaid at latest date shown unless the Treasury give notice of earlier repayment.
[R] Rump stocks (restricted market due to small number of stocks still in issue).

Reliefs

The following is a summary of the main reliefs and exemptions for the year 2003–04. The legislation should be referred to for conditions and exceptions.

Charities

Gains accruing to charities which are both applicable and applied for charitable purposes – extended from 6 April 2002 to donations to Community Amateur Sports Clubs (CASCs)	Exempt

Individuals

Annual exemption (see p 37 for earlier years)	£7,900
Chattel exemption (see p 37 for marginal relief)	£6,000
Compensation (injury to person, profession or vocation)	Exempt
Decorations for valour (acquired otherwise than for money or money's worth)	Gain exempt
Enterprise Investment Scheme (see p 67)	Gain on disposal after relevant three year period exempt to extent full relief given on shares
Foreign currency acquired for personal expenditure	Gain exempt
Gifts for public benefit, works of art, historic buildings etc	No chargeable gain/allowable loss
Gilt-edged stock (see p 40)	No chargeable gain/allowable loss
Married persons living together	No chargeable gain/allowable loss on disposals from one to the other
Motor vehicles	Gain exempt
Principal private residence	Gain exempt
If residence is partly let, exemption for the let part is limited to the smaller of—	(1) exemption on owner-occupied part and (2) £40,000
Qualifying corporate bonds	No chargeable gain (for loans made before 17 March 1998, allowable loss in certain cases if all or part of loss is irrecoverable)
Retirement relief (phased-out over 5 years beginning in 1999–2000: see p 37)	No relief in 2003–04
Hold-over relief for gifts	Restricted to: (1) gifts of business assets (including unquoted shares in trading companies and holding companies of trading groups). Relief is not available on the transfer of shares or securities to a company made after 8 November 1999: FA 2000 s 90 (2) gifts of heritage property (3) gifts to heritage maintenance funds (4) gifts to political parties, and (5) gifts which are chargeable transfers for inheritance tax. Where available, transferee's acquisition cost treated as reduced by held-over gain.
Venture capital trusts (see p 68)	Gain on disposal of shares by original investor exempt if company still a venture capital trust. Exemption applies only to shares acquired up to the permitted maximum of £100,000 per year of assessment.

Reliefs — continued

Businesses

Roll-over relief for replacement of business assets

Qualifying assets:

Buildings and land both occupied and used for the purposes of the trade
Fixed plant and machinery
Ships, aircraft and hovercraft
Satellites, space stations and spacecraft
Goodwill*
Milk and potato quotas*
Ewe and suckler cow premium quotas*
Fish quotas (from 29 March 1999)*
UK oil licences (from 1 July 1999)

The 'replacement' assets must be acquired within 12 months before or 3 years after the disposal of the old asset. Both assets must be within any of the above classes. Holdover relief is available where the new asset is a depreciating asset (having a predictable useful life not exceeding 60 years).

*From 1 April 2002, subject to transitional rules, these items are removed from the list for companies only (as they fall within the intangible assets regime from that date (FA 2002 Sch 29 para 132(5))).

Personal representatives

Annual exemption

Year of death and following 2 years: (See p 37 for earlier years)	£7,900

Allowable expenses

Expenses allowable for the costs of establishing title in computing chargeable gains on disposal of assets in a deceased person's estate: deaths occurring after 5 April 1993 (SP 8/94). (The Revenue accepts computations based either on the scale or on the actual allowable expenditure incurred.)

Gross value of estate	*Allowable expenditure*
Up to £40,000	1.75% of the probate value of the assets sold by the personal representatives
Between £40,001 and £70,000	£700, to be divided between all the assets of the estate in proportion to the probate values and allowed in those proportions on assets sold by the personal representatives
Between £70,001 and £300,000	1% of the probate value of the assets sold
Between £300,001 and £400,000	£3,000, to be divided between all the assets of the estate in proportion to the probate values and allowed in those proportions on assets sold by the personal representatives
Between £400,001 and £750,000	0.75% of the probate value of the assets sold
Exceeding £750,000	Negotiable according to the facts of the particular case

Trustees

Annual exemption see p 37.

Allowable expenses

Expenses allowable in computing chargeable gains of corporate trustees in the administration of trusts and estates: acquisition, disposals and deemed disposals after 5 April 1993 (SP 8/94). (The Revenue accepts computations based either on the scale or on the actual allowable expenditure incurred.)

Transfers of assets to beneficiaries etc	
(a) Quoted stocks and shares	
(i) One beneficiary	£20 per holding
(ii) More than one beneficiary	£20 per holding, divided equally between the beneficiaries
(b) Unquoted shares	As (a) above, plus any exceptional expenditure
(c) Other assets	As (a) above, plus any exceptional expenditure
Actual disposals and acquisitions	
(a) Quoted stocks and shares	Investment fee as charged by the trustee (where a comprehensive annual management fee is charged, the investment fee is taken to be £0.25 per £100 of the sale or purchase moneys)
(b) Unquoted shares	As (a) above, plus actual valuation costs
(c) Other assets	Investment fee (as (a) above), subject to a maximum of £60, plus actual valuation costs
Deemed disposals by trustees	
(a) Quoted stocks and shares	£6 per holding
(b) Unquoted shares	Actual valuation costs
(c) Other assets	Actual valuation costs

Indexation allowance

For corporation tax purposes, an indexation allowance is given as a deduction in calculating gains on disposals from the amount realised (or deemed to be realised) on disposal. The indexation allowance is calculated by multiplying each item of allowable expenditure by:

$$\frac{RD - RI}{RI}$$

where RD = Retail prices index figure for month of disposal
RI = Retail prices index for month of expenditure (or March 1982 if later)

See page 38 for indexation allowances up to April 1998 and taper relief which applies thereafter on disposals made after 5 April 1998 by individuals, trustees and personal representatives. See page 52 for RPI values.

The factors below can be used to calculate the indexation allowance—

Month of disposal

Base Month	1998						1999												2000											
1982	July	Aug	Sept	Oct	Nov	Dec	Jan	Feb	Mar	Apr	May	June	July	Aug	Sept	Oct	Nov	Dec	Jan	Feb	Mar	Apr	May	June	July	Aug	Sept	Oct	Nov	Dec
Mar	1·052	1·061	1·069	1·071	1·069	1·069	1·057	1·061	1·066	1·079	1·085	1·085	1·078	1·083	1·092	1·096	1·098	1·106	1·097	1·108	1·120	1·141	1·149	1·154	1·146	1·146	1·161	1·160	1·166	1·168
Apr	1·011	1·020	1·029	1·030	1·106	1·111	1·104	1·104	1·119	1·117	1·124	1·125	1·111	1·122	1·125	1·136	1·057	1·064	1·056	1·067	1·078	1·099	1·106	1·111	1·104	1·104	1·119	1·117	1·124	1·125
May	·997	1·006	1·014	1·015	1·014	1·014	1·002	1·006	1·010	1·024	1·029	1·029	1·023	1·028	1·036	1·040	1·042	1·050	1·041	1·052	1·063	1·084	1·091	1·096	1·089	1·089	1·104	1·102	1·108	1·110
June	·991	1·000	1·009	1·010	1·009	1·009	·996	1·000	1·005	1·018	1·023	1·023	1·017	1·022	1·031	1·034	1·037	1·044	1·035	1·046	1·057	1·078	1·086	1·090	1·083	1·083	1·098	1·097	1·103	1·104
July	·991	·999	1·008	1·009	1·008	1·008	·996	·999	1·004	1·018	1·023	1·023	1·016	1·021	1·030	1·034	1·036	1·043	1·035	1·046	1·057	1·078	1·085	1·090	1·082	1·082	1·097	1·096	1·102	1·103
Aug	·990	·999	1·007	1·009	1·007	1·007	·995	·999	1·004	1·017	1·022	1·022	1·016	1·021	1·029	1·033	1·035	1·043	1·034	1·045	1·056	1·077	1·084	1·089	1·082	1·082	1·096	1·095	1·101	1·103
Sept	·991	1·000	1·009	1·010	1·009	1·009	·996	1·000	1·005	1·018	1·023	1·023	1·017	1·022	1·031	1·034	1·037	1·044	1·035	1·046	1·057	1·078	1·086	1·090	1·083	1·083	1·098	1·097	1·103	1·104
Oct	·982	·990	·999	1·000	·999	·999	·986	·990	·995	1·008	1·013	1·013	1·007	1·012	1·021	1·024	1·027	1·034	1·025	1·036	1·047	1·068	1·075	1·080	1·073	1·073	1·087	1·086	1·092	1·093
Nov	·972	·980	·989	·990	·989	·989	·977	·980	·985	·999	1·003	1·003	·997	1·002	1·011	1·014	1·017	1·024	1·015	1·026	1·037	1·058	1·065	1·070	1·063	1·063	1·077	1·076	1·082	1·083
Dec	·976	·984	·992	·994	·992	·992	·980	·984	·989	1·002	1·007	1·007	1·001	1·006	1·014	1·018	1·020	1·028	1·019	1·030	1·041	1·062	1·069	1·074	1·066	1·066	1·081	1·080	1·086	1·087
1983																														
Jan	·973	·982	·990	·991	·990	·990	·978	·982	·986	1·000	1·005	1·005	·999	1·003	1·012	1·015	1·018	1·025	1·017	1·028	1·038	1·059	1·066	1·071	1·064	1·064	1·078	1·077	1·083	1·084
Feb	·965	·973	·982	·983	·982	·982	·969	·973	·978	·991	·996	·996	·990	·995	1·003	1·007	1·009	1·016	1·008	1·019	1·030	1·050	1·057	1·062	1·055	1·055	1·070	1·068	1·074	1·076
Mar	·961	·969	·978	·979	·978	·978	·966	·969	·974	·988	·992	·992	·986	·991	1·000	1·003	1·006	1·013	1·004	1·015	1·026	1·046	1·054	1·059	1·051	1·051	1·066	1·065	1·071	1·072
Apr	·934	·942	·951	·952	·951	·951	·939	·942	·947	·960	·965	·965	·959	·964	·972	·975	·978	·985	·977	·987	·998	1·018	1·025	1·030	1·023	1·023	1·037	1·036	1·042	1·043
May	·926	·934	·942	·944	·942	·942	·931	·934	·939	·952	·957	·957	·951	·955	·964	·967	·970	·977	·968	·979	·990	1·010	1·017	1·022	1·014	1·014	1·029	1·027	1·033	1·035
June	·921	·929	·938	·939	·938	·938	·926	·929	·934	·947	·952	·952	·946	·951	·959	·962	·965	·972	·964	·974	·985	1·005	1·012	1·017	1·010	1·010	1·024	1·023	1·028	1·030
July	·911	·919	·927	·929	·927	·927	·916	·919	·924	·937	·941	·941	·936	·940	·948	·952	·954	·961	·953	·964	·974	·994	1·001	1·006	·999	·999	1·013	1·012	1·018	1·019
Aug	·902	·911	·919	·920	·919	·919	·907	·911	·915	·928	·933	·933	·927	·932	·940	·943	·946	·953	·944	·955	·965	·985	·992	·997	·990	·990	1·004	1·003	1·009	1·010
Sept	·894	·902	·910	·911	·910	·910	·899	·902	·907	·920	·924	·924	·918	·923	·931	·935	·937	·944	·936	·946	·957	·977	·984	·988	·981	·981	·995	·994	1·000	1·001
Oct	·887	·895	·904	·905	·904	·904	·892	·895	·900	·913	·917	·917	·912	·916	·924	·928	·930	·937	·929	·939	·950	·970	·977	·981	·974	·974	·988	·987	·993	·994
Nov	·881	·889	·897	·898	·897	·897	·885	·889	·893	·906	·911	·911	·905	·910	·918	·921	·923	·930	·922	·933	·943	·963	·970	·974	·967	·967	·981	·980	·986	·987
Dec	·876	·884	·892	·893	·892	·892	·880	·884	·888	·901	·906	·906	·900	·905	·913	·916	·918	·925	·917	·928	·938	·958	·964	·969	·962	·962	·976	·975	·981	·982
1984																														
Jan	·877	·885	·893	·894	·893	·893	·882	·885	·890	·902	·907	·907	·901	·906	·914	·917	·920	·926	·918	·929	·939	·959	·966	·970	·963	·963	·977	·976	·982	·983
Feb	·869	·877	·885	·886	·885	·885	·874	·877	·882	·895	·899	·899	·893	·898	·906	·909	·912	·919	·911	·921	·931	·951	·958	·962	·955	·955	·969	·968	·974	·975
Mar	·863	·871	·879	·880	·879	·879	·868	·871	·876	·888	·893	·893	·887	·892	·900	·903	·906	·912	·904	·915	·925	·944	·951	·956	·949	·949	·963	·962	·967	·968
Apr	·839	·847	·855	·856	·855	·855	·843	·847	·851	·864	·868	·868	·863	·867	·875	·878	·881	·887	·879	·890	·900	·919	·926	·930	·923	·923	·937	·936	·941	·943
May	·832	·840	·848	·849	·848	·848	·837	·840	·844	·857	·861	·861	·856	·860	·868	·871	·874	·880	·872	·883	·893	·912	·919	·923	·916	·916	·930	·929	·934	·935
June	·827	·835	·843	·844	·843	·843	·832	·835	·840	·852	·856	·856	·851	·855	·863	·867	·869	·876	·868	·878	·888	·907	·914	·918	·911	·911	·925	·924	·929	·930
July	·829	·837	·845	·846	·845	·845	·834	·837	·842	·854	·859	·859	·853	·857	·865	·869	·871	·878	·870	·880	·890	·909	·916	·920	·914	·914	·927	·926	·932	·933
Aug	·812	·820	·828	·829	·828	·828	·817	·820	·825	·837	·841	·841	·836	·840	·848	·851	·854	·860	·852	·862	·872	·891	·898	·902	·896	·896	·909	·908	·914	·915
Sept	·809	·817	·824	·825	·824	·824	·813	·817	·821	·833	·838	·838	·832	·837	·844	·848	·850	·857	·849	·859	·869	·888	·894	·899	·892	·892	·905	·904	·910	·911
Oct	·798	·805	·813	·814	·813	·813	·802	·805	·810	·822	·826	·826	·821	·825	·833	·836	·839	·845	·837	·847	·857	·876	·883	·887	·880	·880	·894	·893	·898	·899
Nov	·792	·800	·808	·809	·808	·808	·797	·800	·804	·816	·821	·821	·815	·820	·827	·831	·833	·839	·832	·842	·852	·870	·877	·881	·875	·875	·888	·887	·892	·893
Dec	·794	·801	·809	·810	·809	·809	·798	·801	·806	·818	·822	·822	·817	·821	·829	·832	·834	·841	·833	·843	·853	·872	·878	·883	·876	·876	·889	·888	·894	·895
1985																														
Jan	·787	·795	·803	·804	·803	·803	·792	·795	·799	·811	·816	·816	·810	·815	·822	·826	·828	·834	·827	·837	·846	·865	·872	·876	·869	·869	·883	·881	·887	·888
Feb	·773	·781	·788	·789	·788	·788	·777	·781	·785	·797	·801	·801	·796	·800	·808	·811	·813	·820	·812	·822	·832	·850	·857	·861	·854	·854	·868	·866	·872	·873
Mar	·756	·764	·772	·773	·772	·772	·761	·764	·768	·780	·784	·784	·779	·783	·791	·794	·796	·803	·795	·805	·815	·833	·839	·844	·837	·837	·850	·849	·855	·856
Apr	·720	·727	·735	·736	·735	·735	·724	·727	·731	·743	·747	·747	·742	·746	·754	·757	·759	·765	·758	·767	·777	·795	·801	·805	·799	·799	·812	·811	·816	·817
May	·712	·719	·727	·728	·727	·727	·716	·719	·724	·735	·739	·739	·734	·738	·746	·749	·751	·757	·750	·759	·769	·787	·793	·797	·791	·791	·803	·802	·808	·809
June	·708	·716	·723	·724	·723	·723	·713	·716	·720	·731	·736	·736	·730	·735	·742	·745	·747	·753	·746	·756	·765	·783	·789	·793	·787	·787	·800	·799	·804	·805
July	·712	·719	·726	·727	·726	·726	·716	·719	·723	·735	·739	·739	·734	·738	·745	·748	·750	·757	·749	·759	·768	·786	·792	·797	·790	·790	·803	·802	·807	·808
Aug	·707	·714	·722	·723	·722	·722	·711	·714	·719	·730	·734	·734	·729	·733	·741	·744	·746	·752	·745	·754	·764	·781	·788	·792	·786	·786	·798	·797	·802	·803
Sept	·708	·715	·723	·724	·723	·723	·712	·715	·719	·731	0·735	·735	·730	·734	·741	·745	·747	·753	·746	·755	·765	·782	·789	·793	·787	·787	·799	·798	·803	·804
Oct	·705	·713	·720	·721	·720	·720	·709	·713	·717	·728	·732	·732	·727	·731	·739	·742	·744	·750	·743	·752	·762	·779	·786	·790	·784	·784	·796	·795	·800	·801
Nov	·699	·707	·714	·715	·714	·714	·704	·707	·711	·722	·726	·726	·721	·725	·733	·736	·738	·744	·737	·746	·756	·773	·780	·784	·778	·778	·790	·789	·794	·795
Dec	·697	·704	·712	·713	·712	·712	·701	·704	·709	·720	·724	·724	·719	·723	·730	·734	·736	·742	·735	·744	·753	·771	·777	·781	·775	·775	·788	·787	·792	·793

Indexation allowance — continued

Month of disposal

Base Month	2001												2002												2003					
1982	Jan	Feb	Mar	Apr	May	June	July	Aug	Sept	Oct	Nov	Dec	Jan	Feb	Mar	Apr	May	June	July	Aug	Sept	Oct	Nov	Dec	Jan	Feb	Mar	Apr	May	June
Mar	1·154	1·165	1·168	1·179	1·193	1·195	1·181	1·190	1·198	1·194	1·185	1·183	1·181	1·188	1·197	1·212	1·218	1·218	1·214	1·220	1·236	1·239	1·243	1·247	1·246	1·257	1·265	1·281	1·285	1·282
Apr	1·111	1·122	1·125	1·136	1·150	1·152	1·138	1·147	1·155	1·151	1·142	1·140	1·138	1·145	1·153	1·168	1·174	1·174	1·171	1·177	1·192	1·195	1·199	1·203	1·201	1·213	1·220	1·236	1·240	1·237
May	1·096	1·107	1·110	1·121	1·134	1·137	1·123	1·132	1·139	1·135	1·127	1·124	1·123	1·129	1·138	1·153	1·159	1·159	1·155	1·161	1·176	1·180	1·183	1·187	1·186	1·197	1·204	1·220	1·224	1·221
June	1·090	1·101	1·104	1·115	1·128	1·131	1·117	1·126	1·133	1·129	1·121	1·118	1·117	1·123	1·132	1·147	1·153	1·153	1·149	1·155	1·170	1·173	1·177	1·181	1·180	1·191	1·198	1·214	1·217	1·215
July	1·090	1·101	1·103	1·114	1·128	1·130	1·117	1·125	1·132	1·129	1·120	1·118	1·117	1·123	1·131	1·146	1·152	1·152	1·148	1·154	1·169	1·173	1·176	1·180	1·179	1·190	1·197	1·213	1·217	1·214
Aug	1·089	1·100	1·103	1·114	1·127	1·129	1·116	1·125	1·132	1·128	1·120	1·117	1·116	1·122	1·131	1·145	1·151	1·151	1·148	1·154	1·168	1·172	1·176	1·179	1·178	1·189	1·197	1·212	1·216	1·214
Sept	1·090	1·101	1·104	1·115	1·128	1·131	1·117	1·126	1·133	1·129	1·121	1·118	1·117	1·123	1·132	1·147	1·153	1·153	1·149	1·155	1·170	1·173	1·177	1·181	1·180	1·191	1·198	1·214	1·217	1·215
Oct	1·080	1·091	1·093	1·104	1·118	1·120	1·107	1·115	1·123	1·119	1·110	1·108	1·107	1·113	1·121	1·136	1·142	1·142	1·138	1·145	1·159	1·163	1·166	1·170	1·169	1·180	1·187	1·203	1·207	1·204
Nov	1·070	1·081	1·083	1·094	1·107	1·110	1·096	1·105	1·112	1·109	1·100	1·098	1·096	1·103	1·111	1·126	1·132	1·132	1·128	1·134	1·149	1·152	1·156	1·159	1·158	1·169	1·176	1·192	1·196	1·193
Dec	1·074	1·085	1·087	1·098	1·111	1·114	1·100	1·109	1·116	1·112	1·104	1·102	1·100	1·106	1·115	1·129	1·136	1·136	1·132	1·138	1·152	1·156	1·160	1·163	1·162	1·173	1·180	1·196	1·200	1·197
1983																														
Jan	1·071	1·082	1·084	1·095	1·109	1·111	1·098	1·106	1·114	1·110	1·101	1·099	1·098	1·104	1·112	1·127	1·133	1·133	1·129	1·135	1·150	1·153	1·157	1·161	1·160	1·170	1·178	1·193	1·197	1·195
Feb	1·062	1·073	1·076	1·086	1·100	1·102	1·089	1·097	1·104	1·101	1·092	1·090	1·089	1·095	1·103	1·118	1·124	1·124	1·120	1·126	1·141	1·144	1·148	1·151	1·150	1·161	1·168	1·184	1·188	1·185
Mar	1·059	1·069	1·072	1·083	1·096	1·098	1·085	1·093	1·101	1·097	1·089	1·086	1·085	1·091	1·099	1·114	1·120	1·120	1·116	1·122	1·137	1·140	1·144	1·148	1·146	1·157	1·164	1·180	1·184	1·181
Apr	1·030	1·041	1·043	1·054	1·067	1·069	1·056	1·064	1·072	1·068	1·060	1·057	1·056	1·062	1·070	1·085	1·091	1·091	1·087	1·093	1·107	1·111	1·114	1·118	1·117	1·127	1·134	1·150	1·153	1·151
May	1·022	1·032	1·035	1·045	1·058	1·061	1·048	1·056	1·063	1·059	1·051	1·049	1·048	1·053	1·062	1·076	1·082	1·082	1·078	1·084	1·098	1·102	1·105	1·109	1·108	1·118	1·126	1·141	1·144	1·142
June	1·017	1·027	1·030	1·040	1·053	1·056	1·043	1·051	1·058	1·054	1·046	1·044	1·043	1·049	1·057	1·071	1·077	1·077	1·073	1·079	1·093	1·097	1·100	1·104	1·103	1·113	1·120	1·136	1·139	1·137
July	1·006	1·016	1·019	1·029	1·042	1·045	1·032	1·040	1·047	1·043	1·035	1·033	1·032	1·038	1·046	1·060	1·066	1·066	1·062	1·068	1·082	1·086	1·089	1·093	1·091	1·102	1·109	1·124	1·128	1·125
Aug	·997	1·008	1·010	1·020	1·033	1·036	1·023	1·031	1·038	1·034	1·026	1·024	1·023	1·029	1·037	1·051	1·057	1·057	1·053	1·059	1·073	1·076	1·080	1·083	1·082	1·093	1·100	1·115	1·118	1·116
Sept	·988	·999	1·001	1·011	1·024	1·027	1·014	1·022	1·029	1·025	1·017	1·015	1·014	1·020	1·028	1·042	1·047	1·047	1·044	1·050	1·064	1·067	1·071	1·074	1·073	1·083	1·090	1·106	1·109	1·107
Oct	·981	·992	·994	1·004	1·017	1·019	1·007	1·015	1·022	1·018	1·010	1·008	1·007	1·012	1·021	1·034	1·040	1·040	1·037	1·043	1·056	1·060	1·063	1·067	1·066	1·076	1·083	1·098	1·102	1·099
Nov	·974	·985	·987	·997	1·010	1·012	1·000	1·008	1·015	1·011	1·003	1·001	1·000	1·005	1·013	1·027	1·033	1·033	1·030	1·035	1·049	1·053	1·056	1·060	1·058	1·069	1·076	1·091	1·094	1·092
Dec	·969	·979	·982	·992	1·005	1·007	·994	1·002	1·009	1·006	·998	·996	·994	1·000	1·008	1·022	1·028	1·028	1·024	1·030	1·044	1·047	1·051	1·054	1·053	1·063	1·070	1·085	1·089	1·086
1984																														
Jan	·970	·981	·983	·993	1·006	1·008	·996	1·004	1·010	1·007	·999	·997	·996	1·001	1·009	1·023	1·029	1·029	1·025	1·031	1·045	1·048	1·052	1·055	1·054	1·065	1·072	1·086	1·090	1·088
Feb	·962	·973	·975	·985	·998	1·000	·987	·995	1·002	·999	·991	·989	·987	·993	1·001	1·015	1·021	1·021	1·017	1·023	1·037	1·040	1·044	1·047	1·046	1·056	1·063	1·078	1·081	1·079
Mar	·956	·966	·968	·979	·991	·994	·981	·989	·996	·993	·985	·982	·981	·987	·995	1·009	1·014	1·014	1·011	1·017	1·030	1·034	1·037	1·041	1·039	1·050	1·057	1·071	1·075	1·073
Apr	·930	·940	·943	·953	·965	·967	·955	·963	·970	·966	·958	·956	·955	·961	·969	·982	·988	·988	·984	·990	1·004	1·007	1·010	1·014	1·013	1·023	1·029	1·044	1·048	1·045
May	·923	·933	·935	·946	·958	·960	·948	·956	·962	·959	·951	·949	·948	·953	·961	·975	·980	·980	·977	·983	·996	·999	1·003	1·006	1·005	1·015	1·022	1·037	1·040	1·038
June	·918	·928	·930	·941	·953	·955	·943	·951	·957	·954	·946	·944	·943	·948	·956	·970	·975	·975	·972	·978	·991	·994	·998	1·001	1·000	1·010	1·017	1·031	1·035	1·032
July	·920	·930	·933	·943	·955	·957	·945	·953	·960	·956	·948	·946	·945	·951	·958	·972	·978	·978	·974	·980	·993	·997	1·000	1·003	1·002	1·012	1·019	1·034	1·037	1·035
Aug	·902	·912	·915	·925	·937	·939	·927	·935	·941	·938	·930	·928	·927	·932	·940	·954	·959	·959	·956	·961	·975	·978	·981	·985	·984	·994	1·000	1·015	1·018	1·016
Sept	·899	·909	·911	·921	·933	·935	·923	·931	·938	·934	·926	·924	·923	·929	·936	·950	·955	·955	·952	·958	·971	·974	·977	·981	·980	·990	·996	1·011	1·014	1·012
Oct	·887	·897	·899	·909	·921	·923	·911	·919	·926	·922	·915	·912	·911	·917	·925	·938	·943	·943	·940	·945	·959	·962	·965	·969	·968	·977	·984	·998	1·002	1·000
Nov	·881	·891	·893	·903	·915	·918	·905	·913	·920	·916	·909	·907	·905	·911	·919	·932	·937	·937	·934	·940	·953	·956	·959	·963	·962	·971	·978	·992	·996	·993
Dec	·883	·893	·895	·905	·917	·919	·907	·915	·921	·918	·910	·908	·907	·913	·920	·933	·939	·939	·936	·941	·954	·958	·961	·964	·963	·973	·980	·994	·997	·995
1985																														
Jan	·876	·886	·888	·898	·910	·912	·900	·908	·914	·911	·903	·901	·900	·906	·913	·926	·932	·932	·929	·934	·947	·951	·954	·957	·956	·966	·973	·987	·990	·988
Feb	·861	·871	·873	·883	·895	·897	·885	·893	·899	·896	·888	·886	·885	·890	·898	·911	·916	·916	·913	·919	·932	·935	·938	·942	·940	·950	·957	·971	·974	·972
Mar	·844	·853	·856	·865	·877	·879	·867	·875	·881	·878	·871	·869	·867	·873	·880	·893	·899	·899	·895	·901	·914	·917	·920	·923	·922	·932	·939	·953	·956	·954
Apr	·805	·815	·817	·826	·838	·840	·828	·836	·842	·839	·832	·830	·828	·834	·841	·854	·859	·859	·856	·861	·874	·877	·880	·883	·882	·892	·898	·912	·915	·913
May	·797	·807	·809	·818	·830	·832	·820	·828	·834	·831	·823	·821	·820	·825	·833	·845	·851	·851	·848	·853	·865	·869	·872	·875	·874	·883	·890	·903	·906	·904
June	·793	·803	·805	·814	·826	·828	·816	·824	·830	·827	·819	·817	·816	·822	·829	·841	·847	·847	·844	·849	·861	·865	·868	·871	·870	·879	·886	·899	·902	·900
July	·797	·806	·808	·818	·829	·831	·820	·827	·833	·830	·823	·821	·820	·825	·832	·845	·850	·850	·847	·852	·865	·868	·871	·874	·873	·883	·889	·903	·906	·904
Aug	·792	·801	·803	·813	·824	·826	·815	·822	·829	·825	·818	·816	·815	·820	·827	·840	·845	·845	·842	·847	·860	·863	·866	·869	·868	·878	·884	·898	·901	·899
Sept	·793	·802	·804	·814	·825	·827	·816	·823	·829	·826	·819	·817	·816	·821	·828	·841	·846	·846	·843	·848	·861	·864	·867	·870	·869	·879	·885	·899	·902	·900
Oct	·790	·799	·801	·811	·822	·824	·813	·820	·827	·823	·816	·814	·813	·818	·826	·838	·843	·843	·840	·845	·858	·861	·864	·867	·866	·876	·882	·896	·899	·897
Nov	·784	·793	·795	·805	·816	·818	·807	·814	·820	·817	·810	·808	·807	·812	·819	·832	·837	·837	·834	·839	·852	·855	·858	·861	·860	·869	·876	·889	·892	·890
Dec	·781	·791	·793	·802	·814	·816	·804	·812	·818	·815	·807	·805	·804	·810	·817	·829	·835	·835	·831	·837	·849	·852	·855	·858	·857	·867	·873	·887	·890	·888

Month of disposal

Base month	1998						1999												2000											
1986	July	Aug	Sept	Oct	Nov	Dec	Jan	Feb	Mar	Apr	May	June	July	Aug	Sept	Oct	Nov	Dec	Jan	Feb	Mar	Apr	May	June	July	Aug	Sept	Oct	Nov	Dec
Jan	·694	·701	·708	·709	·708	·708	·698	·701	·705	·716	·721	·721	·715	·720	·727	·730	·732	·738	·731	·740	·750	·767	·774	·778	·771	·771	·784	·783	·788	·789
Feb	·687	·695	·702	·703	·702	·702	·691	·695	·699	·710	·714	·714	·709	·713	·720	·724	·726	·732	·725	·734	·743	·761	·767	·771	·765	·765	·777	·776	·782	·783
Mar	·685	·692	·700	·701	·700	·700	·689	·692	·696	·708	·712	·712	·707	·711	·718	·721	·723	·730	·722	·732	·741	·759	·765	·769	·763	·763	·775	·774	·779	·780
Apr	·669	·676	·683	·684	·683	·683	·673	·676	·680	·691	·696	·696	·690	·695	·702	·705	·707	·713	·706	·715	·724	·742	·748	·752	·746	·746	·758	·757	·762	·763
May	·666	·673	·680	·681	·673	·680	·681	·680	·680	·670	·673	·677	·688	·692	·692	·687	·691	·699	·702	·704	·710	·703	·712	·721	·738	·745	·749	·743	·743	·755
June	·667	·674	·681	·682	·681	·681	·671	·674	·678	·689	·693	·693	·688	·692	·699	·703	·705	·711	·704	·713	·722	·739	·745	·750	·743	·743	·756	·755	·760	·761
July	·672	·679	·686	·687	·686	·686	·676	·679	·683	·694	·698	·698	·693	·697	·704	·707	·709	·716	·708	·718	·727	·744	·750	·755	·748	·748	·761	·760	·765	·766
Aug	·673	·681	·682	·681	·673	·678	·689	·693	·693	·688	·692	·699	·702	·704	·710	·703	·712	·722	·739	·745	·749	·743	·743	·755	·754	·759	·760	·749	·758	·760
Sept	·658	·665	·672	·673	·672	·672	·662	·665	·669	·681	·685	·685	·680	·684	·691	·694	·696	·702	·695	·704	·713	·730	·736	·741	·734	·734	·747	·746	·751	·752
Oct	·656	·663	·670	·671	·670	·670	·660	·663	·667	·678	·682	·682	·677	·681	·688	·691	·693	·699	·692	·701	·710	·728	·734	·738	·732	·732	·744	·743	·748	·749
Nov	·642	·649	·656	·657	·656	·656	·646	·649	·653	·664	·668	·668	·663	·667	·674	·677	·679	·685	·678	·687	·696	·713	·719	·723	·717	·717	·729	·728	·733	·734
Dec	·636	·643	·650	·651	·650	·650	·640	·643	·647	·658	·662	·662	·657	·661	·668	·671	·673	·679	·672	·681	·690	·707	·714	·718	·712	·712	·724	·723	·728	·729
1987																														
Jan	·630	·637	·644	·645	·644	·644	·634	·637	·641	·652	·656	·656	·651	·655	·662	·665	·667	·673	·666	·675	·684	·701	·707	·711	·705	·705	·717	·716	·721	·722
Feb	·624	·630	·637	·638	·637	·637	·627	·630	·634	·645	·649	·649	·644	·648	·655	·658	·660	·666	·659	·668	·677	·694	·700	·704	·698	·698	·710	·709	·714	·715
Mar4	·620	·627	·634	·635	·634	·634	·624	·627	·631	·642	·646	·646	·641	·645	·652	·655	·657	·663	·656	·665	·674	·691	·697	·701	·695	·695	·707	·706	·711	·712
Apr	·601	·608	·615	·616	·615	·615	·605	·608	·612	·623	·627	·627	·622	·626	·633	·636	·638	·643	·637	·645	·654	·671	·677	·681	·675	·675	·687	·686	·691	·692
May	·600	·606	·613	·614	·613	·613	·604	·606	·610	·621	·625	·625	·620	·624	·631	·634	·636	·642	·635	·644	·653	·669	·675	·679	·673	·673	·685	·684	·689	·690
June	·600	·606	·613	·614	·613	·613	·604	·606	·610	·621	·625	·625	·620	·624	·631	·634	·636	·642	·635	·644	·653	·669	·675	·679	·673	·673	·685	·684	·689	·690
July	·601	·608	·615	·616	·615	·615	·605	·608	·612	·623	·627	·627	·622	·626	·633	·636	·638	·643	·637	·645	·654	·671	·677	·681	·675	·675	·687	·686	·691	·692
Aug	·596	·603	·610	·611	·610	·610	·600	·603	·607	·618	·622	·622	·617	·621	·628	·631	·633	·639	·632	·641	·649	·666	·672	·676	·670	·670	·682	·681	·686	·687
Sept	·592	·599	·605	·606	·605	·605	·596	·599	·603	·613	·617	·617	·612	·616	·623	·626	·628	·634	·627	·636	·645	·661	·667	·671	·665	·665	·677	·676	·681	·682
Oct	·584	·591	·598	·599	·598	·598	·588	·591	·595	·605	·609	·609	·604	·608	·615	·618	·620	·626	·619	·628	·637	·653	·659	·663	·657	·657	·669	·668	·672	·673
Nov	·576	·583	·590	·591	·590	·590	·580	·583	·587	·598	·602	·602	·597	·601	·607	·610	·612	·618	·611	·620	·629	·645	·651	·655	·649	·649	·661	·660	·664	·665
Dec	·578	·585	·591	·592	·591	·591	·582	·585	·589	·599	·603	·603	·598	·602	·609	·612	·614	·620	·613	·621	·630	·647	·652	·656	·651	·651	·662	·661	·666	·667
1988																														
Jan	·578	·585	·591	·592	·591	·591	·582	·585	·589	·599	·603	·603	·598	·602	·609	·612	·614	·620	·613	·621	·630	·647	·652	·656	·651	·651	·662	·661	·666	·667
Feb	·572	·579	·585	·586	·585	·585	·576	·579	·582	·593	·597	·597	·592	·596	·603	·606	·608	·613	·607	·615	·624	·640	·646	·650	·644	·644	·656	·655	·660	·661
Mar	·566	·573	·579	·580	·579	·579	·570	·573	·576	·587	·591	·591	·586	·590	·597	·599	·601	·607	·600	·609	·618	·634	·640	·644	·638	·638	·649	·648	·653	·654
Apr	·547	·554	·554	·555	·554	·554	·544	·547	·551	·561	·565	·565	·560	·564	·571	·574	·576	·581	·575	·583	·592	·608	·613	·617	·612	·612	·623	·622	·627	·628
May	·535	·541	·548	·549	·548	·548	·548	·541	·545	·556'	·559	·559	·555	·558	·565	·568	·570	·575	·569	·577	·586	·602	·607	·611	·605	·605	·617	·616	·621	·621
June	·529	·536	·542	·543	·542	·542	·533	·536	·539	·550	·553	·553	·549	·553	·559	·562	·564	·569	·563	·571	·580	·596	·601	·605	·599	·599	·611	·610	·614	·615
July	·528	·534	·541	·542	·541	·541	·531	·534	·538	·548	·552	·552	·547	·551	·558	·560	·562	·568	·561	·570	·578	·594	·600	·604	·598	·598	·609	·608	·613	·614
Aug	·511	·517	·524	·525	·524	·524	·514	·517	·521	·531	·535	·535	·530	·534	·540	·543	·545	·551	·544	·552	·561	·576	·582	·586	·580	·580	·591	·590	·595	·596
Sept	·504	·510	·517	·518	·517	·517	·507	·510	·514	·524	·528	·528	·523	·527	·533	·536	·538	·543	·537	·545	·554	·569	·575	·578	·573	·573	·584	·583	·588	·589
Oct	·489	·495	·501	·502	·501	·501	·492	·495	·499	·509	·512	·512	·508	·511	·518	·521	·522	·528	·521	·530	·538	·553	·559	·563	·557	·557	·568	·567	·572	·573
Nov	·482	·488	·495	·495	·495	·495	·485	·488	·492	·502	·505	·505	·501	·505	·511	·514	·515	·521	·515	·523	·531	·546	·552	·555	·550	·550	·561	·560	·565	·565
Dec	·478	·484	·490	·491	·490	·490	·481	·484	·488	·498	·501	·501	·497	·500	·507	·510	·511	·517	·510	·519	·527	·542	·548	·551	·546	·546	·557	·556	·560	·561
1989																														
Jan	·468	·475	·481	·482	·481	·481	·472	·475	·478	·488	·492	·492	·487	·491	·497	·500	·502	·507	·501	·509	·517	·532	·538	·541	·536	·536	·547	·546	·550	·551
Feb	·458	·464	·470	·471	·470	·470	·462	·464	·468	·478	·481	·481	·477	·480	·487	·489	·491	·496	·490	·498	·506	·521	·527	·530	·525	·525	·536	·535	·539	·540
Mar	·451	·458	·464	·465	·464	·464	·455	·458	·461	·471	·475	·475	·470	·474	·480	·483	·484	·490	·484	·492	·500	·515	·520	·524	·518	·518	·529	·528	·533	·533
Apr	·426	·432	·438	·439	·438	·438	·430	·432	·436	·445	·449	·449	·444	·448	·454	·457	·458	·464	·458	·465	·473	·488	·493	·497	·492	·492	·502	·501	·506	·507
May	·417	·423	·430	·430	·430	·430	·421	·423	·427	·437	·440	·440	·436	·439	·445	·448	·450	·455	·449	·457	·464	·479	·484	·488	·483	·483	·493	·492	·497	·497
June	·412	·419	·425	·425	·425	·425	·416	·419	·422	·432	·435	·435	·431	·434	·440	·443	·445	·450	·444	·451	·459	·474	·479	·483	·477	·477	·488	·487	·491	·492
July	·411	·417	·423	·424	·423	·423	·415	·417	·421	·430	·434	·434	·429	·433	·439	·442	·443	·448	·442	·450	·458	·473	·478	·481	·476	·476	·487	·486	·490	·491
Aug	·408	·414	·420	·421	·420	·420	·411	·414	·417	·427	·430	·430	·426	·429	·435	·438	·440	·445	·439	·446	·454	·469	·474	·478	·472	·472	·483	·482	·486	·487
Sept	·398	·404	·410	·411	·410	·410	·401	·404	·407	·417	·420	·420	·416	·419	·425	·428	·430	·435	·429	·437	·444	·459	·464	·467	·462	·462	·473	·472	·476	·477
Oct	·387	·393	·399	·400	·399	·399	·391	·393	·397	·406	·409	·409	·405	·409	·414	·417	·419	·424	·418	·426	·433	·448	·453	·456	·451	·451	·461	·460	·465	·466
Nov	·376	·381	·387	·388	·387	·387	·379	·381	·385	·394	·397	·397	·393	·397	·403	·405	·407	·412	·406	·414	·421	·435	·441	·444	·439	·439	·449	·448	·452	·453
Dec	·372	·378	·384	·385	·384	·384	·375	·378	·381	·391	·394	·394	·390	·393	·399	·402	·403	·408	·402	·410	·418	·432	·437	·440	·435	·435	·445	·444	·449	·449
1990																														
Jan	·364	·370	·376	·377	·376	·376	·367	·370	·373	·382	·386	·386	·382	·385	·391	·393	·395	·400	·394	·402	·409	·423	·428	·432	·427	·427	·437	·436	·440	·441
Feb	·356	·362	·368	·369	·368	·368	·359	·362	·365	·374	·378	·378	·374	·377	·383	·385	·387	·392	·386	·394	·401	·415	·420	·423	·418	·418	·428	·428	·432	·433
Mar	·343	·348	·354	·355	·354	·354	·346	·348	·352	·361	·364	·364	·360	·363	·369	·371	·373	·378	·372	·380	·387	·401	·406	·409	·404	·404	·414	·414	·418	·418
Apr	·303	·309	·314	·315	·314	·314	·306	·309	·312	·321	·324	·324	·320	·323	·329	·331	·333	·337	·332	·339	·346	·360	·365	·368	·363	·363	·373	·372	·376	·376
May	·292	·297	·303	·303	·303	·303	·295	·297	·300	·309	·312	·312	·308	·311	·317	·319	·321	·326	·320	·327	·334	·348	·353	·356	·351	·351	·361	·360	·364	·365
June	·287	·292	·298	·298	·298	·298	·290	·292	·295	·304	·307	·307	·303	·306	·312	·314	·316	·320	·315	·322	·329	·343	·347	·350	·346	·346	·355	·354	·358	·359
July	·285	·291	·297	·297	·297	·297	·289	·291	·294	·303	·306	·306	·302	·305	·311	·313	·315	·319	·314	·321	·328	·341	·346	·349	·345	·345	·354	·353	·357	·358
Aug	·272	·278	·283	·284	·283	·283	·276	·278	·281	·290	·293	·293	·289	·292	·297	·300	·301	·306	·301	·308	·315	·328	·333	·336	·331	·331	·340	·340	·343	·344
Sept	·261	·266	·271	·272	·271	·271	·264	·266	·269	·278	·281	·281	·277	·280	·285	·288	·289	·294	·288	·295	·302	·316	·320	·323	·319	·319	·328	·327	·331	·332
Oct	·251	·256	·262	·262	·262	·262	·254	·256	·259	·268	·271	·271	·267	·270	·276	·278	·279	·284	·279	·285	·292	·305	·310	·313	·309	·309	·318	·317	·321	·322
Nov	·254	·259	·265	·265	·265	·265	·257	·259	·262	·271	·274	·274	·270	·273	·278	·281	·282	·287	·282	·288	·295	·308	·313	·316	·312	·312	·321	·320	·324	·325
Dec	·255	·260	·266	·266	·266	·266	·258	·260	·263	·272	·275	·275	·271	·274	·279	·282	·283	·288	·283	·289	·296	·309	·314	·317	·313	·313	·322	·321	·325	·326

Indexation allowance — continued

Month of disposal

Base month

	2001												2002												2003					
1986	Jan	Feb	Mar	Apr	May	June	July	Aug	Sept	Oct	Nov	Dec	Jan	Feb	Mar	Apr	May	June	July	Aug	Sept	Oct	Nov	Dec	Jan	Feb	Mar	Apr	May	June
Jan	·778	·787	·789	·798	·810	·812	·801	·808	·814	·811	·804	·802	·801	·806	·813	·825	·831	·831	·828	·833	·845	·848	·851	·855	·854	·863	·869	·883	·886	·884
Feb	·771	·780	·783	·792	·803	·805	·794	·801	·807	·804	·797	·795	·794	·799	·806	·819	·824	·824	·821	·826	·838	·842	·845	·848	·847	·856	·862	·876	·879	·877
Mar	·769	·778	·780	·790	·801	·803	·792	·799	·805	·802	·795	·793	·792	·797	·804	·816	·822	·822	·818	·824	·836	·839	·842	·845	·844	·854	·860	·873	·876	·874
Apr	·752	·761	·763	·772	·784	·786	·774	·782	·788	·785	·777	·775	·774	·779	·787	·799	·804	·804	·801	·806	·818	·821	·825	·828	·827	·836	·842	·855	·858	·856
May	·754	·758	·760	·769	·780	·782	·771	·778	·784	·781	·774	·772	·771	·776	·783	·796	·801	·801	·798	·803	·815	·818	·821	·824	·823	·832	·839	·852	·855	·853
June	·750	·759	·761	·770	·781	·783	·772	·779	·785	·782	·775	·773	·772	·777	·784	·797	·802	·802	·799	·804	·816	·819	·822	·825	·824	·833	·840	·853	·856	·854
July	·755	·764	·766	·775	·786	·788	·777	·784	·790	·787	·780	·778	·777	·782	·789	·802	·807	·807	·804	·809	·821	·824	·827	·830	·829	·839	·845	·858	·861	·859
Aug	·770	·758	·760	·770	·781	·783	·772	·779	·785	·782	·775	·773	·772	·777	·784	·796	·801	·801	·798	·803	·816	·819	·822	·825	·824	·833	·839	·852	·855	·853
Sept	·741	·750	·752	·761	·772	·774	·763	·770	·776	·773	·766	·764	·763	·768	·775	·787	·792	·792	·789	·794	·807	·810	·813	·816	·815	·824	·830	·843	·846	·844
Oct	·738	·747	·749	·758	·769	·771	·760	·767	·773	·770	·763	·761	·760	·765	·772	·785	·790	·790	·787	·792	·804	·807	·810	·813	·812	·821	·827	·840	·844	·841
Nov	·723	·732	·734	·743	·754	·756	·745	·752	·758	·755	·748	·746	·745	·750	·757	·770	·775	·775	·772	·777	·789	·792	·795	·798	·797	·806	·812	·825	·828	·826
Dec	·718	·727	·729	·738	·749	·751	·740	·747	·753	·750	·743	·741	·740	·745	·752	·764	·769	·769	·766	·771	·783	·786	·789	·792	·791	·800	·806	·819	·822	·820
1987																														
Jan	·711	·720	·722	·731	·742	·744	·733	·740	·746	·743	·736	·734	·733	·738	·745	·757	·762	·762	·759	·764	·776	·779	·782	·785	·784	·793	·799	·812	·815	·813
Feb	·704	·713	·715	·724	·735	·737	·726	·733	·739	·736	·729	·727	·726	·731	·738	·750	·755	·755	·752	·757	·769	·772	·775	·778	·777	·786	·792	·805	·808	·806
Mar	·701	·710	·712	·721	·732	·734	·723	·730	·736	·733	·726	·724	·723	·728	·735	·747	·751	·751	·749	·753	·765	·768	·771	·774	·773	·782	·788	·801	·804	·802
Apr	·681	·690	·692	·700	·711	·713	·702	·709	·715	·712	·705	·703	·702	·707	·714	·726	·731	·731	·728	·733	·745	·748	·750	·753	·752	·761	·767	·780	·783	·781
May	·679	·688	·690	·699	·710	·711	·701	·708	·713	·711	·704	·702	·701	·706	·712	·724	·729	·729	·726	·731	·743	·746	·749	·752	·751	·760	·765	·778	·781	·779
June	·679	·688	·690	·699	·710	·711	·701	·708	·713	·711	·704	·702	·701	·706	·712	·724	·729	·729	·726	·731	·743	·746	·749	·752	·751	·760	·765	·778	·781	·779
July	·681	·690	·692	·700	·711	·713	·702	·709	·715	·712	·705	·703	·702	·707	·714	·726	·731	·731	·728	·733	·745	·748	·750	·753	·752	·761	·767	·780	·783	·781
Aug	·676	·685	·687	·695	·706	·708	·697	·704	·710	·707	·700	·698	·697	·702	·709	·721	·726	·726	·723	·728	·739	·742	·745	·748	·747	·756	·762	·775	·778	·776
Sept	·671	·680	·682	·690	·701	·703	·692	·699	·705	·702	·695	·693	·692	·697	·704	·716	·721	·721	·718	·723	·734	·737	·740	·743	·742	·751	·757	·770	·772	·771
Oct	·663	·672	·673	·682	·693	·695	·684	·691	·697	·694	·687	·685	·684	·689	·696	·707	·712	·712	·709	·714	·726	·729	·732	·735	·734	·742	·748	·761	·764	·762
Nov	·655	·663	·665	·674	·685	·687	·676	·683	·689	·686	·679	·677	·676	·681	·688	·699	·704	·704	·701	·706	·718	·721	·723	·726	·725	·734	·740	·752	·755	·753
Dec	·656	·665	·667	·676	·686	·688	·678	·684	·690	·687	·681	·679	·678	·682	·689	·701	·706	·706	·703	·708	·719	·722	·725	·728	·727	·736	·742	·754	·757	·755
1988																														
Jan	·656	·665	·667	·676	·686	·688	·678	·684	·690	·687	·681	·679	·678	·682	·689	·701	·706	·706	·703	·708	·719	·722	·725	·728	·727	·736	·742	·754	·757	·755
Feb	·650	·659	·661	·669	·680	·682	·671	·678	·684	·681	·674	·672	·671	·676	·683	·694	·699	·699	·696	·701	·713	·716	·718	·721	·720	·729	·735	·747	·750	·748
Mar	·644	·652	·654	·663	·673	·675	·665	·671	·677	·674	·668	·666	·665	·670	·676	·688	·693	·693	·690	·695	·706	·709	·712	·715	·714	·722	·728	·741	·744	·742
Apr	·617	·626	·628	·636	·647	·648	·638	·645	·650	·647	·641	·639	·638	·643	·649	·661	·665	·665	·663	·667	·679	·681	·684	·687	·686	·695	·700	·713	·716	·714
May	·611	·620	·621	·630	·640	·642	·632	·638	·644	·641	·635	·633	·632	·637	·643	·654	·659	·659	·656	·661	·672	·675	·678	·681	·680	·688	·694	·706	·709	·707
June	·605	·614	·615	·624	·634	·636	·626	·632	·638	·635	·629	·627	·626	·630	·637	·648	·653	·653	·650	·655	·666	·669	·672	·674	·674	·682	·688	·700	·703	·701
July	·604	·612	·614	·622	·633	·634	·624	·631	·636	·634	·627	·625	·624	·629	·635	·647	·651	·651	·649	·653	·664	·667	·670	·673	·672	·680	·686	·698	·701	·699
Aug	·586	·594	·596	·604	·614	·616	·606	·613	·618	·615	·609	·607	·606	·611	·617	·628	·633	·633	·630	·635	·646	·649	·652	·654	·653	·662	·667	·679	·682	·680
Sept	·578	·587	·589	·597	·607	·609	·599	·605	·611	·608	·601	·600	·599	·603	·610	·621	·625	·625	·623	·627	·638	·641	·644	·647	·646	·654	·660	·672	·674	·673
Oct	·563	·571	·573	·581	·591	·593	·583	·589	·595	·592	·585	·584	·583	·587	·594	·605	·609	·609	·606	·611	·622	·625	·627	·630	·629	·637	·643	·655	·658	·656
Nov	·555	·564	·565	·574	·584	·585	·575	·582	·587	·585	·578	·576	·575	·580	·586	·597	·602	·602	·599	·604	·615	·617	·620	·623	·622	·630	·635	·647	·650	·648
Dec	·551	·559	·561	·569	·579	·581	·571	·578	·583	·580	·574	·572	·571	·576	·582	·593	·597	·597	·595	·599	·610	·613	·616	·618	·617	·626	·631	·643	·646	·644
1989																														
Jan	·541	·550	·551	·559	·569	·571	·561	·568	·573	·570	·564	·562	·561	·566	·572	·583	·587	·587	·585	·589	·600	·603	·605	·608	·607	·615	·621	·632	·635	·633
Feb	·530	·538	·540	·548	·558	·560	·550	·556	·562	·559	·553	·551	·550	·555	·561	·572	·576	·576	·573	·578	·589	·591	·594	·597	·596	·604	·609	·621	·623	·622
Mar	·524	·532	·533	·541	·551	·553	·543	·549	·555	·552	·546	·544	·543	·548	·554	·565	·569	·569	·566	·571	·581	·584	·587	·589	·589	·597	·602	·614	·616	·614
Apr	·497	·505	·507	·514	·524	·526	·516	·522	·528	·525	·519	·517	·516	·521	·527	·537	·542	·542	·539	·543	·554	·556	·559	·562	·561	·569	·574	·585	·588	·586
May	·488	·496	·497	·505	·515	·517	·507	·513	·518	·516	·510	·508	·507	·511	·517	·528	·532	·532	·530	·534	·544	·547	·550	·552	·551	·559	·564	·576	·578	·577
June	·483	·490	·492	·500	·510	·511	·502	·508	·513	·510	·504	·503	·502	·506	·512	·523	·527	·527	·524	·529	·539	·542	·544	·547	·546	·554	·559	·570	·573	·571
July	·481	·489	·491	·499	·508	·510	·500	·506	·512	·509	·503	·501	·500	·505	·511	·521	·526	·526	·523	·527	·538	·540	·543	·545	·545	·552	·558	·569	·571	·570
Aug	·478	·485	·487	·495	·504	·506	·497	·503	·508	·505	·499	·497	·497	·501	·507	·517	·522	·522	·519	·523	·534	·536	·539	·541	·541	·548	·554	·565	·567	·566
Sept	·467	·475	·477	·485	·494	·496	·486	·492	·497	·495	·489	·487	·486	·491	·497	·507	·511	·511	·509	·513	·523	·526	·528	·531	·530	·538	·543	·554	·557	·555
Oct	·456	·464	·466	·473	·483	·484	·475	·481	·486	·483	·477	·476	·475	·479	·485	·495	·500	·500	·497	·501	·511	·514	·517	·519	·518	·526	·531	·542	·545	·543
Nov	·444	·451	·453	·461	·470	·472	·462	·468	·473	·471	·465	·463	·462	·467	·473	·483	·487	·487	·484	·489	·499	·501	·504	·506	·505	·513	·518	·529	·532	·530
Dec	·440	·448	·449	·457	·466	·468	·459	·465	·470	·467	·461	·460	·459	·463	·469	·479	·483	·483	·481	·485	·495	·497	·500	·503	·502	·509	·514	·525	·528	·526
1990																														
Jan	·432	·439	·441	·449	·458	·459	·450	·456	·461	·459	·453	·451	·450	·454	·460	·470	·474	·474	·472	·476	·486	·489	·491	·494	·493	·500	·505	·516	·519	·517
Feb	·423	·431	·433	·440	·449	·451	·442	·448	·453	·450	·444	·443	·442	·446	·452	·462	·466	·466	·463	·468	·478	·480	·483	·485	·484	·492	·497	·507	·510	·508
Mar	·409	·417	·418	·426	·435	·437	·428	·433	·438	·436	·430	·428	·428	·432	·437	·447	·451	·451	·449	·453	·463	·465	·468	·470	·470	·477	·482	·493	·495	·493
Apr	·368	·375	·376	·384	·392	·394	·385	·391	·396	·393	·388	·386	·385	·389	·395	·404	·408	·408	·406	·410	·420	·422	·424	·427	·426	·433	·438	·448	·451	·449
May	·356	·363	·365	·372	·380	·382	·373	·379	·384	·381	·376	·374	·373	·377	·383	·392	·396	·396	·394	·398	·407	·410	·412	·414	·414	·421	·426	·436	·438	·437
June	·350	·358	·359	·366	·375	·376	·368	·373	·378	·376	·370	·369	·368	·372	·377	·387	·391	·391	·388	·392	·402	·404	·406	·409	·408	·415	·420	·430	·433	·431
July	·349	·356	·358	·365	·374	·375	·367	·372	·377	·375	·369	·368	·367	·371	·376	·386	·390	·390	·387	·391	·401	·403	·405	·408	·407	·414	·419	·429	·431	·430
Aug	·336	·343	·344	·351	·360	·361	·353	·358	·363	·361	·355	·354	·353	·357	·362	·372	·375	·375	·373	·377	·386	·389	·391	·393	·393	·400	·404	·415	·417	·415
Sept	·323	·330	·332	·339	·347	·349	·340	·346	·350	·348	·343	·341	·340	·344	·350	·359	·363	·363	·360	·364	·374	·376	·378	·381	·380	·387	·391	·401	·404	·402
Oct	·313	·320	·322	·328	·337	·338	·330	·335	·340	·338	·332	·331	·330	·334	·339	·348	·352	·352	·350	·354	·363	·365	·368	·370	·369	·376	·381	·391	·393	·391
Nov	·316	·323	·325	·332	·340	·342	·333	·338	·343	·341	·335	·334	·333	·337	·342	·352	·355	·355	·353	·357	·366	·368	·371	·373	·372	·379	·384	·394	·396	·395
Dec	·317	·324	·326	·333	·341	·343	·334	·339	·344	·342	·336	·335	·334	·338	·343	·353	·356	·356	·354	·358	·367	·370	·372	·374	·373	·380	·385	·395	·397	·396

Month of disposal

Base month

	1998						1999												2000											
1991	July	Aug	Sept	Oct	Nov	Dec	Jan	Feb	Mar	Apr	May	June	July	Aug	Sept	Oct	Nov	Dec	Jan	Feb	Mar	Apr	May	June	July	Aug	Sept	Oct	Nov	Dec
Jan	·252	·257	·263	·263	·263	·263	·255	·257	·260	·269	·272	·272	·268	·271	·276	·279	·280	·285	·280	·286	·293	·306	·311	·314	·310	·310	·319	·318	·322	·323
Feb	·245	·251	·256	·257	·256	·256	·248	·251	·254	·262	·265	·265	·261	·264	·270	·272	·273	·278	·273	·280	·286	·299	·304	·307	·303	·303	·312	·311	·315	·316
Mar	·240	·246	·251	·252	·251	·251	·244	·246	·249	·257	·260	·260	·256	·260	·265	·267	·269	·273	·268	·275	·282	·295	·299	·302	·298	·298	·307	·306	·310	·311
Apr	·225	·230	·235	·236	·235	·235	·228	·230	·233	·241	·244	·244	·240	·243	·249	·251	·252	·257	·252	·258	·265	·278	·282	·285	·281	·281	·290	·289	·293	·294
May	·221	·226	·231	·232	·231	·231	·224	·226	·229	·237	·240	·240	·237	·240	·245	·247	·249	·253	·248	·255	·261	·274	·279	·282	·277	·277	·286	·285	·289	·290
June	·216	·221	·226	·227	·226	·226	·218	·221	·224	·232	·235	·235	·231	·234	·239	·242	·243	·248	·242	·249	·256	·268	·273	·276	·271	·271	·280	·280	·283	·284
July	·218	·223	·229	·229	229	·229	·221	·223	·226	·235	·238	·238	·234	·237	·242	·244	·246	·250	·245	·252	·259	·271	·276	·279	·274	·274	·283	·283	·286	·287
Aug	·216	·221	·226	·227	·226	·226	·218	·221	·224	·232	·235	·235	·231	·234	·239	·242	·243	·248	·242	·249	·256	·268	·273	·276	·271	·271	·280	·280	·283	·284
Sept	·211	·216	·221	·222	·221	·221	·214	·216	·219	·227	·230	·230	·227	·230	·235	·237	·238	·243	·238	·244	·251	·264	·268	·271	·267	·267	·276	·275	·279	·279
Oct	·207	·212	·217	·218	·217	·217	·209	·212	·215	·223	·226	·226	·222	·225	·230	·232	·234	·238	·233	·240	·246	·259	·264	·266	·262	·262	·271	·270	·274	·275
Nov	·202	·207	·212	·213	·212	·212	·205	·207	·210	·218	·221	·221	·218	·221	·226	·228	·229	·234	·229	·235	·242	·254	·259	·262	·257	·257	·266	·265	·269	·270
Dec	·201	·206	·211	·212	·211	·211	·204	·206	·209	·217	·220	·220	·217	·220	·225	·227	·228	·233	·228	·234	·241	·254	·258	·261	·256	·256	·265	·265	·268	·269
1992																														
Jan	·202	·207	·212	·213	·212	·212	·205	·207	·210	·218	·221	·221	·218	·221	·226	·228	·229	·234	·229	·235	·242	·254	·259	·262	·257	·257	·266	·265	·269	·270
Feb	·196	·201	·206	·207	·206	·206	·199	·201	·204	·212	·215	·215	·211	·214	·219	·222	·223	·227	·222	·229	·236	·248	·252	·255	·251	·251	·260	·259	·263	·263
Mar	·192	·198	·203	·203	·203	·203	·195	·198	·200	·208	·211	·211	·208	·211	·216	·218	·219	·224	·219	·225	·232	·244	·249	·252	·247	·247	·256	·255	·259	·260
Apr	·174	·179	·184	·185	·184	·184	·177	·179	·182	·190	·193	·193	·189	·192	·197	·200	·201	·205	·200	·207	·213	·226	·230	·233	·228	·228	·237	·236	·240	·241
May	·170	·175	·180	·181	·180	·180	·173	·175	·178	·186	·189	·189	·185	·188	·193	·195	·197	·201	·196	·202	·209	·221	·225	·228	·224	·224	·233	·232	·235	·236
June	·170	·175	·180	·181	·180	·180	·173	·175	·178	·186	·189	·189	·185	·188	·193	·195	·197	·201	·196	·202	·209	·221	·225	·228	·224	·224	·233	·232	·235	·236
July	·174	·179	·184	·185	·184	·184	·177	·179	·182	·190	·193	·193	·189	·192	·197	·200	·201	·205	·200	·207	·213	·226	·230	·233	·228	·228	·237	·236	·240	·241
Aug	·174	·179	·184	·184	·184	·184	·176	·179	·181	·189	·192	·192	·189	·192	·197	·199	·200	·204	·199	·206	·212	·225	·229	·232	·228	·228	·236	·235	·239	·240
Sept	·169	·174	·179	·180	·179	·179	·172	·174	·177	·185	·188	·188	·184	·187	·192	·194	·196	·200	·195	·202	·208	·220	·225	·227	·223	·223	·232	·231	·235	·235
Oct	·165	·170	·175	·176	·175	·175	·168	·170	·173	·181	·184	·184	·180	·183	·188	·190	·192	·196	·191	·197	·204	·216	·220	·223	·219	·219	·227	·227	·230	·231
Nov	·167	·172	·177	·178	·177	·177	·170	·172	·175	·183	·185	·185	·182	·185	·190	·192	·193	·198	·193	·199	·205	·218	·222	·225	·220	·220	·229	·228	·232	·233
Dec	·171	·176	·181	·182	·181	·181	·174	·176	·179	·187	·190	·190	·186	·189	·194	·196	·198	·202	·197	·203	·210	·222	·226	·229	·225	·225	·233	·233	·236	·237
1993																														
Jan	·182	·187	·192	·193	·192	·192	·185	·187	·190	·198	·201	·201	·197	·200	·205	·207	·209	·213	·208	·215	·221	·234	·238	·241	·236	·236	·245	·244	·248	·249
Feb	·174	·179	·184	·185	·184	·184	·177	·179	·182	·190	·193	·193	·189	·192	·197	·200	·201	·205	·200	·207	·213	·226	·230	·233	·228	·228	·237	·236	·240	·241
Mar	·170	·175	·180	·181	·180	·180	·173	·175	·178	·186	·189	·189	·185	·188	·193	·195	·197	·201	·196	·202	·209	·221	·225	·228	·224	·224	·233	·232	·235	·236
Apr	·159	·164	·169	·170	·169	·169	·162	·164	·167	·175	·178	·178	·174	·177	·182	·184	·186	·190	·185	·191	·198	·210	·214	·217	·213	·213	·221	·220	·224	·225
May	·155	·160	·165	·166	·166	·165	·165	·160	·163	·171	·174	·174	·170	·173	·178	·180	·181	·186	·181	·187	·193	·206	·210	·213	·208	·208	·217	·216	·220	·220
June	·156	·161	·166	·167	·166	·166	·159	·161	·164	·172	·174	·174	·171	·174	·179	·181	·182	·187	·182	·188	·194	·206	·211	·213	·209	·209	·218	·217	·221	·221
July	·158	·168	·169	·168	·169	·168	·168	·163	·166	·174	·177	·177	·173	·176	·181	·183	·185	·189	·184	·190	·197	·209	·213	·216	·212	·212	·220	·220	·223	·224
Aug	·154	·159	·163	·164	·163	·163	·156	·159	·161	·169	·172	·172	·168	·171	·176	·178	·180	·184	·179	·185	·192	·204	·208	·211	·207	·207	·215	·214	·218	·219
Sept	·149	·154	·159	·159	·159	·159	·152	·154	·156	·164	·167	·167	·163	·166	·171	·173	·175	·179	·174	·180	·187	·199	·203	·206	·202	·202	·210	·209	·213	·214
Oct	·150	·154	·159	·160	·159	·159	·152	·154	·157	·165	·168	·168	·164	·167	·172	·174	·176	·180	·175	·181	·188	·200	·204	·207	·202	·202	·211	·210	·214	·214
Nov	·151	·156	·161	·162	·161	·161	·154	·156	·159	·167	·169	·169	·166	·169	·174	·176	·177	·181	·177	·183	·189	·201	·206	·208	·204	·204	·213	·212	·215	·216
Dec	·149	·154	·159	·159	·159	·159	·152	·154	·156	·164	·167	·167	·163	·166	·171	·173	·175	·179	·174	·180	·187	·199	·203	·206	·202	·202	·210	·209	·213	·214
1994																														
Jan	·154	·159	·163	·164	·163	·163	·156	·159	·161	·169	·172	·172	·168	·171	·176	·178	·180	·184	·179	·185	·192	·204	·208	·211	·207	·207	·215	·214	·218	·219
Feb	·147	·152	·157	·158	·157	·157	·150	·152	·155	·163	·165	·165	·162	·165	·170	·172	·173	·177	·172	·179	·185	·197	·201	·204	·200	·200	·208	·208	·211	·212
Mar	·144	·149	·154	·154	·154	·154	·147	·149	·152	·159	·162	·162	·159	·161	·166	·168	·170	·174	·169	·175	·182	·194	·198	·201	·196	·196	·205	·204	·208	·208
Apr	·130	·135	·140	·141	·140	·140	·133	·135	·138	·146	·148	·148	·145	·148	·153	·155	·156	·160	·155	·162	·168	·180	·184	·187	·182	·182	·191	·190	·193	·194
May	·126	·131	·136	·137	·136	·136	·129	·131	·134	·142	·144	·144	·141	·144	·149	·151	·152	·156	·151	·158	·164	·176	·180	·182	·178	·178	·187	·186	·189	·190
June	·126	·131	·136	·137	·136	·136	·129	·131	·134	·142	·144	·144	·141	·144	·149	·151	·152	·156	·151	·158	·164	·176	·180	·182	·178	·178	·187	·186	·189	·190
July	·132	·137	·142	·142	·142	·142	·135	·137	·140	·147	·150	·150	·147	·149	·154	·156	·158	·162	·157	·163	·169	·181	·185	·188	·184	·184	·192	·192	·195	·196
Aug	·126	·131	·136	·137	·136	·136	·129	·131	·134	·142	·144	·144	·141	·144	·149	·151	·152	·156	·151	·158	·164	·176	·180	·182	·178	·178	·187	·186	·189	·190
Sept	·124	·129	·134	·134	·134	·134	·127	·129	·132	·139	·142	·142	·139	·141	·146	·148	·150	·154	·149	·155	·161	·173	·177	·180	·176	·176	·184	·183	·187	·188
Oct	·123	·127	·132	·133	·132	·132	·125	·127	·130	·138	·140	·140	·137	·140	·145	·147	·148	·152	·147	·154	·160	·171	·176	·178	·174	·174	·183	·182	·185	·186
Nov	·122	·127	·131	·132	·131	·131	·125	·127	·129	·137	·140	·140	·136	·139	·144	·146	·147	·151	·147	·153	·159	·171	·175	·178	·173	·173	·182	·181	·184	·185
Dec	·116	·121	·126	·127	·126	·126	·119	·121	·124	·132	·134	·134	·131	·134	·138	·140	·142	·146	·141	·147	·153	·165	·169	·172	·168	·168	·176	·175	·179	·179
1995																														
Jan	·116	·121	·126	·127	·126	·126	·119	·121	·124	·132	·134	·134	·131	·134	·138	·140	·142	·146	·141	·147	·153	·165	·169	·172	·168	·168	·176	·175	·179	·179
Feb	·110	·114	·119	·120	·119	·119	·112	·114	·117	·125	·127	·127	·124	·127	·131	·133	·135	·139	·134	·140	·146	·158	·162	·165	·161	·161	·169	·168	·172	·172
Mar	·105	·110	·115	·115	·115	·115	·108	·110	·113	·120	·123	·123	·119	·122	·127	·129	·130	·134	·129	·136	·142	·153	·157	·160	·156	·156	·164	·163	·167	·167
Apr	·094	·099	·103	·104	·103	·103	·097	·099	·101	·109	·111	·111	·108	·111	·115	·117	·119	·123	·118	·124	·130	·142	·146	·148	·144	·144	·152	·152	·155	·156
May	·090	·094	·099	·100	·099	·099	·092	·094	·097	·104	·107	·107	·104	·106	·111	·113	·114	·118	·114	·120	·126	·137	·141	·144	·140	·140	·148	·147	·150	·151
June	·088	·093	·097	·098	·097	·097	·091	·093	·095	·103	·105	·105	·102	·105	·109	·111	·113	·117	·112	·118	·124	·136	·140	·142	·138	·138	·146	·146	·149	·150
July	·093	·098	·103	·103	·103	·103	·096	·098	·101	·108	·111	·111	·107	·110	·115	·117	·118	·122	·117	·123	·129	·141	·145	·148	·144	·144	·152	·151	·154	·155
Aug	·087	·092	·097	·097	·097	·097	·090	·092	·095	·102	·105	·105	·101	·104	·109	·111	·112	·116	·111	·117	·123	·135	·139	·141	·137	·137	·145	·145	·148	·149
Sept	·082	·087	·092	·092	·092	·092	·085	·087	·090	·097	·100	·100	·096	·099	·104	·106	·107	·11[illegible]	·106	·112	·118	·129	·133	·136	·132	·132	·140	·139	·143	·143
Oct	·088	·093	·097	·098	·097	·097	·091	·093	·095	·103	·105	·105	·102	·105	·109	·111	·113	·117	·112	·118	·124	·136	·140	·142	·138	·138	·146	·146	·149	·150
Nov	·088	·093	·097	·098	·097	·091	·091	·093	·095	·103	·105	·105	·102	·105	·109	·111	·113	·117	·112	·118	·124	·136	·140	·142	·138	·138	·146	·146	·149	·150
Dec	·082	·086	·091	·092	·091	·091	·084	·086	·089	·096	·099	·099	·096	·098	·103	·105	·106	·110	·106	·111	·117	·129	·133	·135	·131	·131	·139	·139	·142	·143

Indexation allowance — continued

Month of disposal

Base month	2001												2002												2003					
1991	Jan	Feb	Mar	Apr	May	June	July	Aug	Sept	Oct	Nov	Dec	Jan	Feb	Mar	Apr	May	June	July	Aug	Sept	Oct	Nov	Dec	Jan	Feb	Mar	Apr	May	June
Jan	·314	·321	·323	·329	·338	·339	·331	·336	·341	·339	·333	·332	·331	·335	·340	·349	·353	·353	·351	·355	·364	·366	·369	·371	·370	·377	·382	·392	·394	·392
Feb	·307	·314	·316	·322	·331	·332	·324	·329	·334	·332	·326	·325	·324	·328	·333	·342	·346	·346	·344	·348	·357	·359	·361	·364	·363	·370	·374	·384	·387	·385
Mar	·302	·309	·311	·317	·326	·327	·319	·324	·329	·326	·321	·320	·319	·323	·328	·337	·341	·341	·339	·342	·352	·354	·356	·358	·358	·365	·369	·379	·381	·380
Apr	·285	·292	·294	·301	·309	·310	·302	·307	·312	·310	·304	·303	·302	·306	·311	·320	·324	·324	·322	·325	·334	·337	·339	·341	·340	·347	·352	·361	·364	·362
May	·282	·288	·290	·297	·305	·306	·298	·303	·308	·306	·300	·299	·298	·302	·307	·316	·320	·320	·318	·321	·330	·333	·335	·337	·336	·343	·348	·357	·360	·358
June	·276	·283	·284	·291	·299	·301	·292	·298	·302	·300	·295	·293	·292	·296	·301	·310	·314	·314	·312	·315	·324	·327	·329	·331	·330	·337	·342	·351	·353	·352
July	·279	·286	·287	·294	·302	·303	·295	·300	·305	·303	·297	·296	·295	·299	·304	·313	·317	·317	·315	·318	·327	·330	·332	·334	·333	·340	·345	·354	·357	·355
Aug	·276	·283	·284	·291	·299	·301	·292	·298	·302	·300	·295	·293	·292	·296	·301	·310	·314	·314	·312	·315	·324	·327	·329	·331	·330	·337	·342	·351	·353	·352
Sept	·271	·278	·279	·286	·294	·296	·288	·293	·297	·295	·290	·288	·288	·291	·296	·305	·309	·309	·307	·311	·319	·322	·324	·326	·325	·332	·337	·346	·348	·347
Oct	·266	·273	·275	·281	·289	·291	·283	·288	·292	·290	·285	·283	·283	·286	·292	·301	·304	·304	·302	·306	·315	·317	·319	·321	·321	·327	·332	·341	·343	·342
Nov	·262	·268	·270	·277	·285	·286	·278	·283	·288	·285	·280	·279	·278	·282	·287	·296	·299	·299	·297	·301	·310	·312	·314	·316	·316	·322	·327	·336	·338	·337
Dec	·261	·268	·269	·276	·284	·285	·277	·282	·287	·284	·279	·278	·277	·281	·286	·295	·298	·298	·296	·300	·309	·311	·313	·315	·315	·321	·326	·335	·338	·336
1992																														
Jan	·262	·268	·270	·277	·285	·286	·278	·283	·288	·285	·280	·279	·278	·282	·287	·296	·299	·299	·297	·301	·310	·312	·314	·316	·316	·322	·327	·336	·338	·337
Feb	·255	·262	·263	·270	·278	·280	·271	·277	·281	·279	·274	·272	·271	·275	·280	·289	·293	·293	·291	·294	·303	·305	·307	·310	·309	·315	·320	·329	·332	·330
Mar	·252	·258	·260	·266	·274	·276	·268	·273	·277	·275	·270	·268	·268	·271	·277	·285	·289	·289	·287	·290	·299	·301	·304	·306	·305	·312	·316	·326	·328	·326
Apr	·233	·239	·241	·247	·255	·256	·249	·254	·258	·256	·251	·249	·249	·252	·257	·266	·269	·269	·267	·271	·280	·282	·284	·286	·285	·292	·296	·305	·308	·306
May	·228	·235	·236	·243	·251	·252	·244	·249	·253	·251	·246	·245	·244	·248	·253	·261	·265	·265	·263	·266	·275	·277	·279	·281	·281	·287	·291	·301	·303	·302
June	·228	·235	·236	·243	·251	·252	·244	·249	·253	·251	·246	·245	·244	·248	·253	·261	·265	·265	·263	·266	·275	·277	·279	·281	·281	·287	·291	·301	·303	·302
July	·233	·239	·241	·247	·255	·256	·249	·254	·258	·256	·251	·249	·249	·252	·257	·266	·269	·269	·267	·271	·280	·282	·284	·286	·285	·292	·296	·305	·308	·306
Aug	·232	·238	·240	·246	·254	·256	·248	·253	·257	·255	·250	·248	·248	·251	·256	·265	·269	·269	·266	·270	·279	·281	·283	·285	·284	·291	·295	·305	·307	·305
Sept	·227	·234	·235	·242	·250	·251	·243	·248	·253	·250	·245	·244	·243	·247	·252	·260	·264	·264	·262	·265	·274	·276	·278	·280	·280	·286	·291	·300	·302	·301
Oct	·223	·229	·231	·237	·245	·247	·239	·244	·248	·246	·241	·239	·239	·242	·247	·256	·259	·259	·257	·261	·269	·272	·274	·276	·275	·282	·286	·295	·297	·296
Nov	·225	·231	·233	·239	·247	·248	·241	·246	·250	·248	·243	·241	·241	·244	·249	·258	·261	·261	·259	·263	·271	·273	·276	·278	·277	·283	·288	·297	·299	·298
Dec	·229	·236	·237	·244	·251	·253	·245	·250	·254	·252	·247	·246	·245	·249	·254	·262	·266	·266	·264	·267	·276	·278	·280	·282	·282	·288	·292	·302	·304	·302
1993																														
Jan	·241	·247	·249	·255	·263	·265	·257	·262	·266	·264	·259	·257	·257	·260	·265	·274	·278	·278	·276	·279	·288	·290	·292	·294	·294	·300	·305	·314	·316	·315
Feb	·233	·239	·241	·247	·255	·256	·249	·254	·258	·256	·251	·249	·249	·252	·257	·266	·269	·269	·267	·271	·280	·282	·284	·286	·285	·292	·296	·305	·308	·306
Mar	·228	·235	·236	·243	·251	·252	·244	·249	·253	·251	·246	·245	·244	·248	·253	·261	·265	·265	·263	·266	·275	·277	·279	·281	·281	·287	·291	·301	·303	·302
Apr	·217	·223	·225	·231	·239	·240	·233	·238	·242	·240	·235	·233	·233	·236	·241	·250	·253	·253	·251	·255	·263	·265	·267	·270	·269	·275	·280	·289	·291	·289
May	·213	·219	·220	·227	·235	·236	·228	·233	·237	·235	·230	·229	·228	·232	·237	·245	·249	·249	·247	·250	·259	·261	·263	·265	·264	·271	·275	·284	·286	·285
June	·213	·220	·221	·228	·235	·237	·229	·234	·238	·236	·231	·230	·229	·233	·238	·246	·250	·250	·248	·251	·260	·262	·264	·266	·265	·272	·276	·285	·287	·286
July	·216	·222	·224	·230	·238	·240	·232	·237	·241	·239	·234	·232	·232	·235	·240	·249	·252	·252	·250	·254	·262	·264	·267	·269	·268	·274	·279	·288	·290	·289
Aug	·211	·217	·219	·225	·233	·234	·226	·231	·236	·234	·229	·227	·226	·230	·235	·243	·247	·247	·245	·248	·257	·259	·261	·263	·263	·269	·273	·282	·285	·283
Sept	·206	·212	·214	·220	·228	·229	·221	·226	·230	·228	·223	·222	·221	·225	·230	·238	·242	·242	·240	·243	·252	·254	·256	·258	·257	·264	·268	·277	·279	·278
Oct	·207	·213	·214	·221	·228	·230	·222	·227	·231	·229	·224	·223	·222	·226	·231	·239	·243	·243	·240	·244	·252	·255	·257	·259	·258	·264	·269	·278	·280	·279
Nov	·208	·215	·216	·222	·230	·232	·224	·229	·233	·231	·226	·225	·224	·227	·232	·241	·244	·244	·242	·246	·254	·256	·258	·261	·260	·266	·270	·280	·282	·280
Dec	·206	·212	·214	·220	·228	·229	·221	·226	·230	·228	·223	·222	·221	·225	·230	·238	·242	·242	·240	·243	·252	·254	·256	·258	·257	·264	·268	·277	·279	·278
1994																														
Jan	·211	·217	·219	·225	·233	·234	·226	·231	·236	·234	·229	·227	·226	·230	·235	·243	·247	·247	·245	·248	·257	·259	·261	·263	·263	·269	·273	·282	·285	·283
Feb	·204	·210	·212	·218	·226	·227	·220	·224	·229	·227	·222	·220	·220	·223	·228	·236	·240	·240	·238	·241	·250	·252	·254	·256	·255	·262	·266	·275	·277	·276
Mar	·201	·207	·208	·215	·222	·224	·216	·221	·225	·223	·218	·217	·216	·220	·225	·233	·236	·236	·234	·238	·246	·248	·251	·253	·252	·258	·262	·272	·274	·272
Apr	·187	·193	·194	·200	·208	·209	·202	·207	·211	·209	·204	·202	·202	·205	·210	·218	·222	·222	·220	·223	·232	·234	·236	·238	·237	·243	·248	·257	·259	·257
May	·182	·189	·190	·196	·204	·205	·198	·202	·207	·205	·200	·198	·198	·201	·206	·214	·218	·218	·216	·219	·227	·229	·232	·234	·233	·239	·243	·252	·254	·253
June	·182	·189	·190	·196	·204	·205	·198	·202	·207	·205	·200	·198	·198	·201	·206	·214	·218	·218	·216	·219	·227	·229	·232	·234	·233	·239	·243	·252	·254	·253
July	·188	·194	·196	·202	·210	·211	·203	·208	·213	·210	·206	·204	·203	·207	·212	·220	·224	·224	·222	·225	·233	·235	·238	·240	·239	·245	·249	·258	·260	·259
Aug	·182	·189	·190	·196	·204	·205	·198	·202	·207	·205	·200	·198	·198	·201	·206	·214	·218	·218	·216	·219	·227	·229	·232	·234	·233	·239	·243	·252	·254	·253
Sept	·180	·186	·188	·194	·201	·203	·195	·200	·204	·202	·197	·196	·195	·199	·203	·212	·215	·215	·213	·217	·225	·227	·229	·231	·230	·237	·241	·250	·252	·250
Oct	·178	·185	·186	·192	·200	·201	·194	·198	·202	·200	·196	·194	·194	·197	·202	·210	·213	·213	·211	·215	·223	·225	·227	·229	·229	·235	·239	·248	·250	·249
Nov	·178	·184	·185	·191	·199	·200	·193	·198	·202	·200	·195	·193	·193	·196	·201	·209	·213	·213	·211	·214	·222	·224	·226	·228	·228	·234	·238	·247	·249	·248
Dec	·172	·178	·179	·186	·193	·195	·187	·192	·196	·194	·189	·188	·187	·190	·195	·203	·207	·207	·205	·208	·216	·218	·221	·223	·222	·228	·232	·241	·243	·242
1995																														
Jan	·172	·178	·179	·186	·193	·195	·187	·192	·196	·194	·189	·188	·187	·190	·195	·203	·207	·207	·205	·208	·216	·218	·221	·223	·222	·228	·232	·241	·243	·242
Feb	·165	·171	·172	·178	·186	·187	·180	·184	·189	·187	·182	·180	·180	·183	·188	·196	·199	·199	·197	·201	·209	·211	·213	·215	·214	·221	·225	·233	·236	·234
Mar	·160	·166	·167	·174	·181	·182	·175	·180	·184	·182	·177	·176	·175	·178	·183	·191	·195	·195	·193	·196	·204	·206	·208	·210	·209	·216	·220	·228	·231	·229
Apr	·148	·154	·156	·162	·169	·170	·163	·168	·172	·170	·165	·164	·163	·166	·171	·179	·183	·183	·181	·184	·192	·194	·196	·198	·197	·203	·207	·216	·218	·217
May	·144	·150	·151	·157	·164	·166	·158	·163	·167	·165	·160	·159	·158	·162	·166	·174	·178	·178	·176	·179	·187	·189	·191	·193	·193	·199	·203	·211	·213	·212
June	·142	·148	·150	·156	·163	·164	·157	·162	·166	·164	·159	·158	·157	·160	·165	·173	·176	·176	·174	·178	·186	·188	·190	·192	·191	·197	·201	·210	·212	·210
July	·148	·154	·155	·161	·168	·170	·162	·167	·171	·169	·164	·163	·162	·166	·170	·178	·182	·182	·180	·183	·191	·193	·195	·197	·197	·203	·207	·215	·217	·216
Aug	·141	·147	·149	·155	·162	·163	·156	·161	·165	·163	·158	·157	·156	·159	·164	·172	·175	·175	·173	·177	·185	·187	·189	·191	·190	·196	·200	·209	·211	·209
Sept	·136	·142	·143	·149	·157	·158	·151	·155	·159	·157	·153	·151	·151	·154	·159	·167	·170	·170	·168	·171	·179	·181	·183	·185	·185	·191	·195	·203	·205	·204
Oct	·142	·148	·150	·156	·163	·164	·157	·162	·166	·164	·159	·158	·157	·160	·165	·173	·176	·176	·174	·178	·186	·188	·190	·192	·191	·197	·201	·210	·212	·210
Nov	·142	·148	·150	·156	·163	·164	·157	·162	·166	·164	·159	·158	·157	·160	·165	·173	·176	·176	·174	·178	·186	·188	·190	·192	·191	·197	·201	·210	·212	·210
Dec	·135	·141	·143	·149	·156	·157	·150	·155	·159	·157	·152	·151	·150	·153	·158	·166	·169	·169	·167	·171	·179	·180	·182	·184	·184	·190	·194	·202	·204	·203

Month of disposal

Base month

	1998						1999												2000											
1996	July	Aug	Sept	Oct	Nov	Dec	Jan	Feb	Mar	Apr	May	June	July	Aug	Sept	Oct	Nov	Dec	Jan	Feb	Mar	Apr	May	June	July	Aug	Sept	Oct	Nov	Dec
Jan	·085	·090	·095	·095	·095	·095	·088	·090	·093	·100	·103	·103	·099	·102	·107	·109	·110	·114	·109	·115	·121	·132	·136	·139	·135	·135	·143	·142	·146	·146
Feb	·080	·085	·089	·090	·089	·089	·083	·085	·087	·095	·097	·097	·094	·097	·101	·103	·105	·109	·104	·110	·116	·127	·131	·134	·130	·130	·138	·137	·140	·141
Mar	·076	·081	·085	·086	·085	·085	·079	·081	·087	·090	·093	·093	·090	·092	·097	·099	·100	·104	·100	·106	·112	·123	·127	·129	·125	·125	·133	·133	·136	·137
Apr	·068	·073	·077	·078	·077	·077	·071	·073	·075	·083	·085	·085	·082	·085	·089	·091	·092	·096	·092	·098	·104	·115	·119	·121	·117	·117	·125	·125	·128	·128
May	·066	·071	·075	·076	·075	·075	·069	·071	·073	·080	·083	·083	·080	·082	·087	·089	·090	·094	·090	·095	·101	·112	·116	·119	·115	·115	·123	·122	·126	·126
June	·065	·070	·075	·075	·075	·075	·068	·070	·073	·080	·082	·082	·079	·082	·086	·088	·090	·093	·089	·095	·101	·112	·116	·118	·114	·114	·122	·122	·125	·125
July	·070	·074	·079	·079	·079	·079	·072	·074	·077	·084	·087	·087	·083	·086	·091	·093	·094	·098	·093	·099	·105	·116	·120	·123	·119	·119	·127	·126	·129	·130
Aug	·065	·069	·074	·074	·074	·074	·067	·069	·072	·079	·082	·082	·078	·081	·086	·088	·089	·093	·088	·094	·100	·111	·115	·118	·114	·114	·121	·121	·124	·125
Sept	·060	·064	·069	·070	·069	·069	·062	·064	·067	·074	·077	·077	·073	·076	·081	·083	·084	·088	·083	·089	·095	·106	·110	·112	·109	·109	·116	·116	·119	·120
Oct	·060	·064	·069	·070	·069	·069	·062	·064	·067	·074	·077	·077	·073	·076	·081	·083	·084	·088	·083	·089	·095	·106	·110	·112	·109	·109	·116	·116	·119	·120
Nov	·059	·064	·068	·069	·068	·068	·062	·064	·056	·073	·076	·076	·073	·075	·080	·082	·083	·087	·083	·088	·094	·105	·109	·112	·108	·108	·116	·115	·118	·119
Dec	·056	·060	·065	·065	·065	·065	·058	·060	·063	·070	·073	·073	·069	·072	·076	·078	·080	·084	·079	·085	·091	·102	·106	·108	·104	·104	·112	·111	·115	·115
1997																														
Jan	·056	·060	·065	·065	·065	·065	·058	·060	·063	·070	·073	·073	·069	·072	·076	·078	·080	·084	·079	·085	·091	·102	·106	·108	·104	·104	·112	·111	·115	·115
Feb	·052	·056	·061	·061	·061	·061	·054	·056	·059	·066	·068	·068	·065	·068	·072	·074	·075	·079	·075	·081	·086	·097	·101	·104	·100	·100	·108	·107	·110	·111
Mar	·049	·053	·058	·059	·058	·058	·051	·053	·056	·063	·066	·066	·062	·065	·069	·071	·073	·077	·072	·078	·084	·095	·098	·101	·097	·097	·105	·104	·107	·108
Apr	·043	·047	·052	·052	·052	·052	·045	·047	·050	·057	·060	·060	·056	·059	·063	·065	·067	·070	·066	·072	·077	·088	·092	·095	·091	·091	·099	·098	·101	·102
May	·039	·043	·048	·043	·048	·048	·041	·043	·046	·053	·055	·055	·052	·055	·059	·061	·062	·066	·062	·068	·073	·084	·088	·091	·087	·087	·094	·094	·097	·098
June	·035	·039	·044	·044	·044	·044	·037	·039	·042	·049	·051	·051	·048	·051	·055	·057	·058	·062	·058	·063	·069	·080	·084	·086	·083	·083	·090	·090	·093	·093
July	·035	·039	·044	·044	·044	·044	·037	·039	·042	·049	·051	·051	·048	·051	·055	·057	·058	·062	·058	·063	·069	·080	·084	·086	·083	·083	·090	·090	·093	·093
Aug	·028	·033	·037	·038	·037	·037	·031	·033	·035	·042	·045	·045	·042	·044	·049	·050	·052	·056	·051	·057	·062	·073	·077	·079	·076	·076	·083	·083	·086	·086
Sept	·023	·028	·032	·033	·032	·032	·026	·028	·030	·037	·040	·040	·036	·039	·043	·045	·046	·050	·046	·051	·057	·068	·072	·074	·070	·070	·078	·077	·080	·081
Oct	·022	·026	·031	·031	·031	·031	·024	·026	·029	·036	·038	·038	·035	·038	·042	·044	·045	·049	·045	·050	·056	·066	·070	·073	·069	·069	·076	·076	·079	·080
Nov	·021	·026	·030	·031	·030	·030	·024	·026	·028	·035	·038	·038	·034	·037	·041	·043	·044	·048	·044	·049	·055	·066	·070	·072	·068	·068	·076	·075	·078	·079
Dec	·019	·023	·028	·028	·028	·028	·021	·023	·025	·032	·035	·035	·032	·034	·039	·041	·042	·046	·041	·047	·053	·063	·067	·069	·066	·066	·073	·073	·076	·076
1998																														
Jan	·022	·026	·031	·031	·031	·031	·024	·026	·029	·036	·038	·038	·035	·038	·042	·044	·045	·049	·045	·050	·056	·066	·070	·073	·069	·069	·076	·076	·079	·080
Feb	·017	·021	·026	·026	·026	·026	·019	·021	·024	·031	·033	·033	·030	·032	·037	·039	·040	·044	·039	·045	·051	·061	·065	·067	·064	·064	·071	·070	·074	·074
Mar	·014	·018	·022	·023	·022	·022	·016	·018	·021	·027	·030	·030	·027	·029	·034	·035	·037	·040	·036	·042	·047	·058	·062	·064	·060	·060	·068	·067	·070	·071
Apr	·002	·007	·011	·012	·011	·011	·005	·007	·009	·016	·018	·018	·015	·018	·022	·024	·025	·029	·025	·030	·036	·046	·050	·052	·049	·049	·056	·055	·058	·059
May	·000	·001	·006	·006	·006	·006	·000	·001	·004	·010	·013	·013	·010	·012	·017	·018	·020	·023	·019	·024	·030	·040	·044	·046	·043	·043	·050	·050	·053	·053
June	·000	·002	·006	·007	·006	·006	·000	·002	·004	·011	·013	·013	·010	·013	·017	·019	·020	·024	·020	·025	·031	·041	·045	·047	·043	·043	·051	·050	·053	·054
July	—	·004	·009	·009	·009	·009	·002	·004	·007	·013	·016	·016	·013	·015	·020	·021	·023	·026	·022	·028	·033	·044	·047	·050	·046	·046	·053	·053	·056	·056
Aug	—	—	·004	·005	·004	·004	·000	·000	·002	·009	·012	·012	·009	·011	·015	·017	·018	·022	·018	·023	·029	·039	·043	·045	·042	·042	·049	·048	·051	·052
Sept	—	—	—	·001	·000	·000	·000	·000	·000	·005	·007	·007	·004	·007	·011	·013	·014	·018	·013	·019	·024	·035	·038	·041	·037	·037	·044	·044	·047	·047
Oct	—	—	—	—	·000	·000	·000	·000	·000	·004	·007	·007	·004	·006	·010	·012	·013	·017	·013	·018	·024	·034	·038	·040	·036	·036	·044	·043	·046	·047
Nov	—	—	—	—	—	·000	·000	·000	·000	·005	·007	·007	·004	·007	·011	·013	·014	·018	·013	·019	·024	·035	·038	·041	·037	·037	·044	·044	·047	·047
Dec	—	—	—	—	—	—	·000	·000	·000	·005	·007	·007	·004	·007	·011	·013	·014	·018	·013	·019	·024	·035	·038	·041	·037	·037	·044	·044	·047	·047
1999																														
Jan	—	—	—	—	—	—	—	·002	·004	·011	·013	·013	·010	·013	·017	·019	·020	·024	·020	·025	·031	·041	·045	·047	·043	·043	·051	·050	·053	·054
Feb	—	—	—	—	—	—	—	—	·002	·009	·012	·012	·009	·011	·015	·017	·018	·022	·018	·023	·029	·039	·043	·045	·042	·042	·049	·048	·051	·052
Mar	—	—	—	—	—	—	—	—	—	·007	·009	·009	·006	·009	·013	·015	·016	·020	·015	·021	·026	·037	·040	·043	·039	·039	·046	·046	·049	·049
Apr	—	—	—	—	—	—	—	—	—	—	·002	·002	·000	·002	·006	·008	·009	·013	·008	·014	·019	·030	·033	·036	·032	·032	·039	·039	·042	·042
May	—	—	—	—	—	—	—	—	—	—	—	·000	·000	·000	·004	·005	·007	·010	·006	·011	·017	·027	·031	·033	·030	·030	·037	·036	·039	·040
June	—	—	—	—	—	—	—	—	—	—	—	—	·000	·000	·004	·005	·007	·010	·006	·011	·017	·027	·031	·033	·030	·030	·037	·036	·039	·040
July	—	—	—	—	—	—	—	—	—	—	—	—	—	·002	·007	·008	·010	·013	·009	·015	·020	·030	·034	·036	·033	·033	·040	·039	·042	·043
Aug	—	—	—	—	—	—	—	—	—	—	—	—	—	—	·004	·006	·007	·011	·007	·012	·018	·028	·031	·034	·030	·030	·037	·037	·040	·040
Sept	—	—	—	—	—	—	—	—	—	—	—	—	—	—	—	·002	·003	·007	·002	·008	·013	·023	·027	·029	·026	·026	·033	·032	·035	·036
Oct	—	—	—	—	—	—	—	—	—	—	—	—	—	—	—	—	·001	·005	·001	·006	·011	·022	·025	·028	·024	·024	·031	·031	·034	·034
Nov	—	—	—	—	—	—	—	—	—	—	—	—	—	—	—	—	—	·004	·000	·005	·010	·020	·024	·026	·023	·023	·030	·029	·032	·033
Dec	—	—	—	—	—	—	—	—	—	—	—	—	—	—	—	—	—	—	·000	·001	·007	·017	·020	·023	·019	·019	·026	·026	·029	·029
2000																														
Jan	—	—	—	—	—	—	—	—	—	—	—	—	—	—	—	—	—	—	—	·005	·011	·021	·025	·027	·023	·023	·031	·030	·033	·034
Feb	—	—	—	—	—	—	—	—	—	—	—	—	—	—	—	—	—	—	—	—	·005	·016	·019	·021	·018	·018	·025	·024	·027	·028
Mar	—	—	—	—	—	—	—	—	—	—	—	—	—	—	—	—	—	—	—	—	—	·010	·014	·016	·012	·012	·020	·019	·022	·023
Apr	—	—	—	—	—	—	—	—	—	—	—	—	—	—	—	—	—	—	—	—	—	—	·004	·006	·002	·002	·009	·009	·012	·012
May	—	—	—	—	—	—	—	—	—	—	—	—	—	—	—	—	—	—	—	—	—	—	—	·002	·000	·000	·006	·005	·008	·009
June	—	—	—	—	—	—	—	—	—	—	—	—	—	—	—	—	—	—	—	—	—	—	—	—	·000	·000	·004	·003	·006	·006
July	—	—	—	—	—	—	—	—	—	—	—	—	—	—	—	—	—	—	—	—	—	—	—	—	—	·000	·007	·006	·009	·010
Aug	—	—	—	—	—	—	—	—	—	—	—	—	—	—	—	—	—	—	—	—	—	—	—	—	—	—	·007	·006	·009	·010
Sept	—	—	—	—	—	—	—	—	—	—	—	—	—	—	—	—	—	—	—	—	—	—	—	—	—	—	—	·000	·002	·003
Oct	—	—	—	—	—	—	—	—	—	—	—	—	—	—	—	—	—	—	—	—	—	—	—	—	—	—	—	—	·003	·003
Nov	—	—	—	—	—	—	—	—	—	—	—	—	—	—	—	—	—	—	—	—	—	—	—	—	—	—	—	—	—	·001
Dec	—	—	—	—	—	—	—	—	—	—	—	—	—	—	—	—	—	—	—	—	—	—	—	—	—	—	—	—	—	—

Indexation allowance — continued

Month of disposal

Base month

	2001												2002												2003					
1996	Jan	Feb	Mar	Apr	May	June	July	Aug	Sept	Oct	Nov	Dec	Jan	Feb	Mar	Apr	May	June	July	Aug	Sept	Oct	Nov	Dec	Jan	Feb	Mar	Apr	May	June
Jan	·139	·145	·146	·152	·160	·161	·154	·158	·162	·160	·156	·154	·154	·157	·162	·170	·173	·173	·171	·174	·182	·184	·186	·188	·188	·194	·198	·206	·208	·207
Feb	·134	·140	·141	·147	·154	·156	·148	·153	·157	·155	·150	·149	·148	·152	·156	·164	·168	·168	·166	·169	·177	·179	·181	·183	·182	·188	·192	·201	·203	·201
Mar	·129	·135	·137	·143	·150	·151	·144	·149	·152	·150	·146	·145	·144	·147	·152	·160	·163	·163	·161	·164	·172	·174	·176	·178	·178	·183	·187	·196	·198	·197
Apr	·121	·127	·128	·134	·142	·143	·136	·140	·144	·142	·138	·136	·136	·139	·144	·151	·155	·155	·153	·156	·164	·166	·168	·170	·169	·175	·179	·187	·189	·188
May	·119	·125	·126	·132	·139	·141	·133	·138	·142	·140	·135	·134	·133	·137	·141	·149	·152	·152	·150	·154	·162	·164	·165	·167	·167	·173	·177	·185	·187	·186
June	·118	·124	·125	·131	·139	·140	·133	·137	·141	·139	·135	·133	·133	·136	·141	·148	·152	·152	·150	·153	·161	·163	·165	·167	·166	·172	·176	·184	·186	·185
July	·123	·129	·130	·136	·143	·144	·137	·142	·146	·144	·139	·138	·137	·140	·145	·153	·156	·156	·154	·157	·165	·167	·169	·171	·171	·177	·180	·189	·191	·190
Aug	·118	·123	·125	·131	·138	·139	·132	·137	·140	·138	·134	·133	·132	·135	·140	·148	·151	·151	·149	·152	·160	·162	·164	·166	·165	·171	·175	·184	·185	·184
Sept	·112	·118	·120	·125	·133	·134	·127	·131	·135	·133	·129	·127	·127	·130	·135	·142	·146	·146	·144	·147	·155	·157	·159	·161	·160	·166	·170	·178	·180	·179
Oct	·112	·118	·120	·125	·133	·134	·127	·131	·135	·133	·129	·127	·127	·130	·135	·142	·146	·146	·144	·147	·155	·157	·159	·161	·160	·166	·170	·178	·180	·179
Nov	·112	·118	·119	·125	·132	·133	·126	·131	·135	·133	·128	·127	·126	·129	·134	·142	·145	·145	·143	·146	·154	·156	·158	·160	·159	·165	·169	·177	·179	·178
Dec	·108	·114	·115	·121	·128	·130	·122	·127	·131	·129	·124	·123	·122	·126	·130	·138	·141	·141	·139	·142	·150	·152	·154	·156	·155	·161	·165	·174	·176	·174
1997																														
Jan	·108	·114	·115	·121	·128	·130	·122	·127	·131	·129	·124	·123	·122	·126	·130	·138	·141	·141	·139	·142	·150	·152	·154	·156	·155	·161	·165	·174	·176	·174
Feb	·104	·110	·111	·117	·124	·125	·118	·123	·126	·125	·120	·119	·118	·121	·126	·134	·137	·137	·135	·138	·146	·148	·150	·152	·151	·157	·161	·169	·171	·170
Mar	·101	·107	·108	·114	·121	·122	·115	·120	·124	·122	·117	·116	·115	·118	·123	·131	·134	·134	·132	·135	·143	·145	·147	·149	·148	·154	·158	·166	·168	·167
Apr	·095	·100	·102	·107	·115	·116	·109	·113	·117	·115	·111	·109	·109	·112	·116	·124	·127	·127	·125	·129	·136	·138	·140	·142	·141	·147	·151	·159	·161	·160
May	·091	·096	·098	·103	·110	·112	·105	·109	·113	·111	·106	·105	·105	·108	·112	·120	·123	·123	·121	·124	·132	·134	·136	·138	·137	·143	·147	·155	·157	·156
June	·086	·092	·093	·099	·106	·107	·100	·105	·109	·107	·102	·101	·100	·103	·108	·116	·119	·119	·117	·120	·128	·130	·131	·133	·133	·138	·142	·150	·152	·151
July	·086	·092	·093	·099	·106	·107	·100	·105	·109	·107	·102	·101	·100	·103	·108	·116	·119	·119	·117	·120	·128	·130	·131	·133	·133	·138	·142	·150	·152	·151
Aug	·079	·085	·086	·092	·099	·100	·093	·098	·102	·100	·095	·094	·093	·097	·101	·109	·112	·112	·110	·113	·121	·122	·124	·126	·126	·131	·135	·143	·145	·144
Sept	·074	·080	·081	·087	·094	·095	·088	·092	·096	·094	·090	·089	·088	·091	·095	·103	·106	·106	·104	·107	·115	·117	·119	·121	·120	·126	·129	·137	·139	·138
Oct	·073	·078	·080	·085	·092	·093	·087	·091	·095	·093	·088	·087	·087	·090	·094	·102	·105	·105	·103	·106	·113	·115	·117	·119	·118	·124	·128	·136	·138	·137
Nov	·072	·078	·079	·085	·091	·093	·086	·090	·094	·092	·088	·086	·086	·089	·093	·101	·104	·104	·102	·105	·113	·115	·117	·118	·118	·123	·127	·135	·137	·136
Dec	·069	·075	·076	·082	·089	·090	·083	·088	·091	·089	·085	·084	·083	·086	·091	·098	·101	·101	·099	·103	·110	·112	·114	·116	·115	·121	·124	·133	·134	·133
1998																														
Jan	·073	·078	·080	·085	·092	·093	·087	·091	·095	·093	·088	·087	·087	·090	·094	·102	·105	·105	·103	·106	·113	·115	·117	·119	·118	·124	·128	·136	·138	·137
Feb	·067	·073	·074	·080	·087	·088	·081	·085	·089	·087	·083	·082	·081	·084	·089	·096	·099	·099	·097	·100	·108	·110	·112	·114	·113	·119	·122	·130	·132	·131
Mar	·064	·070	·071	·076	·083	·085	·078	·082	·086	·084	·080	·078	·078	·081	·085	·093	·096	·096	·094	·097	·104	·106	·108	·110	·109	·115	·119	·127	·129	·127
Apr	·052	·058	·059	·065	·071	·073	·066	·070	·074	·072	·068	·066	·066	·069	·073	·081	·084	·084	·082	·085	·092	·094	·096	·098	·097	·103	·106	·114	·116	·115
May	·046	·052	·053	·059	·065	·067	·060	·064	·068	·066	·062	·061	·060	·063	·067	·075	·078	·078	·076	·079	·086	·088	·090	·092	·091	·097	·100	·108	·110	·109
June	·047	·053	·054	·059	·066	·067	·061	·065	·069	·067	·062	·061	·061	·064	·068	·075	·078	·078	·076	·080	·087	·089	·091	·092	·092	·097	·101	·109	·111	·110
July	·050	·055	·056	·062	·069	·070	·063	·067	·071	·069	·065	·064	·063	·066	·071	·078	·081	·081	·079	·082	·090	·091	·093	·095	·094	·100	·104	·112	·113	·112
Aug	·045	·051	·052	·057	·064	·065	·059	·063	·067	·065	·060	·059	·059	·062	·066	·073	·076	·076	·075	·078	·085	·087	·089	·090	·090	·095	·099	·107	·109	·108
Sept	·041	·046	·047	·053	·060	·061	·054	·058	·062	·060	·056	·055	·054	·057	·061	·069	·072	·072	·070	·073	·080	·082	·084	·086	·085	·091	·094	·102	·104	·103
Oct	·040	·046	·047	·052	·059	·060	·053	·058	·061	·060	·055	·054	·053	·057	·061	·068	·071	·071	·069	·072	·080	·081	·083	·085	·084	·090	·094	·102	·103	·102
Nov	·041	·046	·047	·053	·060	·061	·054	·058	·062	·060	·056	·055	·054	·057	·061	·069	·072	·072	·070	·073	·080	·082	·084	·086	·085	·091	·094	·102	·104	·103
Dec	·041	·046	·047	·053	·060	·061	·054	·058	·062	·060	·056	·055	·054	·057	·061	·069	·072	·072	·070	·073	·080	·082	·084	·086	·085	·091	·094	·102	·104	·103
1999																														
Jan	·047	·053	·054	·059	·066	·067	·061	·065	·069	·067	·062	·061	·061	·064	·068	·075	·078	·078	·076	·080	·087	·089	·091	·092	·092	·097	·101	·109	·111	·110
Feb	·045	·051	·052	·057	·064	·065	·059	·063	·067	·065	·060	·059	·059	·062	·066	·073	·076	·076	·075	·078	·085	·087	·089	·090	·090	·095	·099	·107	·109	·108
Mar	·043	·048	·049	·055	·062	·063	·056	·060	·064	·062	·058	·057	·056	·059	·063	·071	·074	·074	·072	·075	·082	·084	·086	·088	·087	·093	·096	·104	·106	·105
Apr	·036	·041	·042	·048	·054	·056	·049	·053	·057	·055	·051	·050	·049	·052	·056	·064	·067	·067	·065	·068	·075	·077	·079	·081	·080	·085	·089	·097	·099	·097
May	·033	·039	·040	·045	·052	·053	·046	·051	·054	·053	·048	·047	·046	·050	·054	·061	·064	·064	·062	·065	·072	·074	·076	·078	·077	·083	·086	·094	·096	·095
June	·033	·039	·040	·045	·052	·053	·046	·051	·054	·053	·048	·047	·046	·050	·054	·061	·064	·064	·062	·065	·072	·074	·076	·078	·077	·083	·086	·094	·096	·095
July	·036	·042	·043	·048	·055	·056	·050	·054	·058	·056	·051	·050	·050	·053	·057	·064	·067	·067	·065	·068	·076	·078	·079	·081	·081	·086	·090	·098	·099	·098
Aug	·034	·039	·040	·046	·053	·054	·047	·051	·055	·053	·049	·048	·047	·050	·054	·062	·065	·065	·063	·066	·073	·075	·077	·079	·078	·083	·087	·095	·097	·095
Sept	·029	·035	·036	·042	·048	·049	·043	·047	·051	·049	·045	·043	·043	·046	·050	·057	·060	·060	·058	·061	·069	·070	·072	·074	·073	·079	·082	·090	·092	·091
Oct	·028	·033	·034	·040	·046	·047	·041	·045	·049	·047	·043	·041	·041	·044	·048	·055	·058	·058	·056	·059	·067	·068	·070	·072	·071	·077	·080	·088	·090	·089
Nov	·026	·032	·033	·038	·045	·046	·040	·044	·047	·046	·041	·040	·040	·043	·047	·054	·057	·057	·055	·058	·065	·067	·069	·071	·070	·076	·079	·087	·089	·088
Dec	·023	·028	·029	·035	·041	·042	·036	·040	·044	·042	·038	·036	·036	·039	·043	·050	·053	·053	·051	·054	·062	·063	·065	·067	·066	·072	·075	·083	·085	·084
2000																														
Jan	·027	·032	·034	·039	·046	·047	·040	·044	·048	·046	·042	·041	·040	·043	·047	·055	·058	·058	·056	·059	·066	·068	·070	·071	·071	·076	·080	·088	·089	·088
Feb	·021	·027	·028	·033	·040	·041	·035	·039	·042	·041	·036	·035	·035	·038	·042	·049	·052	·052	·050	·053	·060	·062	·064	·066	·065	·070	·074	·082	·084	·082
Mar	·016	·021	·023	·028	·034	·036	·029	·033	·037	·035	·031	·030	·029	·032	·036	·043	·046	·046	·045	·048	·055	·056	·058	·060	·059	·065	·068	·076	·078	·077
Apr	·006	·011	·012	·018	·024	·025	·019	·023	·026	·025	·021	·019	·019	·022	·026	·033	·036	·036	·034	·037	·044	·046	·048	·049	·049	·054	·058	·065	·067	·066
May	·002	·008	·009	·014	·021	·022	·015	·019	·023	·021	·017	·016	·015	·018	·022	·029	·032	·032	·030	·033	·040	·042	·044	·046	·045	·050	·054	·062	·063	·062
June	·000	·005	·006	·012	·018	·019	·013	·017	·020	·019	·015	·013	·013	·016	·020	·027	·030	·030	·028	·031	·038	·040	·041	·043	·043	·048	·051	·059	·061	·060
July	·004	·009	·010	·015	·022	·023	·016	·021	·024	·022	·018	·017	·016	·019	·023	·030	·033	·033	·032	·035	·042	·043	·045	·047	·046	·052	·055	·063	·065	·063
Aug	·004	·009	·010	·015	·022	·023	·016	·021	·024	·022	·018	·017	·016	·019	·023	·030	·033	·033	·032	·035	·042	·043	·045	·047	·046	·052	·055	·063	·065	·063
Sept	·000	·002	·003	·008	·015	·016	·009	·013	·017	·015	·011	·010	·009	·012	·016	·023	·026	·026	·024	·027	·034	·036	·038	·040	·039	·044	·048	·055	·057	·056
Oct	·000	·002	·003	·009	·015	·016	·010	·014	·017	·016	·012	·010	·010	·013	·017	·024	·027	·027	·025	·028	·035	·037	·038	·040	·040	·045	·048	·056	·058	·057
Nov	·000	·000	·001	·006	·012	·013	·007	·011	·015	·013	·009	·008	·007	·010	·014	·021	·024	·024	·022	·025	·032	·034	·035	·037	·037	·042	·045	·053	·055	·053
Dec	·000	·000	·000	·005	·012	·013	·006	·010	·014	·012	·008	·007	·006	·009	·013	·020	·023	·023	·021	·024	·031	·033	·035	·037	·036	·041	·045	·052	·054	·053

Month of disposal

Base month

	2001												2002												2003					
2001	Jan	Feb	Mar	Apr	May	June	July	Aug	Sept	Oct	Nov	Dec	Jan	Feb	Mar	Apr	May	June	July	Aug	Sept	Oct	Nov	Dec	Jan	Feb	Mar	Apr	May	June
Jan	—	·005	·006	·012	·018	·019	·013	·017	·020	·019	·015	·013	·013	·016	·020	·027	·030	·030	·028	·031	·038	·040	·041	·043	·043	·048	·051	·059	·061	·060
Feb	—	—	·001	·006	·013	·014	·008	·012	·015	·013	·009	·008	·008	·010	·015	·022	·024	·024	·023	·026	·033	·034	·036	·038	·037	·042	·046	·053	·055	·054
Mar	—	—	—	·005	·012	·013	·006	·010	·014	·012	·008	·007	·006	·009	·013	·020	·023	·023	·021	·024	·031	·033	·035	·037	·036	·041	·045	·052	·054	·053
Apr	—	—	—	—	·006	·008	·001	·005	·009	·007	·003	·002	·001	·004	·008	·015	·018	·018	·016	·019	·026	·028	·029	·031	·031	·036	·039	·047	·049	·047
May	—	—	—	—	—	·001	·000	·000	·002	·001	·000	·000	·000	·000	·002	·009	·011	·011	·010	·013	·020	·021	·023	·025	·024	·029	·033	·040	·042	·041
Jun	—	—	—	—	—	—	·000	·000	·001	·000	·000	·000	·000	·000	·001	·007	·010	·010	·009	·011	·018	·020	·022	·024	·023	·028	·032	·039	·041	·040
Jul	—	—	—	—	—	—	—	·004	·008	·006	·002	·001	·000	·003	·007	·014	·017	·017	·015	·018	·025	·027	·028	·030	·029	·035	·038	·046	·047	·046
Aug	—	—	—	—	—	—	—	—	·003	·002	·000	·000	·000	·000	·003	·010	·013	·013	·01[illegible]	·014	·021	·022	·024	·026	·025	·030	·034	·041	·043	·042
Sep	—	—	—	—	—	—	—	—	—	·000	·000	·000	·000	·000	·000	·006	·009	·009	·007	·010	·017	·019	·021	·022	·022	·027	·030	·038	·040	·038
Oct	—	—	—	—	—	—	—	—	—	—	·000	·000	·000	·000	·001	·008	·011	·011	·009	·012	·019	·021	·022	·024	·024	·029	·032	·040	·041	·040
Nov	—	—	—	—	—	—	—	—	—	—	—	·000	·000	·001	·005	·012	·015	·015	·013	·016	·023	·025	·026	·028	·028	·033	·036	·044	·046	·044
Dec	—	—	—	—	—	—	—	—	—	—	—	—	·000	·002	·006	·013	·016	·016	·014	·017	·024	·026	·028	·029	·029	·034	·037	·045	·047	·046
2002																														
Jan	—	—	—	—	—	—	—	—	—	—	—	—	—	·003	·007	·014	·017	·017	·015	·018	·025	·027	·028	·030	·029	·035	·038	·046	·047	·046
Feb	—	—	—	—	—	—	—	—	—	—	—	—	—	—	·004	·011	·014	·014	·012	·015	·022	·024	·025	·027	·026	·032	·035	·043	·044	·043
Mar	—	—	—	—	—	—	—	—	—	—	—	—	—	—	—	·007	·010	·010	·008	·011	·018	·019	·021	·023	·022	·028	·031	·038	·040	·039
Apr	—	—	—	—	—	—	—	—	—	—	—	—	—	—	—	—	·003	·003	·001	·004	·011	·013	·014	·016	·015	·020	·024	·031	·033	·032
May	—	—	—	—	—	—	—	—	—	—	—	—	—	—	—	—	—	·000	·000	·001	·008	·010	·011	·013	·012	·018	·021	·028	·030	·029
June	—	—	—	—	—	—	—	—	—	—	—	—	—	—	—	—	—	—	·000	·001	·008	·010	·011	·013	·012	·018	·021	·028	·030	·029
July	—	—	—	—	—	—	—	—	—	—	—	—	—	—	—	—	—	—	—	·003	·010	·011	·013	·015	·014	·019	·023	·030	·032	·031
Aug	—	—	—	—	—	—	—	—	—	—	—	—	—	—	—	—	—	—	—	—	·007	·009	·010	·012	·011	·016	·020	·027	·029	·028
Sept	—	—	—	—	—	—	—	—	—	—	—	—	—	—	—	—	—	—	—	—	—	·002	·003	·005	·005	·010	·013	·020	·022	·021
Oct	—	—	—	—	—	—	—	—	—	—	—	—	—	—	—	—	—	—	—	—	—	—	·002	·003	·003	·008	·011	·019	·020	·019
Nov	—	—	—	—	—	—	—	—	—	—	—	—	—	—	—	—	—	—	—	—	—	—	—	·002	·001	·006	·010	·017	·019	·017
Dec	—	—	—	—	—	—	—	—	—	—	—	—	—	—	—	—	—	—	—	—	—	—	—	—	·000	·004	·008	·015	·017	·016
2003																														
Jan	—	—	—	—	—	—	—	—	—	—	—	—	—	—	—	—	—	—	—	—	—	—	—	—	—	·005	·008	·016	·017	·016
Feb	—	—	—	—	—	—	—	—	—	—	—	—	—	—	—	—	—	—	—	—	—	—	—	—	—	—	·003	·011	·012	·011
Mar	—	—	—	—	—	—	—	—	—	—	—	—	—	—	—	—	—	—	—	—	—	—	—	—	—	—	—	·007	·009	·008
Apr	—	—	—	—	—	—	—	—	—	—	—	—	—	—	—	—	—	—	—	—	—	—	—	—	—	—	—	—	·002	·001
May	—	—	—	—	—	—	—	—	—	—	—	—	—	—	—	—	—	—	—	—	—	—	—	—	—	—	—	—	—	·000
June	—	—	—	—	—	—	—	—	—	—	—	—	—	—	—	—	—	—	—	—	—	—	—	—	—	—	—	—	—	—

Note

In the sixty-fourth edition of Whillans's Tax Tables 2002–03 Finance Act Edition the figures for disposals from February to June 2002 relating to acquisitions from May to December 2001 were incorrect. The Inland Revenue provided corrections after that edition had gone to press. The figures were duly corrected in the sixty-fifth, 2003–04 Budget edition.

Retail prices index

	Jan	Feb	Mar	Apr	May	June	July	Aug	Sept	Oct	Nov	Dec
1950	8·73	8·73	8·73	8·81	8·81	8·81	8·81	8·73	8·81	8·89	8·97	8·97
1951	9·03	9·11	9·19	9·35	9·59	9·67	9·72	9·80	9·88	9·96	9·96	10·04
1952	10·20	10·28	10·28	10·44	10·44	10·65	10·65	10·04	9·96	10·11	10·11	10·11
1953	10·11	10·19	10·67	10·34	10·27	10·34	10·34	10·27	10·27	10·27	10·27	10·27
1954	10·27	10·27	10·34	10·42	10·34	10·42	10·62	10·57	10·49	10·57	10·62	10·62
1955	10·70	10·70	10·70	10·77	10·77	11·00	11·00	10·93	11·00	11·15	11·28	11·28
1956	11·25	11·25	11·38	11·56	11·53	11·51	11·48	11·51	11·48	11·56	11·58	11·63
1957	11·74	11·74	11·71	11·76	11·76	11·89	11·99	11·96	11·94	12·04	12·12	12·17
1958	12·17	12·09	12·19	12·32	12·29	12·40	12·19	12·19	12·19	12·29	12·34	12·40
1959	12·42	12·40	12·40	12·32	12·27	12·29	12·27	12·29	12·22	12·29	12·37	12·40
1960	12·37	12·37	12·34	12·40	12·40	12·47	12·50	12·42	12·42	12·52	12·60	12·62
1961	12·62	12·62	12·67	12·75	12·78	12·90	12·90	13·00	13·00	13·00	13·16	13·18
1962	13·21	13·23	13·28	13·46	13·51	13·59	13·54	13·43	13·41	13·41	13·46	13·51
1963	13·56	13·69	13·71	13·74	13·74	13·74	13·66	13·61	13·66	13·71	13·74	13·76
1964	13·84	13·84	13·89	14·02	14·14	14·20	14·20	14·25	14·25	14·27	14·37	14·42
1965	14·47	14·47	14·52	14·80	14·85	14·90	14·90	14·93	14·93	14·96	15·01	15·08
1966	15·11	15·11	15·13	15·34	15·44	15·49	15·41	15·51	15·49	15·51	15·61	15·64
1967	15·67	15·67	15·67	15·79	15·79	15·84	15·74	15·72	15·69	15·86	15·92	16·02
1968	16·07	16·15	16·20	16·50	16·50	16·58	16·58	16·60	16·63	16·70	16·76	16·96
1969	17·06	17·16	17·21	17·41	17·39	17·47	17·47	17·41	17·47	17·59	17·64	17·77
1970	17·90	18·00	18·10	18·38	18·43	18·48	18·63	18·61	18·71	18·91	19·04	19·16
1971	19·42	19·54	19·70	20·13	20·25	20·38	20·51	20·53	20·56	20·66	20·79	20·89
1972	21·01	21·12	21·19	21·39	21·50	21·62	21·70	21·88	22·00	22·31	22·38	22·48
1973	22·64	22·79	22·92	23·35	23·52	23·65	23·75	23·83	24·03	24·51	24·69	24·87
1974	25·35	25·78	26·01	26·89	27·28	27·55	27·81	27·83	28·14	28·69	29·20	29·63
1975	30·39	30·90	31·51	32·72	34·09	34·75	35·11	35·31	35·61	36·12	36·55	37·01
1976	37·49	37·97	38·17	38·91	39·34	39·54	39·62	40·18	40·71	41·44	42·03	42·59
1977	43·70	44·24	44·56	45·70	46·06	46·54	46·59	46·82	47·07	47·28	47·50	47·76
1978	48·04	48·31	48·62	49·33	49·61	49·99	50·22	50·54	50·75	50·98	51·33	51·76
1979	52·52	52·95	53·38	54·30	54·73	55·67	58·07	58·53	59·11	59·72	60·25	60·68
1980	62·18	63·07	63·93	66·11	66·72	67·35	67·91	68·06	68·49	68·92	69·48	69·86
1981	70·29	70·93	71·99	74·07	74·55	74·98	75·31	75·87	76·30	76·98	77·78	78·28
1982	78·73	78·76	79·44	81·04	81·62	81·85	81·88	81·90	81·85	82·26	82·66	82·51
1983	82·61	82·97	83·12	84·28	84·64	84·84	85·30	85·68	86·06	86·36	86·67	86·89
1984	86·84	87·20	87·48	88·64	88·97	89·20	89·10	89·94	90·11	90·67	90·95	90·87
1985	91·20	91·94	92·80	94·78	95·21	95·41	95·23	95·49	95·44	95·59	95·92	96·05
1986	96·25	96·60	96·73	97·67	97·85	97·79	97·52	97·82	98·30	98·45	99·29	99·62
1987	100·00	100·40	100·60	101·80	101·90	101·90	101·80	102·10	102·40	102·90	103·40	103·30
1988	103·30	103·70	104·10	105·80	106·20	106·60	106·70	107·90	108·40	109·50	110·00	110·30
1989	111·00	111·80	112·30	114·30	115·00	115·40	115·50	115·80	116·60	117·50	118·50	118·80
1990	119·50	120·20	121·40	125·10	126·20	126·70	126·80	128·10	129·30	130·30	130·00	129·90
1991	130·20	130·90	131·40	133·10	133·50	134·10	133·80	134·10	134·60	135·10	135·60	135·70
1992	135·60	136·30	136·70	138·80	139·30	139·30	138·80	138·90	139·40	139·90	139·70	139·20
1993	137·90	138·80	139·30	140·60	141·10	141·00	140·70	141·30	141·90	141·80	141·60	141·90
1994	141·30	142·10	142·50	144·20	144·70	144·70	144·00	144·70	145·00	145·20	145·30	146·00
1995	146·00	146·90	147·50	149·00	149·60	149·80	149·10	149·90	150·60	149·80	149·80	150·70
1996	150·20	150·90	151·50	152·60	152·90	153·00	152·40	153·10	153·80	153·80	153·90	154·40
1997	154·40	155·00	155·40	156·30	156·90	157·50	157·50	158·50	159·30	159·50	159·60	160·00
1998	159·50	160·30	160·80	162·60	163·50	163·40	163·00	163·70	164·40	164·50	164·40	164·40
1999	163·40	163·70	164·10	165·20	165·60	165·60	165·10	165·50	166·20	166·50	166·70	167·30
2000	166·60	167·50	168·40	170·10	170·70	171·10	170·50	170·50	171·70	171·60	172·10	172·20
2001	171·10	172·00	172·20	173·10	174·20	174·40	173·30	174·00	174·60	174·30	173·60	173·40
2002	173·30	173·80	174·50	175·70	176·20	176·20	175·90	176·40	177·60	177·90	178·20	178·50
2003	178·40	179·30	179·90	181·20	181·50	181·30						

Corporation tax

Rates of corporation tax and advance corporation tax

Financial year	1995	1996	1997	1998	1999	2000	2001	2002	2003
Corporation tax (full rate)	33%	33%	31%	31%	30%	30%	30%	30%	30%
Advance corporation tax: from 6 April	¼	¼	¼	¼	—*	—	—	—	—
Tax credit: from 6 April	20%†	20%†	20%†	20%†	10%†	10%†	10%†	10%†	10%†

The full rate of corporation tax will remain at 30% for the financial year beginning on 1 April 2004 (FA 2003 s 133).

* Advance corporation tax is abolished from 6 April 1999.

† Individual shareholders not subject to tax at the higher rate will have no further tax to pay. The abolition of the repayment of the tax credit to charities is phased in over five years at 21% for 1999–2000, 17% for 2000–01, 13% for 2001–02, 8% for 2002–03 and 4% for 2003–04.

Starting and small companies' rates (TA 1988 ss 13, 13AA)

Financial year:	1997	1998	1999	2000	2001	2002	2003
Starting rate	—	—	—	10%	10%	0%	0%
first relevant amount*	—	—	—	£10,000	£10,000	£10,000	£10,000
second relevant amount*	—	—	—	£50,000	£50,000	£50,000	£50,000
marginal relief fraction	—	—	—	1/40	1/40	19/400	19/400
effective marginal rate†	—	—	—	22.5%	22.5%	23.75%	23.75%
Small companies' rate	21%	21%	20%	20%	20%	19%	19%
lower relevant amount*	£300,000	£300,000	£300,000	£300,000	£300,000	£300,000	£300,000
upper relevant amount*	£1,500,000	£1,500,000	£1,500,000	£1,500,000	£1,500,000	£1,500,000	£1,500,000
marginal relief fraction	1/40	1/40	1/40	1/40	1/40	11/400	11/400
effective marginal rate†	33.5%	33.5%	32.5%	32.5%	32.5%	32.75%	32.75%

* Reduced proportionally for accounting periods of less than 12 months. Associated companies: divide limits by total number of associated companies (including the company in question).

1) The starting and the small companies' rate apply to *basic profits* ("I") where *profits* ("P") do not exceed the first (in the case of the starting rate) and lower (small companies' rate) relevant amounts.

2) Where *profits* ("P") exceed the first or lower relevant amounts but not the second or upper relevant amounts, corporation tax on *basic profits* ("I") is reduced by—

$$(\text{second or upper relevant amount} - P) \times \frac{I}{P} \times \text{fraction}$$

For the purposes of 1) and 2) above:

P = profits as finally computed for corporation tax purposes *plus* franked investment income *excluding* franked investment income from UK companies in the same group or from UK companies owned by a consortium of which the recipient is a member (TA 1988 s 13(7) amended by FA 1998 Sch 3 para 7 for distributions made after 5 April 1999).

I = profits on which corporation tax is actually borne (income plus chargeable gains).

† Where there is no franked investment income, an alternative to the above formula is to apply the starting or small companies' rate up to the first or lower relevant amount and the marginal rate to the balance of the profits.

Corporate venturing scheme (FA 2000 s 63, Schs 15, 16; FA 2001 s 64, Sch 16)

	1.4.00–6.3.01	7.3.01 onwards
Rate of corporation tax relief	20%	20%
Minimum percentage of investee company's ordinary share capital held by individuals	20%	20%
Investing company's maximum stake in investee company	30%	30%
Minimum investment period	3 years	3 years
Minimum percentage of invested money employed in qualifying business within 12 months	100%	80%

Companies can obtain corporation tax relief on amounts invested in new ordinary unquoted shares in small higher-risk trading companies.

Research and development (FA 2000 ss 68, 69, Schs 19, 20; FA 2002 s 53, Sch 12; FA 2003 s 168, Sch 31)

Minimum threshold on spending[1]	£10,000
Large companies (from 1 April 2002) Rate of corporation tax relief	125%
Small and medium-sized companies (from 1 April 2000) Rate of corporation tax relief Maximum turnover limit	150% £25 million

[1] The threshold is reduced from £25,000 to £10,000 from 9 April 2003 for large companies and from a date to be announced for SMEs.

Companies not yet in profit or which have not yet started to trade can claim the relief up front.

See also the 100% capital allowance for research and development, p 56.

Research into vaccines and medicines for the prevention and treatment of specified diseases: extra 50% relief from 22 April 2003 (FA 2002 s 54, Schs 13, 14; FA 2003 s 168, Sch 31).

Community Investment Tax Relief see page 69.

Urban Regeneration Companies see page 67.

Capital allowances

Rates

Agricultural and forestry land

Expenditure incurred after		% Rate
Initial allowance	31 March 1986	Nil
	31 October 1992[1]	20
	31 October 1993	Nil
Writing-down allowance	31 March 1986	4

Note:

[1] Initial allowances were temporarily reintroduced for 1 year in respect of capital expenditure on agricultural buildings or works. The allowances applied to buildings or works constructed under a contract entered into between 1 November 1992 and 31 October 1993, and brought into use for the purposes of the farming trade by 31 December 1994. See CAA 1990 s 124A.

Dredging

Expenditure incurred after		% Rate
Initial allowance	31 March 1986	Nil
Writing-down allowance	5 November 1962	4

Industrial buildings and structures

Expenditure[1] incurred after		% Rate
Initial allowance		
Generally:	31 March 1986	Nil
	31 October 1992[2]	20
	31 October 1993	Nil
Exceptions:		
Enterprise zones	within 10 years of site being included in zone[3]	100
Writing-down allowance		
Generally:	5 April 1946	2
	5 November 1962[4]	4
Exception:		
Enterprise zones	within 10 years of site being included in zone[5]	25

Notes:

[1] The amount qualifying for allowance is the price paid for the relevant interest *minus* (i) the value of the land element and (ii) any value attributable to elements over and above those which would feature in a normal commercial lease negotiated in the open market: FA 1995 s 100 confirming previous practice.

[2] Initial allowances were temporarily reintroduced for 1 year in respect of capital expenditure on industrial buildings and qualifying hotels. The allowances applied to buildings constructed under, or bought unused under, a contract entered into after 31 October 1992 and before 1 November 1993, and brought into use in qualifying trade by 31 December 1994. Balance of relief by 4% pa writing-down allowance. All or part of the initial allowance could be disclaimed. See CAA 1990 ss 2A, 10C.

[3] CAA 2001 s 306. Includes expenditure on qualifying hotels. See p 56 for a list of enterprise zones.

[4] Includes expenditure on qualifying hotels (other than in an enterprise zone).
Also includes expenditure on the construction of toll roads incurred for accounting periods or basis periods ending after 5 April 1991.

[5] CAA 2001 s 310. Includes expenditure on qualifying hotels. See p 56 for a list of enterprise zones.

Films

From 10 March 1992, pre-production expenditure on films produced with sufficient EU content is relieved as it occurs. 100% write-off is available for expenditure incurred after 1 July 1997 and before 2 July 2005 on a qualifying British film completed after 1 July 1997. See F(No 2)A 1992 ss 41, 42; F(No 2)A 1997 s 48; FA 2001 s 72; Statement of Practice SP1/98. The rules are amended for certain films completed after 16 April 2002 and to certain acquisition expenditure incurred after 29 June 2002 (FA 2002 ss 99–101).

Flat conversions

Expenditure incurred after		% Rate
Initial allowance	10 May 2001[1]	100

Note:

[1] Expenditure incurred on renovating or converting vacant or storage space above commercial properties to provide low value flats for rent (CAA 2001 ss 393A–393W; FA 2001 s 67, Sch 19).

Know-how

Writing-down allowance

Expenditure incurred after 31 March 1986: annual 25% writing-down allowance (reducing balance basis).

Plant and machinery Expenditure incurred	after	before	% Rate
First-year allowance (FYA)			
Generally:	31 October 1993[1]		Nil
Exceptions:			
Small and medium-sized businesses	1 July 1997[2]	2 July 1998	50
	1 July 1998[3]		40
Small and medium-sized businesses in Northern Ireland *only*	11 May 1998[4]	12 May 2002	100
Small businesses: ICT	31 March 2000[5]	1 April 2004	100
Energy-saving plant or machinery	31 March 2001[6]		100
New low-emission cars and refuelling equipment	16 April 2002[7]	1 April 2008	100
Environmentally beneficial plant or machinery	31 March 2003[8]		100
Writing-down allowance (WDA)			
Generally:	26 October 1970[9]		25
Exception:			
Leasing to non-residents	31 October 1993[9]		10
FYA: long-life assets			
Generally:	25 November 1996		Nil
Exceptions:			
Small and medium-sized businesses	1 July 1997[2]	2 July 1998	12
	1 July 1998		Nil
WDA: long-life assets[10]	25 November 1996[9]		6

Notes:

[1] First-year allowances available universally had been generally abolished for expenditure after 31 March 1986 but were reintroduced temporarily at the rate of 40% for expenditure in the 12 months to 31 October 1993. Thereafter, first-year allowances have been specifically targeted as below.

[2] Qualifying expenditure incurred by *qualifying businesses* during the year ended 1 July 1998. The higher FYA does not apply to certain expenditure including that on plant and machinery for leasing, motor cars, ships or railway assets. After the first year, allowances revert to the normal writing-down rate of 25% (or 6% for long-life assets). Qualifying businesses are, broadly, those which satisfy any two of the following conditions: (*a*) turnover £11,200,000 or less (*b*) assets £5,600,000 or less (*c*) not more than 250 employees (CAA 1990 ss 22(3C)(6B), 22A).

[3] *Small and medium-sized businesses*: 40% first-year allowances for qualifying expenditure incurred after 1 July 1998. The conditions for relief are similar to those outlined in footnote 2 above, but long-life assets do not qualify (see footnote 10 below) (CAA 2001 ss 44, 46–49).

[4] The conditions for relief are similar to those outlined in footnote 2 above, but long-life assets and goods vehicles used in freight haulage businesses do not qualify (CAA 2001 ss 40–43, 46).

[5] *ICT (information and communications technology)*: 100% first-year allowances for *small businesses* buying computers or investing in e-commerce and new information technology. The allowance is extended to 31 March 2004 (FA 2003 s 165). Small businesses are, broadly, those which satisfy any two of the following conditions: (*a*) turnover £2,800,000 or less (*b*) assets £1,400,000 or less (*c*) not more than 50 employees (CAA 2001 ss 45, 46).

[6] *Energy-saving plant or machinery*: 100% first-year allowances are available for investment by *any* business in designated energy-saving plant and machinery in accordance with the Government's Energy Technology Product List (CAA 2001 ss 45A–45C; FA 2001 s 65, Sch 17; SI 2001/2541). For expenditure incurred after 16 April 2002, the List is extended, and the 100% allowance is available where the asset is for leasing, letting or hire (CA 2001 s 46). The product lists are available at www.eca.gov.uk.

[7] For expenditure incurred after 16 April 2002 and before 1 April 2008, the allowance is given on (a) cars which are either electrically propelled or emit not more than 120g/km of carbon dioxide, registered after 16 April 2002 and (b) plant and machinery to refuel vehicles with natural gas or hydrogen fuels. The allowance is also available where the asset is to be leased, let or hired (CAA 2001 ss 45D, 45E, 46).

[8] *Environmentally beneficial plant or machinery*: 100% first-year capital allowances are available for expenditure after 31 March 2003 by *any* business on new and unused designated technologies and products which satisfy the relevant environmental criteria in accordance with the Government's technologies or products lists (FA 2003 s 167, Sch 30). The product lists are available at www.eca.gov.uk.

[9] CAA 2001 s 56.

[10] On reducing balance basis. Applies to plant or machinery with an expected working life, when new, of 25 years or more. Applies where expenditure on long-life assets in a year is £100,000 or more (in the case of companies the de minimis limit is £100,000 divided by one plus the number of associated companies). Transitional provisions apply to maintain a 25% allowance for expenditure incurred before 1 January 2001 under a contract entered into before 26 November 1996 and to expenditure on second-hand plant or machinery if old rules applied to vendor. It does not apply to plant or machinery in a building used wholly or mainly as, or for purposes ancillary to, a dwelling-house, retail shop, showroom, hotel or office, cars, or sea-going ships and railway assets acquired before 1 January 2011 (CAA 2001 ss 90–104, Sch 3 para 20).

Cars: See p 56 and **Expensive cars** p 63.

Leased assets: First-year allowances are not available for expenditure after 31 October 1993 on the provision of leased plant or machinery (but see notes 6 and 7 above). Writing-down allowances are available.

Mineral extraction (CA 2001 s 418)

	Expenditure incurred after	% Rate
Initial allowance	31 March 1986	Nil

Writing-down allowance

Expenditure incurred after 31 March 1986: annual writing-down allowance on reducing balance basis—10% for certain pre-trading expenditure and expenditure on the acquisition of a mineral asset, otherwise 25%.

Motor cars available for private use

	Expenditure incurred after	% Rate
Writing-down allowance (WDA)	11 March 1992	25%[1]

(1) Restricted to £3,000 for cars costing more than £12,000 and bought outright, on hire purchase or by way of a lease with an option to purchase (CAA 2001 ss 74, 75).

(2) The requirement that expenditure on cars costing £12,000 or less goes into a separate pool was removed from the start of the chargeable period which includes 1 April 2000 (corporation tax) or 6 April 2000 (income tax) or the start of the chargeable period which includes 1 (or 6) April 2001 at the option of the taxpayer (CAA 1990 s 41; FA 2000 s 74).

See also note 7, p 55 and **Expensive cars**, p 63.

Patent rights (CA 2001 s 472)

Writing-down allowance

Expenditure incurred before 1 April 1986 spread equally over 17 years or, if less
- (a) the period for which the rights are acquired, or
- (b) 17 years less the number of complete years from the commencement of the patent to the acquisition.

Expenditure incurred after 31 March 1986: annual 25% writing-down allowance (reducing balance basis).

Research and development (formerly scientific research)*

	Expenditure incurred after	% Rate
Allowance in year 1	5 November 1962	100

Note: Land and houses are excluded from 1 April 1985.

*See also corporation tax relief, p 53.

Enterprise zones

The following areas have been designated as enterprise zones. The designation applies for 10 years from the commencement date. Previous enterprise zones, the designation of which has lapsed, are not shown.

Area	*Commencement date*
Dearne Valley	3 November 1995
East Midlands (North East Derbyshire)	3 November 1995
East Midlands (Bassetlaw)	16 November 1995
East Midlands (Ashfield)	21 November 1995
East Durham	29 November 1995
Tyne Riverside (North Tyneside)	19 February 1996
Tyne Riverside (North Tyneside and South Tyneside)	21 October 1996

Time limits for capital allowances claims see p 26.

Income tax

Starting, basic and higher rates and rate applicable to trusts

Band of taxable income £	Band £	Rate %	Tax £	Cumulative tax £
2003–04				
0–1,960	1,960	10	196.00	196.00
1,961–30,500	28,540	22	6,278.80	6,474.80
over 30,500	—	40	—	—
2002–03				
0–1,920	1,920	10	192.00	192.00
1,921–29,900	27,980	22	6,155.60	6,347.60
over 29,900	—	40	—	—
2001–02				
0–1,880	1,880	10	188.00	188.00
1,881–29,400	27,520	22	6,054.40	6,242.40
over 29,400	—	40	—	—
2000–01				
0–1,520	1,520	10	152.00	152.00
1,521–28,400	26,880	22	5,913.60	6,065.60
over 28,400	—	40	—	—
1999–2000				
0–1,500	1,500	10	150	150
1,501–28,000	26,500	23	6,095	6,245
over 28,000	—	40	—	—
1998–99				
0–4,300	4,300	20	860	860
4,301–27,100	22,800	23	5,244	6,104
over 27,100	—	40	—	—
1997–98				
0–4,100	4,100	20	820	820
4,101–26,100	22,000	23	5,060	5,880
over 26,100	—	40	—	—

Taxation of savings: From 6 April 1999, savings income is chargeable at the rates of 10% (if within the starting rate band), 20% and/or 40% (TA 1988 s 1A; FA 2000 s 32). From 6 April 1996 to 5 April 1999, savings income was chargeable at the rates of 20% and 40%.

Savings income includes interest from banks and building societies, interest distributions from authorised unit trusts, interest on gilts and other securities including corporate bonds, purchased life annuities and discounts.

Where income does not exceed the basic rate limit, there will be no further tax to pay on savings income from which the 20% tax rate has been deducted, and any tax over-deducted is repayable. Higher rate taxpayers are liable to pay tax at 40% on that part of their savings income falling above the higher rate limit.

From 6 April 1999, savings income is generally treated as the second top slice of income behind dividends.

Non-taxpayers may apply to have interest paid without deduction of tax where their total income is expected to be covered by personal allowances. Taxpayers who are entitled to a refund of tax deducted from interest can claim the refund using form R40. The Revenue have launched a *Taxback* website page to simplify repayments: www.inlandrevenue.gov.uk/taxback.

Taxation of dividends: UK and foreign dividends (except those foreign dividends taxed under the remittance basis) form the top slice of taxable income. From 6 April 1999, special rates apply to dividend income following the reduction of the tax credit to 10%. Where income does not exceed the basic rate limit the rate is 10% so that the liability is met by the tax credit. Higher rate taxpayers are liable to pay tax at 32.5% on that part of their dividend income falling above the basic rate limit. For 1993–94 to 1998–99 inclusive, dividend income was chargeable at the 20% and 40% rates as for savings income above.
See FA 1999 s 22; TA 1988 s 1A.

Rate applicable to trusts: 1996–97 onwards: 34%.

Schedule F trust rate: 1999–2000 onwards: 25%.

Construction industry sub-contractors rate of deduction at source: 2000–01 onwards: 18%, 1999–2000 and before: basic rate of tax.

Table of income tax reliefs

	2003-04	2002-03
Personal allowance (under 65)	£4,615	£4,615
Married couple's allowance[1] (from 6 April 2000 available only where either spouse is aged 65 or over at 5 April 2000, see Age allowance below) Monthly reduction in year of marriage	— —	— —
Children's tax credit[2] Baby rate[3]	— —	£5,290 £10,490
Age allowance Abatement of relief by £1 for every £2 income over	£18,300	£17,900
Personal allowance (under 75)	£6,610	£6,100
Not beneficial if individual's total income exceeds	£22,290	£20,870
Married couple's allowance (elder spouse under 75) either spouse born before 6 April 1935	£5,565	£5,465
Minimum married couple's allowance where income exceeds limit[1]	£2,150	£2,110
Not beneficial if husband: under 65 and his total income exceeds 65-74 and his total income exceeds	 £25,130 £29,120	 £24,610 £27,580
Personal allowance (75 and over)	£6,720	£6,370
Not beneficial if individual's total income exceeds	£22,510	£21,410
Married couple's allowance[1] (either spouse 75 or over)	£5,635	£5,535
Minimum married couple's allowance where income exceeds limit[1]	£2,150	£2,110
Not beneficial if husband: under 65 and his total income exceeds 65-74 and his total income exceeds 75 or over and his total income exceeds	 £25,270 £29,260 £29,480	 £24,750 £27,720 £28,260
Widow's bereavement allowance[1] (available only where the death occurred before 6 April 2000 and the wife had not remarried before that date)	—	—
Additional relief for children[1]	—	—
Blind person	£1,510	£1,480
Mortgage interest relief Limit on amount available for relief Relief restricted to	 — —	 — —
Life assurance relief For contracts made before 14 March 1984 *only*, given by deduction	12·5%	12·5%
NI Class 2 Small earnings exception	£4,095	£4,025
NI Class 4 Band Amount payable to upper limit Charge on earnings above upper limit	£4,615–£30,940 £26,325 @ 8% £2,106 1%	£4,615–£30,420 £25,805 @ 7% £1,806·35 —
Starting rate (before 1999–2000, lower rate) of tax Band	10% £1,960	10% £1,920
Basic rate of tax Band	22% £28,540	22% £27,980

[1] Relief is restricted to 10% of figure quoted from 1999–2000 and 15% from 1995–96 to 1998–99 and is given as a reduction in tax liability.

[2] The relief is withdrawn at the rate of £2 for every £3 of income chargeable to income tax at the higher rate and is restricted to 10% of the resulting figure. From 2003–04 the allowance has been replaced by the Child Tax Credit which is paid direct to the main carer.

[3] From 6 April 2002 the amount per claimant is higher for the year of birth. From 2003–04 the allowance has been replaced by the Child Tax Credit which is paid direct to the main carer.

2001-02	2000-01	1999-2000	1998-99	1997-98
£4,535	£4,385	£4,335	£4,195	£4,045
—	—	£1,970	£1,900	£1,830
—	—	£164·16	£158·33	£152·50
£5,200	—	—	—	—
—	—	—	—	—
£17,600	£17,000	£16,800	£16,200	£15,600
£5,990	£5,790	£5,720	£5,410	£5,220
£20,510	£19,810	£19,570	£18,630	£17,950
£5,365	£5,185	£5,125	£3,305	£3,185
£2,070	£2,000	£1,970	£1,900	£1,830
£24,190	£23,370	£23,110	£19,010	£18,310
£27,100	£26,180	£25,880	£21,440	£20,660
£6,260	£6,050	£5,980	£5,600	£5,400
£21,050	£20,330	£20,090	£19,010	£18,310
£5,435	£5,255	£5,195	£3,345	£3,225
£2,070	£2,000	£1,970	£1,900	£1,830
£24,330	£23,510	£23,250	£19,090	£18,390
£27,240	£26,320	£26,020	£21,520	£20,740
£27,780	£26,840	£26,540	£21,900	£21,100
—	£2,000	£1,970	£1,900	£1,830
—	—	£1,970	£1,900	£1,830
£1,450	£1,400	£1,380	£1,330	£1,280
—	—	£30,000	£30,000	£30,000
—	—	10%	10%	15%
12·5%	12·5%	12·5%	12·5%	12·5%
£3,955	£3,825	£3,770	£3,590	£3,480
£4,535–£29,900	£4,385–£27,820	£7,530–£26,000	£7,310–£25,220	£7,010–£24,180
£25,365 @ 7%	£23,435 @ 7%	£18,470 @ 6%	£17,910 @ 6%	£17,170 @ 6%
£1,775·55	£1,640·45	£1,108·20	£1,074·60	£1,030·20
—	—	—	—	—
10%	10%	10%	20%	20%
£1,880	£1,525	£1,500	£4,300	£4,100
22%	22%	23%	23%	23%
£27,520	£26,880	£26,500	£22,800	£22,000

Car benefits

From 6 April 2002: The income tax charge is based on a percentage of the car's price graduated according to the level of the car's carbon dioxide emissions measured in grams per kilometre (g/km) and rounded down to the nearest 5 g/km: ITEPA 2003 ss 114–148, 169; FA 2003 s 138.

CO_2 emissions in grams per kilometre				*% of list price*	
2002/03	**2003/04**	**2004/05**	**2005/06**	*Petrol*	*Diesel*
165	155	145	140	15%	18%
170	160	150	145	16%	19%
175	165	155	150	17%	20%
180	170	160	155	18%	21%
185	175	165	160	19%	22%
190	180	170	165	20%	23%
195	185	175	170	21%	24%
200	190	180	175	22%	25%
205	195	185	180	23%	26%
210	200	190	185	24%	27%
215	205	195	190	25%	28%
220	210	200	195	26%	29%
225	215	205	200	27%	30%
230	220	210	205	28%	31%
235	225	215	210	29%	32%
240	230	220	215	30%	33%
245	235	225	220	31%	34%
250	240	230	225	32%	35%
255	245	235	230	33%	35%
260	250	240	235	34%	35%
265	255	245	240	35%	35%

Cars registered after 28 February 2001

For cars registered on or after 1 March 2001, the definitive CO_2 emissions figure is recorded on the vehicle registration document. For cars first registered between 1 January 1998 and 28 February 2001, the Vehicle Certification Agency supply relevant information on their website at www.vcacarfueldata.org.uk and in their free, twice-yearly edition of the 'New Car Fuel Consumption & Emission Figures' booklet.

Cars registered after 31 December 1997 with no CO_2 emission figures

Cylinder capacity of car	*Appropriate percentage*
1,400cc or less	15%
Over 1,400cc up to 2,000cc	25%
Over 2,000cc	35%
Electrically propelled vehicle	9%

Cars registered before 1 January 1998 with no CO_2 emission figures

Cylinder capacity of car	*Appropriate percentage*
1,400cc or less	15%
Over 1,400cc up to 2,000cc	22%
Over 2,000cc	32%
No cylinder capacity	*Appropriate percentage*
Electrically propelled vehicle	15%
Other vehicles	32%

Notes

List price of car:

(1) Includes any optional accessories supplied with the car when first made available to the employee and any further accessories costing £100 or more (ITEPA 2003 ss 122–131).

(2) Reduced by capital contributions made by the employee (up to a maximum of £5,000) (ITEPA 2003 s 132).

(3) Capped at £80,000 (ITEPA 2003 s 121).

(4) Classic cars (aged 15 years or more and with a market value of £15,000 or more at the end of the year of assessment): substitute market value at end of year of assessment if this is higher than the adjusted list price. £80,000 cap and reduction for capital contributions apply (ITEPA 2003 s 147).

Automatic car made available to a disabled driver: CO_2 figure reduced to that for an equivalent manual car (ITEPA 2003 s 138).

Car unavailable for part of year: Value of the benefit is reduced proportionately (ITEPA 2003 s 143).

**Note:* Also used to calculate the national insurance contributions payable by employers on the benefit of cars they provide for the private use of their employees, see p 87.

1994–1995 to 2001–02

Basic cash equivalent 1999–2000 to 2001–02

List price of car plus extra qualifying accessories[1] *less* capital contributions[2] by employee[3,4].

Multiplied by –
35% where business mileage is under 2,500[5] miles.
25% where business mileage is at least 2,500[5] but less than 18,000[5] miles.
15% where business mileage is 18,000[5] miles or more[6].

Adjustments

1. Reduce cash equivalent by –
   ¼ where car is 4 years old or more at end of year of assessment.
2. Reduce adjusted cash equivalent in **1** proportionately where car is not available throughout year of assessment.
3. Reduce adjusted cash equivalent in **2** by amount of payments by employee for private use.

Basic cash equivalent 1994–95 to 1998–99

35% x (list price of car plus extra qualifying accessories[1] *less* capital contributions[2] by employee[3])[4].

Adjustments

1. Reduce *basic cash equivalent* by –
   1/3 where business mileage is at least 2,500[5] but less than 18,000[5] miles
   2/3 where business mileage is 18,000[5] miles or more[6].
2. Reduce *adjusted cash equivalent* in **1** by –
   1/3 where car is 4 years old or more at end of year of assessment.
3. Reduce *adjusted cash equivalent* in **2** proportionately where car is not available throughout year of assessment.
4. Reduce *adjusted cash equivalent* in **3** by amount of payments by employee for private use.

[1] Excluding an accessory provided after car was made available if it was provided before 1 August 1993 or its list price was less than £100. From 6 April 1995 accessories designed for use only by disabled people are also excluded. From 1998–99 to 2001–02 where a car is manufactured so as to be capable of running on road fuel gas, its price is proportionately reduced by so much of that price as is reasonably attributable to it being manufactured in that way. Where a new car is converted to run on road fuel gas, the equipment is not regarded as an accessory.
[2] Up to £5,000.
[3] List price as adjusted capped at £80,000.
[4] Classic cars (aged 15 years or more and with a market value of £15,000 or more at end of year of assessment): substitute market value at end of year of assessment if this is higher than adjusted list price. £80,000 cap and reduction for capital contributions apply.
[5] Mileage figures are reduced proportionately where car is not available for whole year.
[6] For second and subsequent cars there is no reduction if business mileage is under 18,000 miles; **from 1999–2000** reduce basic cash equivalent to 25% if business mileage is 18,000 miles or more (from 1994–95 to 1998–99 the basic cash equivalent was reduced by 1/3).

Vans: private use including fuel

(ITEPA 2003 ss 114–118, 154–166, 168)

	Under 4 years old[1]	4 years old or more[1]
1993-94 onwards: Vehicle weight up to 3,500 kgs	£500	£350

[1] At the end of the relevant year of assessment.

The Inland Revenue has issued a consultation document on 8 May 2003 proposing to change the way in which vans are taxed from 2003/04 to simplify the current system, take into account the type of private use and to account for the environmental impact of the vans in line with the company car regime.

Bus services

From 6 April 2002 onwards: No taxable benefit in respect of the provision of works buses with a seating capacity of 9 or more, provided to employees (or their children) to travel to and from work (ITEPA 2003 s 242). (From 6 April 1999 to 5 April 2002 the minimum seating capacity was 12.)

From 6 April 2002 there is no tax or NIC charge where employees are carried free or at reduced rates on employer-subsidised local bus services (ITEPA 2003 s 243).

Cycles and cyclist's safety equipment

From 6 April 1999 onwards: No taxable benefit in respect of the provision to employees of bicycles or cycling safety equipment for travel to and from work (ITEPA 2003 s 244).

Parking facilities

No taxable benefit for work place provision of car parking spaces, or, from 6 April 1999, parking for bicycles or motorcycles (ITEPA 2003 s 237).

Car fuel benefits

(ITEPA 2003 ss 149–153; TA 1988 s 158)

2003–04[1]					
CO_2 emissions grams per kilometre	**Petrol** £	**Diesel** £	CO_2 emissions grams per kilometre	**Petrol** £	**Diesel** £
155	2,160	2,592	210	3,744	4,176
160	2,304	2,736	215	3,888	4,320
165	2,448	2,880	220	4,032	4,464
170	2,592	3,024	225	4,176	4,608
175	2,736	3,168	230	4,320	4,752
180	2,880	3,312	235	4,464	4,896
185	3,024	3,456	240	4,608	5,040
190	3,168	3,600	245	4,752	5,040
195	3,312	3,744	250	4,896	5,040
200	3,456	3,888	255	5,040	5,040
205	3,600	4,032			

2002–03		
Cylinder capacity: (non-diesel cars)	1,400 cc or less	£2,240
	Over 1,400 cc up to 2,000 cc	£2,850
	Over 2,000 cc	£4,200
Cylinder capacity: (diesel cars)	2,000 cc or less	£2,850
	Over 2,000 cc	£4,200
No internal combustion engine		£4,200
2001–02		
Cylinder capacity: (non-diesel cars)	1,400 cc or less	£1,930
	Over 1,400 cc up to 2,000 cc	£2,460
	Over 2,000 cc	£3,620
Cylinder capacity: (diesel cars)	2,000 cc or less	£2,460
	Over 2,000 cc	£3,620
No internal combustion engine		£3,620
2000–01		
Cylinder capacity: (non-diesel cars)	1,400 cc or less	£1,700
	Over 1,400 cc up to 2,000 cc	£2,170
	Over 2,000 cc	£3,200
Cylinder capacity: (diesel cars)	2,000 cc or less	£2,170
	Over 2,000 cc	£3,200
No internal combustion engine		£3,200
1999–2000		
Cylinder capacity: (non-diesel cars)	1,400 cc or less	£1,210
	Over 1,400 cc up to 2,000 cc	£1,540
	Over 2,000 cc	£2,270
Cylinder capacity: (diesel cars)	2,000 cc or less	£1,540
	Over 2,000 cc	£2,270
No internal combustion engine		£2,270
1998–99		
Cylinder capacity: (non-diesel cars)	1,400 cc or less	£1,010
	Over 1,400 cc up to 2,000 cc	£1,280
	Over 2,000 cc	£1,890
Cylinder capacity: (diesel cars)	2,000 cc or less	£1,280
	Over 2,000 cc	£1,890
No internal combustion engine		£1,890

From 2003–04, the same percentage figure on page 60 used to calculate the car benefit charge for the company car, which is directly linked to the car's CO_2 emissions, is used to calculate the benefit charge for fuel provided for private motoring. The relevant percentage figure is multiplied by £14,400 for 2003–04.

The benefit is reduced to nil if the employee is required to, and does, make good all fuel provided for private use. There is no taxable benefit where the employer only provides fuel for business travel. From 2003–04, the charge is proportionately reduced where the employee stops receiving free fuel part way through the tax year, but where free fuel is subsequently provided in the same tax year, the full year's charge is payable.

The benefit is proportionately reduced where a car is not available or is incapable of being used for part of a year (being at least 30 days).

Advisory fuel rates for company cars

Engine size	*Cost per mile*		
From 2002–03[1]	*Petrol*	*Diesel*	*LPG*
1,400cc or less	10p	9p	6p
1,401–2,000cc	12p	9p	7p
Over 2,000cc	14p	12p	9p

Notes

[1] The advisory fuel rates can be used to negotiate dispensations for mileage payments from 28 January 2002 where employers:
 (a) reimburse employees for business travel in their company cars; or
 (b) require employees to repay the cost of fuel used for private travel.
(In the case of (b) the figures may be used for private travel from 6 April 2001.)

[2] Payments at these rates give rise to no income tax or Class 1 NIC liability. The table figures will be accepted for VAT purposes.

[3] Other rates may be used if the employer can demonstrate that they are justified.

[4] The rates will be reviewed if fuel prices vary by more than 10% from the prices used when the rates were set. The rates will continue to apply from 6 April 2003 until further notice.

Authorised mileage rates: cars and vans

2002–03 and 2003–04	**Rate per mile**[1]
Annual business mileage up to 10,000 miles	40p
Each additional mile over 10,000 miles	25p
Each passenger making same business trip	5p

Business mileage	*Engine size* Up to 1,000cc	1,001–1,500cc	1,501–2,000cc	Over 2,000cc	One rate[3]
2001–02[2]					
Up to 4,000 miles	40p	40p	45p	63p	—
Excess over 4,000 miles	25p	25p	25p	36p	—
1997–98 to 2000–01:[2,4]					
Up to 4,000 miles	28p	35p	45p	63p	40p
Excess over 4,000 miles	17p	20p	25p	36p	22·5p

[1] ITEPA 2003 ss 229–236. Except in the case of the rate applying in respect of passengers, if the employer pays less than the statutory rate, the employee can claim tax relief on the difference.

[2] Employees using their own car may claim these rates as a tax-free allowance or as a deduction whether or not their employer operates the scheme (1995) SWTI 1879.

[3] Where the same rate of mileage allowance is paid irrespective of the engine size, a fixed rate based on the average of the two middle bands is used.

[4] Subject to transitional relief.

Authorised mileage rates: pedal cycles and motorcycles

	Pedal cycles Rate per mile	**Motorcycles Rate per mile**
2002–03 and 2003–04	20p	24p
2000–01 and 2001–02	12p	24p
1999–2000	12p	—

When the employee is not paid by the employer for using the pedal cycle or motorcycle the employee is able to claim the appropriate rate per mile (or on the balance up to the appropriate rate per mile if the employer pays less than this rate) ITEPA 2003 ss 230–232.

Expensive cars: restricted allowances

Restriction on deduction for hire charge

(TA 1988 ss 578A, 578B)

Contracts made after 10 March 1992

If a car with a retail price when new of more than £12,000 is acquired under a rental lease the maximum allowable deduction in computing Schedule D Case I or II profits is —

$$\frac{£12{,}000 + P}{2P} \times R$$

P = retail price of car when new
R = annual rental

Capital allowances see p 56.

Charities

Gift aid

(FA 2002 s 58; FA 2000 ss 39, 40; FA 1990 s 25; FA 1998 s 48)

The gift aid scheme gives higher rate relief for an individual donor and corporation tax relief for a corporate donor. The charity claims repayment of basic rate income tax on the grossed up amount of the donation.

From 6 April 2000 for individuals and from 1 April 2000 for companies, gift aid was extended to all donations to charity, including one-off gifts, made by UK-taxpayers. There is no minimum limit for donations. Donors (who may be resident or non-resident) have to make a declaration that they are UK taxpayers if the charity is to claim the repayment of basic rate income tax on the gift. One declaration can cover a series of donations to the same charity. Donors are able to join the scheme by phone or the internet. It is no longer necessary for companies to deduct income tax from their donations and for the recipient charity to claim back the tax.

From 6 April 2002, gift aid was extended to gifts to Community Amateur Sports Clubs (CASCs).

Before 6 April 2000 the minimum amount which could be donated by gift aid was £250.

Covenants

(FA 2000 s 41)

Because of the extension of the gift aid scheme from 6 April 2000, charitable covenants are in effect treated as regular donations by gift aid. For payments under a charitable covenant falling due before 6 April 2000 to be tax-effective, the covenant had to be for a period capable of exceeding three years (there are no monetary limits). With the introduction of the extended gift aid provisions, however, the separate tax relief for payments under covenants is withdrawn and all relief for such payments falling due on or after 6 April 2000 is given under the gift aid scheme.

Payroll giving

(ITEPA 2003, ss 713–715; SI 1986 No 2211; FA 2000 s 38; FA 2003 s 146)

Under the payroll giving scheme, employees authorise their employer to deduct charitable donations from their pay and receive tax relief on their donation at their top rate of tax. The government will add a supplement to donations from 6 April 2000 to 5 April 2004 (an extension of one year having been provided by FA 2003 s 146).

Before 6 April 2000, there was a maximum amount which could be donated in this way of £1,200.

Gifts in kind

Relief available for gifts by traders to educational establishments of plant or machinery either manufactured and sold or used for the purposes of the trade (TA 1988 s 84; CAA 2001 s 63(2)–(4)).
Millennium Gift Aid Scheme, tax relief introduced by FA 1998 s 47 for businesses to donate goods to help education projects and projects undertaken for medical purposes in eighty 'low income countries' from 31 July 1998. From 27 July 1999, this relief was extended by FA 1999 s 55 to donations of goods or plant and machinery to any type of charity (TA 1988 s 83A; CAA 2001 s 63(2)–(4), and from 6 April 2002 to such donations to Community Amateur Sports Clubs (CASCs) (FA 2002 s 58)).

Gifts of real property

From 6 April 2002 (individuals) and 1 April 2002 (companies), income or corporation tax relief is available for gifts of freehold or leasehold property which a charity agrees to accept (FA 2002 s 97).

Gifts of shares and securities

From 6 April 2000, relief is available where a person disposes of listed shares and securities, unit trust units, AIM shares, etc to a charity by way of a gift or sale at an undervalue. The amount deductible from total income is the market value of the shares etc on the date of disposal plus incidental disposal costs less any consideration or value of benefits received by the donor or a connected person. This is in addition to any capital gains tax relief (TA 1988 s 587B; FA 2000 s 43).

Tax return giving: For gifts made after 5 April 2003 under gift aid, donors may elect to have the donation treated as though made in the previous year of assessment (FA 2002 s 98).

From April 2004, taxpayers can nominate a charity (from a published list of participating charities) to receive all or part of any tax repayments due to them, the nomination to be made on the self-assessment tax return.

Inheritance tax relief see p 81.

Capital gains tax see p 41.

Fixed rate expenses

For most classes of industry fixed rate allowances for the upkeep of tools and special clothing have been agreed between the Revenue and the trade unions concerned. Alternatively, the individual employee may claim as a deduction his or her actual expenses (ITEPA 2003, s 367). The rates are published by the Treasury and are as previously set out in Concession A1.

Industry code	*Industry*	*Occupation*	*Deduction from 1995–96*
10	Agriculture	All workers	70
100	Aluminium	*(a)* Continual casting operators, process operators, de-dimplers, driers, drill punchers, dross unloaders, firemen, furnace operators and their helpers, leaders, mouldmen, pourers, remelt department labourers, roll flatteners *(b)* Cable hands, case makers, labourers, mates, truck drivers and measurers, storekeepers *(c)* Apprentices *(d)* All other workers	130 60 45 100
330	Banks	Uniformed bank employees	40
90	Brass and Copper	All workers	100
270	Building	*(a)* Joiners and carpenters *(b)* Cement works and roofing felt and asphalt labourers *(c)* Labourers and navvies *(d)* All other workers	105 55 40 85
250	Building Materials	*(a)* Stone-masons *(b)* Tilemakers and labourers *(c)* All other workers	85 40 55
190	Clothing	*(a)* Lacemakers, hosiery bleachers, dyers, scourers and knitters, knitwear bleachers and dyers *(b)* All other workers	45 30
150	Constructional Engineering	*(a)* Blacksmiths and their strikers, burners, caulkers, chippers, drillers, erectors, fitters, holders up, markers off, platers, riggers, riveters, rivet heaters, scaffolders, sheeters, template workers, turners, welders *(b)* Banksmen, labourers, shop-helpers, slewers, straighteners *(c)* Apprentices and storekeepers *(d)* All other workers	115 60 45 75
170	Electrical and Electricity Supply	*(a)* Those workers incurring laundry costs only (generally CEGB employees) *(b)* All other workers	25 90
110	Engineering	*(a)* Pattern makers *(b)* Labourers, supervisory and unskilled workers *(c)* Apprentices and storekeepers *(d)* Motor mechanics in garage repair shops *(e)* All other workers	120 60 45 100 100
Not known	Fire service	Uniformed fire fighters and fire officers	60
220	Food	All workers	40
20	Forestry	All workers	70
240	Glass	All workers	60
Not known	Healthcare	*(a)* Ambulance staff on active service *(b)* Nurses and midwives, chiropodists, dental nurses, occupational, speech and other therapists, phlebotomists, physiotherapists, radiographers *(c)* Plaster room orderlies, hospital porters, ward clerks, sterile supply workers, hospital domestics, hospital catering staff *(d)* Laboratory staff, pharmacists, pharmacy assistants *(e)* Uniformed ancillary staff maintenance workers, grounds staff, drivers, parking attendants and security guards, receptionists and other uniformed staff	110 70 60 45 45
280	Heating	*(a)* Pipe fitters and plumbers *(b)* Coverers, laggers, domestic glaziers, heating engineers and their mates *(c)* All gas workers, all other workers	100 90 70
50	Iron Mining	*(a)* Fillers, miners and underground workers *(b)* All other workers	100 75
70	Iron and Steel	*(a)* Day labourers, general labourers, stockmen, time keepers, warehouse staff and weighmen *(b)* Apprentices *(c)* All other workers	60 45 120

Fixed rate expenses — continued

Industry code	*Industry*	*Occupation*	*Deduction from 1995–96*
210	Leather	*(a)* Curriers (wet workers), fellmongering workers, tanning operatives (wet) *(b)* All other workers	55 40
140	Particular Engineering	*(a)* Pattern makers *(b)* All chainmakers; cleaners, galvanisers, tinners and wire drawers in the wire drawing industry; tool-makers in the lock making industry *(c)* Apprentices and storekeepers *(d)* All other workers	120 100 45 60
355	Police Force	Uniformed police officers (ranks up to and including Chief Inspector)	55
160	Precious Metals	All workers	70
230	Printing	*(a)* Letterpress Section Electrical engineers (rotary presses), electrotypers, ink and roller makers, machine minders (rotary), maintenance engineers (rotary presses) and stereotypers *(b)* Bench hands (P & B), compositors (Lp), readers (Lp), T & E Section wire room operators, warehousemen (Ppr box) *(c)* All other workers	105 30 70
320	Prisons	Uniformed prison officers	55
300	Public Service	(i) Dock and Inland Waterways *(a)* Dockers, dredger drivers, hopper steerers *(b)* All other workers (ii) Public Transport *(a)* Garage hands (including cleaners) *(b)* Conductors and drivers	55 40 55 40
60	Quarrying	All workers	70
290	Railways	(See the appropriate category for craftsmen, e.g. engineers, vehicle builders etc.) All other workers	70
30	Seamen	*(a)* Carpenters (Seamen) — Passenger liners *(b)* Carpenters (Seamen) — Cargo vessels, tankers, coasters and ferries *(c)* Other seamen — Passenger liners *(d)* Other seamen — Cargo vessels, tankers, coasters and ferries	165 130 nil nil
120	Shipyards	*(a)* Blacksmiths and their strikers, boilermakers, burners, carpenters, caulkers, drillers, furnacemen (platers), holders up, fitters, platers, plumbers, riveters, sheet iron workers, shipwrights, tubers, welders *(b)* Labourers *(c)* Apprentices and storekeepers *(d)* All other workers	115 60 45 75
200	Textile Prints	All workers	60
180	Textiles	*(a)* Carders, carding engineers, overlookers (all), technicians in spinning mills *(b)* All other workers	85 60
130	Vehicles	*(a)* Builders, railway wagon etc. repairers, and railway wagon lifters *(b)* Railway vehicle painters and letterers, railway wagon etc. builders' and repairers' assistants *(c)* All other workers	105 60 40
260	Wood & Furniture	*(a)* Carpenters, cabinet makers, joiners, wood carvers and woodcutting machinists *(b)* Artificial limb makers (other than in wood), organ builders and packing case makers *(c)* Coopers not providing own tools, labourers, polishers and upholsterers *(d)* All other workers	115 90 45 75

1) 'Industry code' is an industry identification term used for Inland Revenue computer purposes.
2) The expressions 'all workers' and 'all other workers' refer only to manual workers who have to bear the cost of upkeep of tools and special clothing. They do not extend to other employees such as office staff.

Investment reliefs

Enterprise investment scheme

(Shares issued after 31 December 1993: TA 1988 ss 289–312; FA 1997 Sch 8 as revised from 1998–99 by FA 1998 ss 70, 71, 74, Sch 13 and as amended from 1999–2000 by FA 1999 ss 71–73, Schs 7, 8; FA 2000 s 64, Sch 17; FA 2001 s 63, Sch 15.)

Relief on investment

Maximum investment:	From 1998–99 1994–95	£150,000 £100,000
Minimum investment:	From 1993–94	£500
Maximum carryback to preceding year	From 1998–99 1994–95	½ amount invested between 6 April and 5 October (maximum £25,000) ½ amount invested between 6 April and 5 October (maximum £15,000)
Rate of relief	From 1993–94	20% (given as a reduction in income tax liability)

Other reliefs

(a) A gain on a disposal of shares on which EIS relief has been given and not withdrawn is exempt from capital gains tax.

(b) Reinvestment relief (ie deferral relief under TCGA 1992 Sch 5B) is available for gains on assets where the disposal proceeds are reinvested in eligible shares in a qualifying company. (CGT taper relief is calculated in accordance with the combined periods of ownership of the first and second investments (and any subsequent qualifying periods of reinvestment) where the shares in the first EIS company were issued after 5 April 1998 and disposed of after 5 April 1999: TCGA 1992 Sch 5BA.)

(c) A loss on a disposal of shares on which EIS relief has been given may be relieved against income tax or capital gains tax.

Main conditions for relief

1 The relief is available for subscriptions in cash to new ordinary fully paid-up shares in a qualifying company with no present or future right of redemption and no present or future preferential right to dividends or to the company's assets on a winding-up, throughout a five-year period from the date of issue.

2 The investor must hold the shares for three years from the date of issue (or from the commencement of trade, if later) where shares are issued after 5 April 2000. (The previous limit was five years from date of issue.) The investor must not be connected with the issuing company at any time in the period beginning two years before the issue of the shares and ending immediately before the third anniversary of the issue date (or, if later, the date of commencement of trade) (for shares issued after 5 April 2000). He must not receive value from the company at any time in the period beginning one year before the issue date and ending immediately before the third anniversary of the issue date (or, if later, the date of commencement of trade) (for shares issued after 6 March 2001 and also as regards value received after that date in respect of shares issued on or before that date). From 7 March 2001 such receipts may be ignored where the amount is insignificant or if equivalent replacement value is given.

3 The money subscribed must be used wholly for the purpose of a qualifying business activity within 12 months of the share issue date (or, where the company commences a qualifying trade within 12 months of the share issue date, within 12 months of the commencement). From 7 March 2001 only 80% of the money subscribed has to be used in a qualifying business within that time limit, though the remainder must be used within the subsequent 12 months.

4 The business activity must be carried on wholly or mainly in the UK for three years after the share issue date (or after the commencement of the trade, if later), unless there is a bona fide liquidation or receivership.

5 Throughout the period beginning with the share issue date and ending three years after that date (or, if later, three years after the date on which its qualifying business activity commences), the company must

(a) exist for a qualifying purpose;

(b) have fully paid up capital; and

(c) not be controlled by another company, or control another company (apart from a qualifying subsidiary).

Under the provisions of FA 1997 Sch 8, a parent company may qualify if non-qualifying activities do not form a substantial part of the group's activities *as a whole.*

Before 7 March 2001 it was a condition for relief that the company be unquoted throughout the three-year period. From that date it is necessary only that the company be unquoted at the time the shares are issued, provided that there are at that time no arrangements for the company to cease to be unquoted.

6 For shares issued after 1 July 1997, no arrangement must exist before or at the time of issue for the disposal of shares in the company, the disposal of the company's assets, the ending of the company's trade or a guarantee of the shareholders' investment.

Urban Regeneration Companies

Relief is available from 1 April 2003 for expenditure incurred by businesses in making contributions to designated Urban Regeneration Companies (TA 1988 s 79B; FA 2003 s 180).

Corporate venturing scheme see p 53.

Venture capital trusts

(TA 1988 ss 332A, 842AA, Sch 15B, Sch 28B; TCGA 1992 ss 151A, 151B, Sch 5C; FA 1997 Sch 9; FA 1998 ss 70, 72, 73, Sch 12; FA 1999 ss 69, 70; FA 2000 s 65, Sch 18; FA 2002 s 109, Sch 33.)

Relief on investment

Maximum annual investment:	From 1995–96	£100,000
Rate of relief:	From 1995–96	20%[1]

[1] Given as a reduction in income tax liability. The rate of relief is an amount equal to the 'lower rate' of income tax for the year of assessment in respect of which the claim is made (TA 1988 Sch 15B para 1). The lower rate of income tax is 20% as defined by TA 1988 ss 1A, 832(1); FA 1999 s 22.

Other reliefs

(a) Dividends on shares within investment limit exempt from income tax (unless the investor's main purpose is tax avoidance – from 9 March 1999).
(b) Gains on share disposals exempt from capital gains tax (subject to investment limit).
(c) Reinvestment relief is available for gains on assets where the disposal proceeds are reinvested in a venture capital trust.

Main conditions for relief

1 The investment must be in new eligible shares: that is, ordinary shares which, in the five-year period from the issue date, carry no present or future preferential right to dividends or to a return of assets on the winding-up of the trust and no present or future right to redemption.
2 The investor must be an individual, aged 18 or over. He or she must hold the shares for three years from the date of issue where the shares are issued after 5 April 2000. (The previous minimum holding period was five years.)
3 The trust must satisfy the following conditions for approval by the Revenue –
   (a) it must not be a close company;
   (b) its income must be derived wholly or mainly (at least 70%) from investments in shares or securities;
   (c) at least 70% by value of its investments must comprise 'qualifying holdings' (newly issued shares in unquoted companies carrying on qualifying trades – the provisions relating to parent companies are relaxed by FA 1997). Special provisions apply where a company in which the VCT has invested goes into bona fide liquidation or receivership, or where the company is sold, merges or undergoes a capital reconstruction;
   (d) at least 30% by value of its qualifying holdings must comprise 'eligible shares' (see above);
   (e) it may not hold more than 15% by value of its total investment portfolio in any one company;
   (f) each class of its shares must be quoted on the Stock Exchange;
   (g) it must distribute at least 85% of the income derived from shares and securities and 100% of income derived from other sources in each accounting period;
   (h) at least 10% of the total investment in any one company must be held in ordinary, non-preferential shares (accounting periods ending after 1 July 1997);
   (i) no part of a qualifying holding may consist of securities relating to a guaranteed loan (accounting periods ending after 1 July 1997).

Business expansion scheme

(Shares issued before 1 January 1994: TA 1988 ss 289–312 as originally enacted)

Relief on investment

Maximum investment:	£40,000[1]
Minimum investment:	£500
Maximum carryback to preceding year:	½ amount invested between 6 April and 5 October (maximum £5,000)
Rate of relief:	Up to 40%[2]

[1] Applied to total enterprise investment and business expansion scheme investments for 1993–94.
[2] Given as a deduction from total income.

Other reliefs

Capital gains relief: gains on the first disposal of shares on which BES relief has not been withdrawn are exempt from capital gains tax.
Loss relief (shares issued after 18 March 1986): none.

Main conditions for relief

As for the enterprise investment scheme (see above), except that the investor had to be UK resident and ordinarily resident in the year in which the shares were issued and the company had to be UK resident throughout the three-year period from the share issue date. There was no time limit for using the funds raised.

Community investment tax credit

(FA 2002 s 57, Sch 16)

Investments made after 16 April 2002 by an individual or company in an accredited community development finance institution (CDFI) are eligible for tax relief. The investment may be by a loan to the CDFI or by a subscription for shares in or securities of a CDFI. Tax relief may be claimed for the tax year in which the investment is made and each of the four subsequent years. Relief for each year is the smaller of:

(a) 5% of the invested amount, or
(b) the amount which reduces the investor's income tax liability for the year to nil.

Individual savings accounts

(TA 1988 s 333; FA 1998 s 75; SI 1998/1870; SI 1998/1871; SI 1998/1869; SI 1998/1872; SI 2000/809; SI 2001/908)

The overall annual subscription limit will remain at £7,000 and the cash limit will remain at £3,000 until 2005–06 inclusive.

(From 6 April 1999)

Overall annual subscription limit	1999–2000 to 2005–06 6 April 2006 onwards	£7,000 £5,000
Cash limit	1999–2000 to 2005–06 6 April 2006 onwards	£3,000 £1,000
Life insurance limit	6 April 1999 onwards	£1,000

Reliefs

(a) Investments under the scheme are free from income tax and capital gains tax.
(b) 10% tax credit paid until 5 April 2004 on dividends from UK equities.
(c) Withdrawals may be made without loss of tax relief.

Main conditions for relief

1 The account can include three components:
   (a) cash (including National Savings),
   (b) life insurance,
   (c) stocks and shares.
2 Savers are subject to the subscription limits set out above. If the subscription limit is reached in a year, no further subscriptions can be made in that year, irrespective of any amounts withdrawn.
3 Accounts must be administered by a single manager or by separate managers for each component.

Tax-exempt special savings accounts

(Accounts opened **before 6 April 1999**: TA 1988 ss 326A–326C; FA 1998 s 78)

Reliefs

Interest and bonuses payable on the account over a five-year period from the date on which it was opened are exempt from income tax.

Main conditions for relief

1 No capital may be withdrawn from the account during the initial five-year period.
2 TESSAs could be opened until 5 April 1999. Payments into them may be made for the full five-year period. After five years the account ceases to be tax exempt, but the capital (ie a maximum of £9,000) may be reinvested in full within six months in an ISA. The capital in a TESSA that matured between 6 January 1999 and 5 April 1999 could be transferred into an ISA after 5 April 1999 rather than invested into another TESSA before that date.

Personal equity plans

(Subscriptions made **before 6 April 1999**: TA 1988 s 333; FA 1998 s 76; SI 1989/469; S1 1998/1869)

Reliefs

(a) Dividends on shares held in a plan are exempt from income tax.
(b) Interest on plan investments is exempt from income tax if reinvested; interest on cash deposits is paid gross.
(c) Gains on the disposal of assets held in a plan are exempt from capital gains tax.
(d) PEPs held at 5 April 1999 can be held outside the new ISA, but with the same tax advantages as the ISA: (1998) SWTI 388; FA 1998 ss 75, 76.
(e) 10% tax credits paid until 5 April 2004 on dividends from UK equities.

Loan benefits and official rate of interest

A director, or an employee earning £8,500 or more a year, who receives a loan by reason of his or her employment may be charged to tax on the cash equivalent of the benefit for the year (ITEPA 2003 ss 173–191).

There is no charge to tax if either:

(a) all the beneficial loans provided by reason of the employment; or
(b) all the beneficial loans, excluding loans qualifying for tax relief, do not exceed £5,000.

The cash equivalent is calculated using the difference between the interest paid (if any) and the official rate of interest.

In January 2000 it was announced that the official rate of interest will be set, in advance, for the whole of the following tax year (although this policy will not be followed if typical mortgage rates fall sharply during the year). Under this policy, the official rate of interest remained at 6.25% for 1999–00, 2000–01 and 2001–02: (2000) SWTI 95, (2001) SWTI 192. The rate was reduced to 5% from 6 January 2002 following reductions in mortgage rates. It remained at this rate for 2002–03 and it is intended to keep it at this rate for 2003–04: (2002) SWTI 1800.

The official rate of interest is set out below.

Date	*Rate*
From 6 January 2002	5%
6 March 1999–5 January 2002	6.25%
6 August 1997–5 March 1999	7.25%
6 November 1996–5 August 1997	6.75%

Average official rate of interest	**1998–99**	**1999–00**	**2000–01**	**2001–02**	**2002–03**	**2003–04**
	7·16%	6·25%	6·25%	5·94%	5%	5%

Note
Loans made on commercial terms by employers who lend predominantly to the general public are generally exempt.

Foreign currency loans

Currency	*Date*	*Rate*
Swiss franc	From 6 July 1994	5·5%
Japanese yen	From 6 June 1994	3·9%

Loans of equipment

Computer equipment: No taxable benefit in respect of loan to employees (provided loans are not restricted to directors or senior staff) of computer equipment for private home use, the value of the equipment and related expenses not to exceed £2,500 (ITEPA 2003 s 320).

Bicycles and cycle safety equipment: No taxable benefit arises from 6 April 1999 in respect of loan to employees of bicycles and cycling safety equipment for travel to and from work (ITEPA 2003 s 244).

Equipment for disabled employees: No taxable benefit from 9 July 2002 in respect of equipment and facilities provided by employers (such as hearing aids and wheelchairs) to allow disabled employees to perform their duties of employment (the Revenue has indicated it will not pursue past liabilities) (SI 2002/1596).

Maintenance payments

From 6 April 2000: Relief for maintenance payments was withdrawn from 6 April 2000, *except* where either party to the marriage was born before 6 April 1935. In this case *only*, relief continues to be given under the rules for arrangements made after 15 March 1988 even if the obligation existed on or before that date. Under these rules the payer can claim tax relief in respect of the lesser of (a) the amount of the payments in the year concerned and (b) the minimum amount of the married couple's allowance for the year concerned (£2,110 for 2002–03). From 1999–2000 the relief has been given at the rate of 10% on the relevant amount.

The payment must be made to the divorced or separated spouse. It is made gross and is not taxable in the hands of the recipient. (TA 1988 ss 347A, 347B.)

Mobile telephones

6 April 1999 onwards: no taxable benefit

Cash equivalent of benefit from 6 April 1991 to 5 April 1999 £200

National Savings Bank interest

First £70 of interest on deposits (other than investment deposits) is exempt (TA 1988 s 325).

PAYE and national insurance thresholds

	1997–98	1998–99	1999–00	2000–01	2001–02	2002–03	2003–04
PAYE[1]: Weekly	£78·00	£80·50	£83·00	£84·00	£87·00	£89·00	£89·00
Monthly	£337·00	£350·00	£361·00	£365·00	£378·00	£385·00	£385·00
National Insurance[2]: Weekly	£62·00	£64·00	£66·00	£76·00	£87·00	£89·00	£89·00
Monthly	£269·00	£278·00	£286·00	£329·00	£378.00	£385·00	£385·00

[1] From 1999–2000 these are also the earnings thresholds for employers for national insurance contributions.
[2] For employees only from 1999–2000.

Profit-related pay schemes

(TA 1988 ss 169–184, Sch 8; FA 1997 s 61; FA 1998 s 62)

Limit on tax-free pay

Profit period beginning	*Exempt amount*
After 31 December 1999	no relief
1 January 1999–31 December 1999	lowest of: profit-related pay, 20% of earnings and £1,000
1 January 1998–31 December 1998	lowest of: profit-related pay, 20% of earnings and £2,000
1 April 1991–31 December 1997	lowest of: profit-related pay, 20% of earnings and £4,000
Earnings within PAYE (excluding benefits) plus profit-related pay.	

Relocation expenses and benefits

Qualifying removal benefits and expenses

The statutory relief covers the following expenses and benefits (ITEPA 2003 ss 271–289), subject to an £8,000 limit—

(a) *disposal expenses and benefits* (legal and advertising expenses in connection with the disposal of accommodation, penalty for redeeming a mortgage, auctioneers' and estate agents' fees, disconnection of public utilities, rent, maintenance and insurance costs while the property is unoccupied);

(b) *acquisition expenses and benefits* (legal expenses in connection with the acquisition of an interest in a new main residence, loan fees, mortgage indemnity insurance costs, survey and land registry fees, stamp duty, connection of public utilities). (NB: similar expenses and benefits are covered in respect of abortive acquisitions, if the property would have been the employee's new residence but the acquisition does not proceed either for reasons outside the employee's control or because he or she reasonably declines to proceed);

(c) *transportation of domestic belongings* (including insurance costs);

(d) *travelling and subsistence expenses and benefits* (for temporary visits to new residence before relocation; travel from old residence to new place of work or from new residence to old place of work where date of move and relocation of work do not coincide; subsistence and travel costs of child under 19 relocating before or after parents for educational reasons; benefit of a car or van for use in connection with the relocation where it is not otherwise available for private use);

(e) *bridging loan expenses and cheap bridging loans* (relief is given on any charge to interest at the official rate on a beneficial loan to the extent that the aggregate value of other qualifying benefits and expenses falls short of the maximum exempt amount);

(f) *duplicate expenses and benefits in respect of new residence* (replacement domestic items).

Rent-a-room scheme

Subject to a maximum, gross annual receipts from letting furnished accommodation in the only or main home are exempt from tax. If the receipts exceed the maximum, the taxpayer can pay tax on the gross receipts after deduction of expenses or on the amount by which the receipts exceed the maximum, without relief for the actual expenses. An individual's maximum is halved if during the basis period for the year some other person received income from letting accommodation in that property. (F(No 2)A 1992 Sch 10).

	Maximum amount
6 April 1997 onwards	£4,250
6 April 1992–5 April 1997	£3,250

Personal pension schemes, stakeholder pensions and retirement annuities

1 July 1988: Retirement annuity contracts were replaced by personal pension schemes, although retirement annuity premiums may continue to be paid, and tax relief obtained (TA 1988 ss 618–629). There are provisions for the carrying back (TA 1988 s 619) and the carrying forward (TA 1988 s 625) of relief, and these are not affected by FA 2000.

6 April 2001: The personal pension scheme rules were adapted to accommodate the stakeholder pensions provisions (TA 1988 ss 630–655, FA 2000 s 61, Sch 13). From that date, personal pension and stakeholder pension contributions are subject to the same rules.

6 April 2005: Major changes to the pension scheme rules are proposed.

Tax relief on contributions

Retirement annuities: Premiums continue to be deducted from or set off against relevant earnings (TA 1988 s 619). The amount of relief available is based on a percentage of net relevant earnings (see maximum amount, below).

Personal pension schemes: Before 6 April 2001, premiums were deducted from or set off against relevant earnings (TA 1988 s 639, as enacted). The amount of relief available was based on a percentage of net relevant earnings (see maximum amount, below).

Personal pension schemes/stakeholder pensions:

Contributions not exceeding the earnings threshold:

(1) Contributions of up to £3,600 gross ('the earnings threshold') may be paid into a stakeholder pension by anyone who is not a member of an occupational pension scheme, regardless of the amount (if any) of their earnings (TA 1988 s 632A).
(2) An individual who is a member of an occupational pension scheme but who is not a controlling director and whose total annual remuneration is no more than £30,000 is allowed to pay into both an occupational scheme and a stakeholder pension and will receive tax relief on an annual contribution of up to £3,600 (gross) into the stakeholder pension (TA 1988 s 632B).

Contributions exceeding the earnings threshold:

(1) Contributions in excess of the earnings threshold may be made. Tax relief is given on contributions up to a maximum based on a percentage of net relevant earnings (see maximum percentage below).
(2) For the purpose of supporting contributions in excess of the earnings threshold, a tax year for which evidence of relevant earnings can be provided may be nominated as the basis year and contributions based on the amount of those earnings may be paid in each of the next 5 years (TA 1988 s 646B). The provisions enable an individual to make pension contributions for up to 5 years after the relevant earnings ceased, by reference to the net relevant earnings of a basis year which may be any one of the 6 tax years preceding the first year for which there are no relevant earnings (TA 1988 s 646D).

Carry-back of relief:

Carry-back of relief is provided for in TA 1988 s 641A. There is no carry forward of relief (FA 2000 Sch 13 para 19).

Basic and higher rate relief:

From 6 April 2001, contributions are payable net of basic rate tax relief. Tax relief at the higher rate is given by extending the basic rate band by the amount of the contribution paid in the year of assessment (TA 1988 s 639, as amended by FA 2000 Sch 13 para 15).

From 2001–02, relief for contributions is given up to a maximum which is the greater of:

(a) the 'earnings threshold'; and
(b) the 'maximum percentage' of net relevant earnings for the year

(TA 1988 s 640, as amended by FA 2000 Sch 13 para 16). For the purposes of calculating the maximum percentage, net relevant earnings are subject to an earnings cap (TA 1988 s 640A).

Earnings threshold: from 6 April 2001 onwards £3,600 (TA 1988 s 630(1), as amended)

Maximum amount

Personal pension schemes/ stakeholder pensions (TA 1988 s 640)		
	Age in years at beginning of year of assessment	*Maximum percentage*
	35 and below	17½
	36 to 45	20
	46 to 50	25
	51 to 55	30
	56 to 60	35
	61 or more	40
Earnings cap	£	
2003–04	99,000	
2002–03	97,200	
2001–02	95,400	
2000–01	91,800	
1999–00	90,600	
1998–99	87,600	

Retirement annuities (TA 1988 s 626)

Age in years at beginning of year of assessment	*Maximum percentage*
50 and below	17½
51 to 55	20
56 to 60	22½
61 or more	27½

Life insurance element (TA 1988 s 640(3), as amended)

The maximum amount of contributions in respect of life insurance on which tax relief can be given is limited to a percentage of net relevant earnings (retirement annuities; personal pension contracts taken out before 6 April 2001) or of total amount of relevant pension contributions (personal pensions/stakeholder pension contracts taken out after 5 April 2001).

	Maximum percentage of net relevant earnings
Retirement annuities (contracts for dependants or life insurance)	5%
Personal pension schemes (contract of life insurance made before 6 April 2001)	5%
	Maximum percentage of total relevant pension contributions
Personal pension schemes/stakeholder pensions Contract of life insurance made after 5 April 2001	10%

Approval of contracts – early retirement ages

Trades and professions for which an early retirement age has been agreed by the Revenue under TA 1988 s 620(4)(c) for the purpose of the approval of retirement annuity contracts are set out below. Under the personal and stakeholder pensions legislation, individuals may not take benefits from their pension arrangements before the age of 50. The trades and professions listed below for which the Revenue has approved an earlier retirement age of 30, 35, 40 or 45 have been approved under TA 1988 s 634(3)(b) for the purposes of personal pension schemes and stakeholder pensions.

Retirement age	*Profession or occupation*		
30	downhill skiers		
35	athletes	ice hockey players	table tennis players
	badminton players	models	tennis players (including real tennis players)
	boxers	national hunt jockeys	wrestlers
	cyclists	rugby league players	
	dancers	rugby union players	
	footballers	squash players	
40	cricketers	golfers	speedway drivers
	divers (saturation, deep sea and free swimming)	motorcycle riders (motorcross or road racing)	trapeze artists
		motor racing drivers	WPBSA snooker players
45	flat racing jockeys	members of the reserve forces	
50	circus animal trainers	off-shore riggers (mechanical fitters, pipe fitters, riggers, platers, welders and roustabouts)	rugby league referees
	croupiers	Royal Navy reservists	territorial army members
	interdealer brokers		TV newsreaders
	martial arts instructors		
	moneybroker dealers		
55	air pilots	inshore fishermen	psychiatrists (who are also maximum part-time specialists employed within the NHS solely in the treatment of the mentally disordered)
	brass instrumentalists	midwives (female)	singers
	distant water trawlermen	moneybroker dealer managers and directors responsible for dealers	
	firemen (part-time)	nurses (female)	
	health visitors (female)	physiotherapists (female)	

Share schemes

Inland Revenue share schemes web page: www.inlandrevenue.gov.uk/shareschemes

Share incentive plans

(TCGA 1992 ss 236A, 238A, Schs 7C, 7D Pt 1; ITEPA 2003 ss 488–515, Sch 2; FA 2003 s 139, Sch 21)
Applications for approval of Share Incentive Plans could be made from 28 July 2000.

Free share plan

2000–01 onwards	*annual maximum*	£3,000

Partnership share plan

2000–01 to 2002–03	*monthly maximum*	£125 or 10% of monthly salary if lower
2003–04 onwards	*annual maximum*	£1,500 or 10% of annual salary if lower

Matching shares

2000–01 onwards	*Maximum number of shares given by employer to employee for each partnership share bought*	2

Reliefs

Where the conditions of the scheme are complied with –

(a) Free share plans: employers can give shares to employees free of income tax and national insurance contributions. (Some or all of these shares may be awarded for reaching performance targets.)
(b) Partnership share plans: employees may allocate part of their pre-tax salary to buy shares in their employing company without income tax or national insurance contributions being payable.
(c) Generally, all shares held in a plan for five years, will be free of income tax and national insurance contributions.
(d) No capital gains tax is payable on the withdrawal of shares from the plan and they are deemed to be acquired at their market value at that time.
(e) There is no stamp duty charge when the employee buys shares from trustees of the plan (FA 2000 Sch 8 para 116A; FA 2001 s 95; ITEPA 2003 Sch 6 para 257).
(f) If shares are taken out of a plan within between three and five years, income tax and national insurance contributions will be payable on the lower of their initial value and their value on leaving the plan.
(g) Dividends paid on the shares are tax free (up to a £1,500 annual limit) provided they are used to acquire additional shares in the company.
(h) The costs of the plan will be deductible from profits for tax purposes.

Enterprise management incentives

(TCGA 1992 s 238A, Sch 7D Pt 4; ITEPA 2003 ss 527–541, Sch 5)

With effect from 28 July 2000, independent trading companies with gross assets not exceeding £15 million may grant share options then worth up to £100,000 to an eligible employee. The total value of shares in respect of which unexercised qualifying options exist must not exceed £3 million. (For options granted before 11 May 2001 the number of employees who could hold options at any one time was limited to 15, giving an overall limit of £1.5 million.)

Reliefs

Where the conditions of the scheme are complied with –

(a) There is no charge to tax or NICs when the option is granted provided the option to acquire the shares is not at less than their market values at that date, and there is no charge on exercise providing the option is exercised within ten years.
(b) Capital gains tax will be payable when the shares are sold, but business assets taper relief (see p 37) will be available and will begin to run from the date on which the options are granted.

Company share option plans

(TCGA 1992 s 238A, Sch 7D Pt 3; ITEPA 2003 ss 521–526, Sch 4; FA 2003 s 139, Sch 21)

Limit on value of shares under option held by employee at any one time

From 29 April 1996	£30,000

Reliefs

Where the conditions of the scheme are complied with, no tax charge arises on the employee in respect of –

(a) the grant of an option to acquire shares;
(b) the exercise of the option;[1] or
(c) any increase in the value of the shares.

Capital gains tax is chargeable on disposal of the shares: the CGT base cost is the consideration given by the employee for both the shares and the option.

[1] The option must be exercised between 3 and 10 years after the grant (or may be exercised less than 3 years after the grant where the individual ceases to be an employee due to injury, disablement, redundancy or retirement). For options granted before 9 April 2003, the options must be exercised between 3 and 10 years after the grant (without exception) and not less than 3 years after a previous exempt exercise of another option under the same or another approved company share option scheme.

Approved save as you earn (SAYE) share option schemes

(TCGA 1992 s 238A, Sch 7D Pt 2; ITEPA 2003 ss 516–520, Sch 3; FA 2003 s 139, Sch 21)

The scheme is linked to an approved savings scheme, on which interest and bonuses are exempt from tax, to provide funds for the acquisition of shares when the option is exercised at the end of a 3 or 5–year contract. A 5–year contract may offer the option of repayment on the 7th anniversary.

Monthly contributions to SAYE scheme

Minimum	£5–£10[1]
Maximum	£250

[1] The company may choose a minimum savings contribution between £5 and £10.

Reliefs

Where the conditions of the scheme are complied with, no income tax charge arises on the employee in respect of –

(a) the grant of an option to acquire shares at a discount of up to 20% of the share price at time of the grant;
(b) the exercise of the option; or
(c) any increase in the value of the shares.

Capital gains tax is chargeable on disposal of the shares: the CGT base cost is the consideration given by the employee for both the shares and the option.

Bonus and interest payments on termination

Contracts joined from	**1.9.02**	**1.10.01 to 31.8.02**	**1.10.98 to 30.9.01**
3–year contract			
bonus rate	1·8 × monthly payments	2 × monthly payments	2·75 × monthly payments
effective interest rate	3·18%	3·67%	4·83%
interest rate on termination after 1 but less than 3 years	2% simple interest	2% simple interest	3% simple interest
5–year contract			
bonus rate	5·7 × monthly payments	6·2 × monthly payments	7·5 × monthly payments
effective interest rate	3·57%	3·99%	4·65%
interest rate on termination after 1 but less than 5 years	2% simple interest	2% simple interest	3% simple interest
7–year contract			
bonus rate	11 × monthly payments	11·9 × monthly payments	13·5 × monthly payments
effective interest rate	3·69%	4·07%	4·52%
interest rate on termination after 5 but less than 7 years	2% compound interest	2% compound interest	3% compound interest

A new mechanism for adjusting the bonus rates for the 3, 5 and 7-year SAYE contracts was introduced from 1 October 2001 and the rates will in future be adjusted automatically on an annual basis from 1 September by linking them to the 3, 5 and 7-year market swap rates. The mechanism will allow bonus rates to be adjusted during the 12-month period if there is a dramatic rise or fall in the market reference swap rates. Existing employees who entered SAYE contracts before the implementation of the new mechanism will continue to receive the bonus and interest rates in force when they joined the scheme.

Approved profit sharing schemes

(TA 1988 ss 186, 187, Sch 9, 10)

NOTE: The income tax relief in respect of awards of shares under approved profit sharing schemes was withdrawn for awards of shares made after 31 December 2002: FA 2000 s 49.)

Annual limit on shares appropriated

From 1991–92:	Greater of £3,000 or 10% of salary, up to £8,000

Schedule E charge on early disposal or receipt of capital from shares

Time of disposal or capital receipt	*Percentage charge*[1]
Before 3rd anniversary of appropriation	100%[2]

[1] Calculated on the appropriate percentage of the initial market value of the shares when appropriated (or the sales proceeds if less).

[2] The charge is reduced to 50% where the employee reaches the retirement age specified in the scheme rules or leaves the employment due to injury, disability or redundancy before the shares are sold or capital is received.

Reliefs

Where the conditions of the scheme are satisfied, no tax charge arises on the employee in respect of –

(a) the value of the shares at the time of appropriation;

(b) any increase in the value of the shares; or

(c) any gain on the disposal of the shares (although capital gains tax is chargeable on any gain over the market value on appropriation).

Executive share option schemes

(TA 1988 ss 185, 187, Sch 9)

NOTE: The income tax relief in respect of the grant and exercise of options under executive schemes was withdrawn with effect for options granted after 17 July 1995, subject to transitional provisions (see Revenue Press Release dated 28 November 1995). In general, options granted under an approved scheme after 16 July 1995 qualify for tax relief only if they meet the conditions for approved company share option plans (see above).

Limit on market value of unexercised options

Greater of £100,000 or 4 times emoluments subject to PAYE (excluding benefits).

Reliefs

Where the conditions of the scheme are satisfied, no tax charge arises on the employee in respect of –

(a) the grant or exercise of the option; or

(b) any increase in value of the shares.

Capital gains tax is chargeable on disposal of the shares: the CGT base cost is the consideration given by the employee for both the shares and the option.

Tax credits

Child tax credit and working tax credit

From 6 April 2003 the Working Families' Tax Credit, the Disabled Person's Tax Credit and the Children's Tax Credit have been replaced by two new tax credits – the Child Tax Credit (CTC) and the Working Tax Credit (WTC). The tax credits are awarded on an annual basis and do not form part of the taxable income. They are payable based on the income of the claimant or joint claimants. CTC and the childcare element of WTC is paid direct to the main carer by the Inland Revenue. WTC, apart from any childcare cost element, is paid through the employer or direct to a self-employed person by bank credit.

Child tax credit	**2003–2004 Annual amount**	**2003–04 Weekly equivalent**
	£	£
Family element[1]	545	10.45
Family element – child under age of 1[1]	1,090	20.90
Child element (for each child or young person)	1,445	27.75
Addition for disabled child or young person	2,155	41.30
Enhancement for severe disabled child or young person	865	16.60

Working tax credit	**2003–2004 Annual amount**	**2003–04 Weekly equivalent**
	£	£
Basic element	1,525	29.20
Lone parent and couples element	1,500	28.80
30-hour element	620	11.90
Disability element	2,040	39.15
Severe disability element	865	16.60
50 plus element – 16 to 29 hours worked	1,045	20.00
50 plus element – 30 or more hours worked[2]	1,565	30.00
Childcare element (up to 70% of eligible costs)		
– maximum eligible cost for 1 child		135.00
– maximum eligible cost for 2 or more children		200.00

Income thresholds	**2003–2004 Annual amount**	**2003–04 Weekly equivalent**
First income threshold	£5,060	£97
First withdrawal rate	37%	–
Second income threshold	£50,000	£958·90
Second withdrawal rate	1 in 15	–
First threshold for those entitled to Child Tax Credit only	£13,230	£253·76

[1] Only one family element available per family. Families are entitled to the family element and the baby addition in the first year of the child's life.
[2] Where an individual qualifies for the 50 plus (30+ hours) payment, they cannot also qualify for the 50 plus (16–29 hours) payment.

Working families' and disabled person's tax credits

The Working Families' Tax Credit (WFTC) and the Disabled Person's Tax Credit (DPTC) were introduced in October 1999 to replace Family Credit and Disability Working Allowance. The tax credits have been payable to working families depending on their circumstances from 5 October 1999 and from April 2000 to April 2003 were administered by employers and paid through the PAYE system. The credits do not form part of taxable income and normally last for 26 weeks.

Weekly rates 9.4.02–7.4.03[1]	**WFTC**	**DPTC**
	£	£
Adult credit – single	60.00/62.50	62.10
– couples/lone parents	–	92.80/95.30
– working 30 hours	11.65	11.65
Child credit – under 16	26.45	26.45
– 16–18	27.20	27.20
Disabled child tax credit	35.50	35.50
Enhanced disability tax credit – lone parent/couple	16.25	16.25
– single person	–	11.25
– child[2]	46.75	46.75
Childcare credit (70% of eligible costs) – 1 child (max)	135.00	135.00
– 2 or more children (max)	200.00	200.00
Earnings at which credit is reduced by 55% – single	–	73.50
– couples/lone parents	94.50	94.50
Capital – upper limit	8,000	16,000
– amount disregarded	3,000	3,000

[1] Higher rates apply from June 2001 and June 2002 respectively.
[2] Includes the disabled child tax credit for relevant awards starting from April 2001.

Taxable earnings – income from employment

(ITEPA 2003 ss 14–43)

	Services performed			
Persons domiciled in UK	Wholly in UK	Partly in UK	Partly abroad	Wholly abroad
Non-resident	All	That part	None	None
Resident but not ordinarily resident	All	That part	Remittances	Remittances
Resident and ordinarily resident	All	All[1]	All[1]	All[1]
Persons domiciled outside UK	UK employer Foreign employer	As for person domiciled in UK. *Non-resident* All UK earnings. *Resident (not ordinarily resident)*—All UK earnings. (Remittances for duties performed outside UK.) *Resident (and ordinarily resident)* All earnings. (Remittances if all duties performed outside UK.)		

[1] Before 17 March 1998, exempt if qualifying period of over 364 days mostly abroad. The relief for seafarers continues after that date (FA 1998 s 63; ITEPA 2003 ss 378–385). Special relief for employees forced to return early from Kuwait or Iraq who had intended to work abroad for over 364 days.
It was further announced in the Budget Speech made on 9 April 2003 that the Government is reviewing the residence and domicile rules as they affect the tax liabilities of individuals; a background paper having been published on the same day (Budget 2003 PN 01).

Termination payments

Exempt lump sum payments

(a) Payments in connection with the cessation of employment on the death, injury or disability of the employee.

(b) Payments under unapproved retirement benefits schemes where the employee has been taxed on the actual or notional contributions to provide the benefit.

(c) Payments under approved retirement benefits schemes which can properly be regarded as a benefit earned by past service.

(d) Certain payments of terminal grants to members of the armed forces.

(e) Certain benefits under superannuation schemes for civil servants in Commonwealth overseas territories.

(f) Payments in respect of foreign service where the period of foreign service comprises –

- (i) 75% of the whole period of service; or
- (ii) the whole of the last 10 years of service; or
- (iii) where the period of service exceeded 20 years, one-half of that period, including any 10 of the last 20 years.

Otherwise, a proportion of the payment is exempt, as follows –

$$\frac{\text{length of foreign service}}{\text{length of total service}} \text{ x amount otherwise chargeable}$$

(g) The first £30,000 of genuine ex gratia payments (where there is no 'arrangement' by the employer to make the payment): ITEPA 2003 ss 401–413.

(h) Statutory redundancy payments (included in computing £30,000 limit in (f) above).

Inheritance tax

Delivery of accounts: due dates

Type of transfer	*Due date*
Chargeable lifetime transfers	Later of – (a) 12 months after the end of the month in which the transfer took place; and (b) 3 months after the date on which the person delivering the account became liable
PETs which become chargeable	12 months after the end of the month in which the transferor died
Gifts with reservation chargeable on death	12 months after the end of the month in which the death occurred
Transfers on death	Later of – (a) 12 months after the end of the month in which the death occurred; and (b) 3 months after the date on which the personal representatives first act or the person liable first has reason to believe that he is liable to deliver an account
National heritage property	6 months after the end of the month in which the chargeable event occurred

Delivery of accounts: excepted transfers, estates and settlements

Date of transfer or death	6 April 1996–5 April 1998	6 April 1998–5 April 2000	6 April 2000–5 April 2002	6 April 2002–5 April 2003	After 5 April 2003
Excepted transfers:	*Value below:*	*Value below:*	*Value below:*	*Value below:*	*Value below:*
Total chargeable transfers since 6 April	£10,000	£10,000	£10,000	£10,000	£10,000
Total chargeable transfers during last 10 years	£40,000	£40,000	£40,000	£40,000	£40,000
Excepted estates:					
Total gross value	£180,000[1]	£200,000[1]	£210,000[1]	£220,000[1]	£240,000[1]
Total gross value of property outside UK	£30,000	£50,000	£50,000	£75,000	£75,000
Aggregate value of 'specified transfers'[2]	£50,000	£75,000	£75,000	£100,000	£100,000
Settled property passing on death	—	—	—	£100,000	£100,000

Excepted estates: No account need be delivered where the deceased died domiciled in the UK, provided there was no chargeable lifetime transfers in the 7 years before death other than 'specified transfers' not exceeding the above limits.

Where the deceased was never domiciled in the UK, no account need be delivered for deaths after 5 April 2002 provided the value of the estate in the UK is wholly attributable to cash and quoted shares and securities not exceeding £100,000.

Notes:

[1] This limit applies to the aggregate gross value of the estate and of 'specified transfers' within 7 years before death.

[2] 'Specified transfers' are transfers of cash, quoted shares and securities and, after 6 April 2002, interests in or over land (including furnishings and chattels disposed of at the same time to the same donee).

Excepted settlements: No account need be delivered of property comprised in excepted settlements where a chargeable event occurs after 5 April 2002. 'Excepted settlements' is one comprising solely of cash not exceeding £1,000 and in which there is no interest in possession. The trustees must be UK resident throughout the life of the trust and there must be no related settlements.

Rates of tax

From 15 March 1988 onwards

Tax rates on cumulative gross transfers	*% rate on gross*
Gross transfers on death	
Up to cumulative chargeable transfer limit	0
Over cumulative chargeable transfer limit	40
Gross lifetime transfers	
Up to cumulative chargeable transfer limit	0
Over cumulative chargeable transfer limit	20

Grossing-up rate on net transfers	*Rate on net fraction*
Net transfers on death not bearing own tax	
Up to cumulative chargeable transfer limit	nil
For each £ over chargeable transfer limit	⅔
Net lifetime transfers	
Up to cumulative chargeable transfer limit	nil
For each £ over chargeable transfer limit	¼

Cumulative chargeable transfer limits

Period	*Limit*
	£
2003–04	255,000
2002–03	250,000
2001–02	242,000
2000–01	234,000
1999–2000	231,000
1998–99	223,000
1997–98	215,000
1996–97	200,000
1995–96	154,000
10.3.92–5.4.95	150,000
6.4.91–9.3.92	140,000
1990–91	128,000
1989–90	118,000
15.3.88–5.4.89	110,000

Reliefs

The following is a summary of the main reliefs and exemptions for 2003–04 under the Inheritance Tax Act 1984. The legislation should be referred to for conditions and exceptions.

Agricultural property

Transfer with vacant possession (or right to obtain it within 12 months); transfer on or after 1 September 1995, of land let (or treated as let) on or after that date.	100% of agricultural value
Any other case	50% of agricultural value

(Under IHTA 1984 s 124C, as inserted by FA 1997 s 94, land managed according to terms of certain Habitat Schemes is treated as farm land, and qualifies for relief after 26 Nov. 1996.)

Charges arising and transfers occurring after 9 March 1992 and before 1 September 1995:

Transfer with vacant possession (or right to obtain within 12 months)	100% of agricultural value
Most other cases	50% of agricultural value

Note: The 100% relief is extended in limited circumstances by Concession F17.

Annual exemption

From 6 April 1981	£3,000

Business property

Unincorporated business Unquoted shares (including shares in AIM or USM companies) (held for 2 years or more)[1] Unquoted securities which alone, or together with other such securities and unquoted shares, give the transferor control of the company (held for 2 years or more)[1] Settled property used in life tenant's business	100%	Controlling holding in fully quoted companies Land, buildings, machinery or plant used in business of company or partnership	50%

[1] Tax charges arising and transfers occurring after 5 April 1996. 10 March 1992–5 April 1996 minority holding of shares or securities of up to 25% in unquoted or USM company qualified for 50% relief; larger holdings qualified for 100% relief.

Charities, gifts to

From 15 March 1983	Exempt

Community Amateur Sports Clubs (CASCs), gifts to

From 6 April 2002	Exempt

Marriage gifts

Made by: parent	£5,000
remoter ancestor	£2,500
party to marriage	£2,500
other person	£1,000

Political parties, gifts to

From 15 March 1988	Exempt

Quick succession relief

Estate increased by chargeable transfer followed by death within 5 years

Death within first year	100%
Each additional year: decreased by	20%

Small gifts to same person

From 6 April 1981	£250

Spouses with separate domicile (one not being in the UK)

Total exemption	£55,000

Tapering relief

The value of the estate on death is taxed as the top slice of cumulative transfers in the 7 years before death. Transfers on or within 7 years of death are taxed on their value at the date of the gift on the death rate scale, but using the scale in force at the date of death, subject to the following taper—

Years between gift and death	*Percentage of full charge at death rates*
0–3	100
3–4	80
4–5	60
5–6	40
6–7	20

Penalties see p 20.

National insurance & State benefits

Taxable and non-taxable state benefits

State benefits of an income nature are in principle taxable in the same way as other sources of income, but the majority of such benefits are not in fact taxed.

Benefits taxed as earned income

Bereavement allowance[1]
Carer's allowance[2]
Incapacity benefit[3]
Industrial death benefit pensions
Jobseeker's allowance[4]
Retirement pension[2]
Statutory adoption pay
Statutory maternity pay
Statutory paternity pay
Statutory sick pay
Widowed parents' allowance[2 and 5]

Notes:
[1] Replaced widow's pension from 9 April 2001. Paid up to 52 weeks.
[2] Invalid care allowance before 6 April 2003. Child dependency additions are not taxable (see (2) below).
[3] Payments made during the initial 28-week period, and that part of the benefit which represents a child addition, are exempt (see below).
[4] In practice limited to the smaller of the jobseeker's allowance 'personal allowance' (for a couple or single person as appropriate) and the weekly amount to which the claimant is entitled: IR41 Income tax and jobseekers.
[5] Replaced widowed mother's allowance from 9 April 2001.

Benefits which are not taxed

(1) *Short-term benefits*
Adoption pay
Maternity allowance

(2) *Benefits in respect of children*
Child benefit
Child dependency additions paid with retirement pension, widows' benefit, incapacity benefit, invalidity benefit, carer's allowance, severe disablement allowance, higher-rate industrial death benefit, unemployability supplement and sickness (or, formerly, unemployment benefit) if beneficiary over pension age
Child tax credit
Child's special allowance
Guardian's allowance
One-parent benefit

(3) *Industrial injury benefits*
Constant attendance allowance
Industrial death benefit
Industrial injuries disablement benefit
Pneumoconiosis and miscellaneous disease benefits
Reduced earnings allowance

(4) *War disablement benefits*
Constant attendance allowance
Disablement pension
Severe disablement allowance

(5) *Other benefits*
Attendance allowance
Bereavement payment
Christmas bonus
Cold weather payments
Council tax benefit
Disability living allowance
Disability working allowance (replaced by disabled person's tax credit from 5 October 1999)
Disabled person's tax credit (replaced by child tax credit and working tax credit from 6 April 2003)
Earnings top-up
Housing benefit
Incapacity benefit (initial 28-week period *only*)
Income support
Jobfinder's grant
Redundancy payment
Social fund payments
Television licence payment
Vaccine damage (lump sum)
War pensions
Widow's payment (replaced by bereavement payment from 9 April 2001)
Winter fuel payment
Working families' tax credit (replaced by child tax credit and working tax credit from 6 April 2003)
Working tax credit

Taxable benefits – rates from 7 April 2003

	Qualifying average weekly earnings	Rate	Maximum no weeks paid
Statutory adoption pay[1]	£77	lower of 90% of average weekly earnings and £100	26
Statutory maternity pay[1]	6.4.03–19.7.03 £75 20.7.03–5.4.04 £77	first six weeks: 90% of average weekly earnings after first six weeks: lower of 90% of average weekly earnings and £100	26
Statutory paternity pay[1]	6.4.03–19.7.03 £75 20.7.03–5.4.04 £77	lower of 90% of average weekly earnings and £100	2
Statutory sick pay	£77	£64.35 daily rate is the weekly rate divided by number of qualifying days in week (commencing on the Sunday) in which day to be paid occurs	–

[1] For babies expected, or where children are matched or start to live with adoptive parents, after 5 April 2003

Taxable benefits

	Weekly 8.4.02 onwards £	Total 2002–03 (52 weeks) £	Weekly 7.4.03 onwards £	Total 2003–04 (52 weeks) £
Retirement pensions				
Single person	75.50	3,926.00	77.45	4,027.40
Married couple:				
both contributors—each	75.50	3,926.00	77.45	4,027.40
wife non-contributor—addition	45.20	2,350.40	46.35	2,410.20
wife non-contributor—joint	120.70	6,276.40	123.80	6,437.60
Age addition (over 80)—each	0.25	13.00	0.25	13.00
Bereavement benefits[1]				
Bereavement allowance —standard	75.50	3,926.00	77.45	4,027.40
Widowed parent's allowance	75.50	3,926.00	77.45	4,027.40
Non-contributory retirement pension				
Single person (category C or D)	45.20	2,350.40	46.35	2,410.20
Married couple (category C)	72.20	3,754.40	74.05	3,850.60
Married couple (category D—over 80)	90.40	4,700.80	92.70	4,820.40
Age addition	0.25	13.00	0.25	13.00
Incapacity benefit				
Long-term	70.95	3,689.40	72.15	3,751.80
Increased for age: Higher rate	14.90	774.80	15.15	787.80
Lower rate	7.45	387.40	7.60	395.20
Short-term[2] (under pension age) higher rate	63.25	—	64.35	—
(over pension age) higher rate	70.95	—	72.15	—
Invalidity allowance when paid with retirement pension				
Higher rate	14.90	774.80	15.15	787.80
Middle rate	9.50	494.00	9.70	504.40
Lower rate	4.75	247.00	4.85	252.20
Industrial death benefit				
Widow's pension:				
Higher permanent rate	75.50	3,926.00	77.45	4,027.40
Lower permanent rate	22.65	1,177.80	23.24	1,208.48
Widower's pension	75.50	3,926.00	77.45	4,027.40
Carer's allowance[3]				
Each qualifying individual	42.45	2,207.40	43.15	2,243.80
Earnings limit	75.00	—	77.00	—
Adult dependency increase	25.35	1,318.20	25.80	1,341.60
Jobseeker's allowance				
Single: under 18	32.50	—	32.90	—
18 to 24	42.70	—	43.25	—
25 or over	53.95	—	54.65	—

[1] Paid to widows and widowers for up to 52 weeks.

[2] Lower rate (tax-free) paid up to week 28 (see below). Higher rate (taxable) paid weeks 29 to 52. New claims cannot be made by persons over pensionable age.

[3] Invalid care allowance before April 2003.

Child dependency additions (from 7.4.03): £9·55 a week where higher rate child benefit payable
£11·35 a week for each other child (tax free).

The Revenue generally apply the basis of 52 weeks at the new rate. In certain cases, however, it may be to the advantage of the recipient to calculate the amount actually received within the year of assessment where this includes one week at the old rate.

Non-taxable benefits – rates from 7 April 2003

Attendance allowance:	Higher rate	£57·20 a week
	Lower rate	£38·30 a week
Child benefit:	£16·05 for eldest eligible child (couple)	
	£17·55 for eldest eligible child (lone parent, existing claimants only)	
	£10·75 (each) for other eligible children	
Disability living allowance:		
Care component:	Higher rate	£57·20 a week
	Middle rate	£38·30 a week
	Lower rate	£15·15 a week
Mobility component:	Higher rate	£39·95 a week
	Lower rate	£15·15 a week
Incapacity benefit:		
Short term (under pension age)	Lower rate	£54·40 a week
Short term (over pension age)	Lower rate	£69·20 a week
Maternity allowance:	Lower earnings limit	£100·00 a week (average)
	Standard rate	£100·00 a week
	Earnings threshold	£30·00 a week (average)
	Lower rate	90% average weekly earnings (at least £100)
Bereavement payment:	£2,000 lump sum (Paid to widows and widowers.)	

Contributions

From 6 April 2003

Class 1

Lower earnings limit	£77 a week; £334 a month; £4,004 a year
Earnings threshold (employees and employers)	£89 a week; £385 a month; £4,615 a year
Upper earnings limit	£595 a week; £2,579 a month; £30,940 a year

	Not contracted out	Contracted out	
Employees' contributions[1]			
Weekly earnings: £89·01–£595	11%	9·4%[2]	
Over £595	1%	1%	
Employers' contributions[2]		*Salary-related schemes*	*Money purchase schemes*
Weekly earnings: £89·01–£595	12·8%	9·3%	11·8%
Over £595	12·8%	12·8%	12·8%

[1] Employees' rates are nil for children under 16, men over 65 and women over 60. Rates for married women and widows with valid certificates of election are reduced to 4·85% for earnings between £89·01 and £595 pw but the 1% rate still applies to amounts above £595. Normal employers' contributions are payable. NICs are not payable on the first £89 of earnings pw.

[2] Employers receive a rebate of 3·5% for salary-related schemes and 1% for money purchase schemes on earnings from £77 to £89 pw. A rebate of 1·6% on earnings from £77 to £89 pw is given to employees (or employers to the extent that insufficient contributions have been paid for offset). NICs are not payable on the first £89 of earnings pw.

Class 1A and Class 1B:	12·8%
Class 2 (self-employed):	Flat rate £2 a week Volunteer development workers £3·85 a week Share fishermen £2·65 a week Small earnings exception £4,095 a year
Class 3 (voluntary contributions):	£6·95 a week
Class 4 (self-employed):	profits £4,615–£30,940 a year: 8% over £30,940: 1% Exempt if pensionable age reached by beginning of tax year

6 April 2002–5 April 2003

Class 1

Lower earnings limit	£75 a week; £325 a month; £3,900 a year
Earnings threshold (employees and employers)	£89 a week; £385 a month; £4,615 a year
Upper earnings limit	£585 a week; £2,535 a month; £30,420 a year

	Not contracted out	Contracted out	
Employees' contributions[1]			
Weekly earnings: £89·01–£585	10%	8·4%[2]	
Over £585	no additional liability	no additional liability	
Employers' contributions[2]		*Salary-related schemes*	*Money purchase schemes*
Weekly earnings: £89·01–£585	11·8%	8·3%	10·8%
Over £585	11·8%	11·8%	11·8%

[1] Employees' rates are nil for children under 16, men over 65 and women over 60. Rates for married women and widows with valid certificates of election are reduced to 3·85% for earnings between £89·01 and £585 pw. Normal employers' contributions are payable. NICs are not payable on the first £89 of earnings pw.

[2] Employers receive a rebate of 3·5% for salary-related schemes and 1% for money purchase schemes on earnings from £75 to £89 pw. A rebate of 1·6% on earnings from £75 to £89 pw is given to employees (or employers to the extent that insufficient contributions have been paid for offset). NICs are not payable on the first £89 of earnings pw.

Class 1A and Class 1B:	11·8%
Class 2 (self-employed):	Flat rate £2 a week Volunteer development workers £3·75 a week Share fishermen £2·65 a week Small earnings exception £4,025 a year
Class 3 (voluntary contributions):	£6·85 a week
Class 4 (self-employed):	7% of profits between £4,615 and £30,420 a year Exempt if pensionable age reached by beginning of tax year

6 April 2001–5 April 2002

Class 1

Lower earnings limit	£72 a week; £312 a month; £3,744 a year
Employees' earnings (primary) threshold	£87 a week; £378 a month; £4,535 a year
Employers' earnings (secondary) threshold	£87 a week; £378 a month; £4,535 a year
Upper earnings limit	£575 a week; £2,492 a month; £29,900 a year

	Not contracted out	Contracted out	
Employees' contributions[1]			
Weekly earnings: £87·01–£575	10%	8·4%[2]	
Over £575	no additional liability	no additional liability	
Employers' contributions[2]		*Salary-related schemes*	*Money purchase schemes*
Weekly earnings: £87·01–£575	11·9%	8·9%	11·3%
Over £575	11·9%	11·9%	11·9%

[1] Employees' rates are nil for children under 16, men over 65 and women over 60. Rates for married women and widows with valid certificates of election are reduced to 3·85% for earnings between £87·01 and £575 pw. Normal employers' contributions are payable. NICs are not payable on the first £87 of earnings pw.
[2] Employers receive a rebate of 3% for salary-related schemes and 0·6% for money purchase schemes on earnings from £72 to £87 pw. A rebate of 1·6% on earnings from £72 to £87 pw is given to employees (or employers to the extent that insufficient contributions have been paid for offset). NICs are not payable on the first £87 of earnings pw.

Class 1A and Class 1B:	11·9%
Class 2 (self-employed):	Flat rate £2 a week Volunteer development workers £3·60 a week Share fishermen £2·65 a week Small earnings exception £3,955 a year
Class 3 (voluntary contributions):	£6·75 a week
Class 4 (self-employed):	7% of profits between £4,535 and £29,900 a year Exempt if pensionable age reached by beginning of tax year

6 April 2000–5 April 2001

Class 1

Lower earnings limit	£67 a week; £291 a month; £3,484 a year
Employees' earnings (primary) threshold	£76 a week; £329 a month; £3,952 a year
Employers' earnings (secondary) threshold	£84 a week; £365 a month; £4,385 a year
Upper earnings limit	£535 a week; £2,319 a month; £27,820 a year

	Not contracted out	Contracted out	
Employees' contributions[1]			
Weekly earnings: £76·01–£535	10%	8·4%[2]	
Over £535	no additional liability	no additional liability	
Employers' contributions[2]		*Salary-related schemes*	*Money purchase schemes*
Weekly earnings: £84·01–£535	12·2%	9·2%	11·6%
Over £535	12·2%	12·2%	12·2%

[1] Employees' rates are nil for children under 16, men over 65 and women over 60. Rates for married women and widows with valid certificates of election are reduced to 3·85% for earnings between £76·01 and £535 pw. Normal employers' contributions are payable. NICs are not payable on the first £76 of earnings pw.
[2] Employers receive a rebate of 3% for salary-related schemes and 0·6% for money purchase schemes on earnings from £67 to £84 pw. A rebate of 1·6% on earnings from £67 to £76 pw is given to employees (or employers to the extent that insufficient contributions have been paid for offset). Employers' NICs are not payable on the first £84 of earnings pw. Employees' NICs are not payable on the first £76 of earnings pw.

Class 1A and Class 1B:	12·2%
Class 2 (self-employed):	Flat rate £2 a week Volunteer development workers £3·35 a week Share fishermen £2·65 a week Small earnings exception £3,825 a year
Class 3 (voluntary contributions):	£6·55 a week
Class 4 (self-employed):	7% of profits between £4,385 and £27,820 a year Exempt if pensionable age reached by beginning of tax year

Contributions — continued

6 April 1999–5 April 2000

Class 1			
Lower earnings limit		£66 a week; £286 a month; £3,432 a year	
Employers' earnings (secondary) threshold		£83 a week; £361 a month; £4,335 a year	
Upper earnings limit		£500 a week; £2,167 a month; £26,000 a year	
	Not contracted out	**Contracted out**	
Employees' contributions[1]			
Weekly earnings: £66·01–£500	10%	8·4%	
Over £500	no additional liability	no additional liability	
Employers' contributions[2]		*Salary-related schemes*	*Money purchase schemes*
Weekly earnings: £83·01–£500	12·2%	9·2%	11·6%
Over £500	12·2%	12·2%	12·2%

[1] Employees' rates are nil for children under 16, men over 65 and women over 60. Rates for married women and widows with valid certificates of election are reduced to 3·85% for earnings between £66·01 and £500 pw. Normal employers' contributions are payable. NICs are not payable on the first £66 of earnings pw.
[2] Employers receive a rebate of 3% for salary-related schemes and 0·6% for money purchase schemes on earnings from £66 to £83 pw. Employers' NICs are not payable on the first £83 of earnings pw. Employees' NICs are not payable on the first £66 of earnings pw.

Class 1A and Class 1B:	12·2%
Class 2 (self-employed):	Flat rate £6·55 a week Volunteer development workers £3·30 a week Share fishermen £7·20 a week Small earnings exception £3,770 a year
Class 3 (voluntary contributions):	£6·45 a week
Class 4 (self-employed):	6% of profits between £7,530 and £26,000 a year Exempt if pensionable age reached by beginning of tax year

6 April 1998–5 April 1999

Class 1

Lower earnings limit:	£64 a week £278 a month £3,328 a year	**Upper earnings limit: (employees only)**	£485 a week £2,102 a month £25,220 a year

	Employees from 6.4.98		**Employers from 6.4.98**		
Not contracted out	*On first £64*	*Remainder*	*(Rate applying to all earnings)*		
Earnings: £ 64·00–£109·99	2%	10%	3%		
£110·00–£154·99	2%	10%	5%		
£155·00–£209·99	2%	10%	7%		
£210·00–£485·00	2%	10%	10%		
Over £485	no additional liability		10%		
Contracted out	*On first £64*	*Remainder*	*On first £64*	*Remainder* SR[1]	MP[2]
Earnings: £ 64·00–£109·99	2%	8·4%	3%	Nil	1·5%
£110·00–£154·99	2%	8·4%	5%	2	3·5%
£155·00–£209·99	2%	8·4%	7%	4	5·5%
£210·00–£485·00	2%	8·4%	10%	7	8·5%
Over £485	no additional liability		10% 10%	7% (to £485) 10% (over £485)	8·5% (to £485) 10% (over £485)
Reduced rate for married women and widows with valid certificate of election	3·85% (earnings to £485)		(As above)		
Men over 65 and women over 60	Nil		(As above)		
Children under 16	Nil		Nil		

Class 1A:	10%
Class 2 (self employed):	Flat rate: £6·35 a week Volunteer development workers £3·20 a week Share fishermen £7 a week Small earnings exception £3,590 a year
Class 3 (voluntary contributions):	£6·25 a week
Class 4 (self-employed):	6% of profits between £7,310 and £25,220 a year Exempt if pensionable age reached by beginning of year of assessment

[1] Rates apply to salary-related schemes. [2] Rates apply to money-purchase schemes.

Employers' contributions: benefits in kind

From *6 April 2000,* **Class 1A** national insurance contributions are payable by employers (at 12·8% for 2003–04) on most taxable benefits in kind, excluding benefits:

(1) which are covered by a dispensation; or
(2) included in a PAYE settlement agreement; or
(3) provided for employees not earning more than £8,500 pa (including benefits in kind and expenses payments); or
(4) otherwise not required to be included on a PIID; or
(5) on which Class 1 national insurance contributions were due.

Expenses payments and certain benefits are not liable to Class 1A national insurance contributions.

Before 6 April 2000, national insurance contributions were payable by employers only where the benefits in kind were of cars and free fuel provided for the private use of employees (where the latter were liable to the income tax charge on cars). The benefit of cars and free fuel continues to be chargeable (see above).

From *6 April 1999,* **Class 1B** contributions are payable by employers (at 12·8% for 2003–04) by reference to the value of any items included in a PAYE settlement agreement (PSA) which would otherwise be earnings for Class 1 or Class 1A, including the amount of tax paid. Income tax and Class 1B contributions on a PSA are payable by 19 October after the end of the tax year to which the PSA relates.

Benefits subject to Class 1 and Class 1A national insurance contributions		
Benefit	**NICs Class**	**PAYE or P11D**
Assets/gifts given to employees	1A	P11D
Assets loaned to employees	1A	P11D
Car fuel supplied for private motoring	1A	P11D
Cars or vans available for private use	1A	P11D
Christmas gifts: – cash	1	PAYE
– benefits	1A	P11D
Clothing and uniforms		
– cash payment for clothing that can be worn at any time	1	PAYE
– cash payment for clothing that can only be worn at work or non-durable items such as tights or stockings	–	PAYE
– clothing provided by employer that can be worn at any time	1A	P11D
Credit cards and tokens – personal expenses not reimbursed	1	PAYE
Entertaining – non-business staff expenses/allowances	1A	P11D
– staff expenses where employee contracts	1	P11D
Living accommodation (beneficial)	1A	P11D
Loans – at low interest or interest-free	1A	P11D
– written off	1	P11D
Medical insurance or treatment provided in the UK by employer	1A	P11D
Notional payments	1	PAYE
Payments in kind convertible to cash	1	PAYE
Payments of employees personal liabilities	1	PAYE
Personal incidental expense payments	1	P11D
Prize money	1	PAYE
Relocation payments – qualifying over £8,000	1A	P11D
– non-qualifying benefits	1A	P11D
– non-qualifying expenses	1	P11D
Round sum allowances (not identified as business expense)	1	PAYE
Services supplied	1A	P11D
Telephone rental and private calls – employee subscribes	1	P11D
– employer subscribes	1A	P11D

National insurance contributions leaflets

Leaflets regarding National Insurance contributions are issued by the Inland Revenue. They are available from the Inland Revenue website: http://www.inlandrevenue.gov.uk and can be obtained from local Inland Revenue offices (including those which were Contributions Agency offices before 1 April 1999) except where indicated:

‡Inland Revenue National Insurance Contributions Office, Services to Pension Industry, Barton Park View, Newcastle Upon Tyne NE98 1ZZ (Tel: 08459 150 150).
Further leaflets are available, including rates and tables within the PAYE and NIC Employer's Annual Pack, which can be ordered online or from the orderline on 08457 646 646.

National Insurance

Leaflet	*Date*	*Title*
CA01	2003	National insurance contributions for employees
CA02	2003	National insurance contributions for self-employed people with small earnings
CA04	2003	Class 2 and Class 3: direct debit – the easier way to pay
CA07	2003	Unpaid and late-paid contributions
CA08	2003	Voluntary contributions
CA09	2003	National insurance contributions for widows or widowers
CA10	2003	National insurance contributions for divorcees
CA11	2003	Share fishermen
CA12	2001	Training for further employment and your National Insurance record
CA13	2003	National insurance contributions for married women with reduced elections
CA14‡	2002	Termination of contracted-out employment: manual for salary related pension schemes and salary related parts of mixed benefits schemes
CA14A‡	2002	Termination of contracted-out employment: manual for money purchase pension schemes and money purchase parts of mixed benefits schemes
CA14C‡	1999	Contracted-out guidance for SR pension schemes and SR overseas schemes
CA14D‡	1999	Contracted-out guidance for money purchase pension schemes and money purchase overseas schemes
CA14E‡	1999	Contracted-out guidance for mixed benefit pension schemes and mixed benefit overseas schemes
CA14F‡	2003	Technical guidance on contracted-out decision making and appeals
CA15‡	1999	Cessation of contracted-out pension schemes manual
CA16‡	2002	Appropriate personal pension scheme manual – procedural guidance
CA16A‡	2002	Appropriate personal pension scheme manual – guidance for scheme managers
CA17‡	2002	Employees' guide to minimum contributions
CA19‡	2003	Using the accrued GMP liability service
CA20‡	2003	Using the contracted-out contributions/earnings information service
CA21‡	2003	Using the National Insurance number/date of birth checking service
CA22‡	2002	Contracted-out data transactions using magnetic media
CA23	2001	National insurance contributions for mariners
CA24	2001	National insurance contributions for masters and employers of mariners
CA25	2002	Agencies and people working through agencies
CA26	2003	National insurance contributions for examiners, moderators and invigilators, lecturers, teachers and instructors
CA30	2003	Statutory Sick Pay manual for employers
CA33	2003	Employer's manual on Class 1A NICs on cars and fuel
CA42	2003	Foreign going mariner's and deep-sea fisherman's contributions for employers
CA43‡	2003	Tables: contracted-out contributions and minimum payments for employers with contracted out money purchase schemes
CA44	2003	National insurance for company directors
CA47	2002	Charter for national insurance contributors
CA50	1999	Making your year end return on tape or disk
CA51/52	2003	Submitting year end returns on magnetic media – Technical guide
CA65	2003	NIC for people working for embassies, consulates and overseas employers
CA70	2000	Magnetic media transmission of data
CA72	2003	National insurance contributions – deferring payments
CA72A	2003/04	Application for deferment of payment of Class 1 contributions
CA72B	2003/04	Application for deferment of payment of Class 2 and Class 4 contributions
CA75	2001	Resolving benefit involved cases
CA76	2001	National insurance abroad – a guide for employers of employees from abroad
CA78A	2001	International services employers' pack
CA82	2001	If you think our decision is wrong
CA84‡	2002	Stakeholder pension scheme manual
CA85	2003	Contracted-out stakeholder pension scheme manual
CA86	2003	Employees' guide to statutory sick pay
CA87	2000	National insurance contributions and the Welsh language
CA88	2002	Payroll cleansing: what is it and what can it do for you?
CA89	2001	Payroll cleansing employer's pack
CA90	2000	Convention on social security between the UK and the Republic of Korea
CA91	2001	Agreement between the UK and Japan on social security
CA92‡	2003	Services to the pension industry – an information guide
CA1437/A	2001	Employer's guide to centralised payments of national insurance contributions
CA1583	2003	Notification of termination of contracted-out employment – split of protected rights
CA1889	2003	Notification of termination and change of responsibility from a contracted-out salary related scheme or salary related part of a mixed benefit scheme
CA1892	2003	Transfer
CA1893	2003	Notification of a change of responsibility from a contracted-out money purchase scheme or the money purchase part of a mixed benefit scheme
CA1894	2003	Notification of termination of contracted-out employment and change of responsibility from a contracted-out money purchase scheme or the money purchase part of a mixed benefit scheme
CWG2	2003	Employer's further guide to PAYE and NICs
CWG5	2003	Class 1A NICs and benefits in kind – a guide for employers
P/SE/1	2001	Starting your own business
CWL2	2003	NIC for self-employed people, Class 2 and Class 4
IR37	2003	Appeals against tax (see also correction)
IR 56	1999	Employed or self-employed? A guide for tax and national insurance
IR 148	2001	Are your workers employed or self-employed? – construction workers
NE1	1999	First steps as a new employer
NI38	2001	Social security abroad
NI132	2002	National insurance for employers of people working abroad
OCSS1	2003	NICO. Our customer service standards

Stamp duties

Rates of duty

(FA 1963 s 55; FA 1999 s 111, Sch 13; FA 2000 ss 114, 116; FA 2003 ss 55, 56, 125, Schs 4, 5, 20)

Stamp duty land tax

Applies to contracts entered into, or varied, after 10 July 2003 and completed, or leases granted, on or after 1 December 2003 (subject to further consultation on lease duty).

On land transactions[1]

Residential property		*Non-residential or mixed property*	
Not exceeding £60,000	Nil	Not exceeding £150,000	Nil
£60,001–£250,000	1%	£151,001–£250,000	1%
£250,001–£500,000	3%	£250,001–£500,000	3%
£500,001 or more	4%	£500,001 or more	4%

Lease granted for a premium
The same duty is payable as above for land transactions. The nil rate, however, only applies where the rent under the lease does not exceed £600 p.a.

Lease rentals
On net present value of rent over term of lease (applying a discount rate of 3·5%)

Residential property		*Non-residential or mixed property*	
Not exceeding £60,000	Nil	Not exceeding £150,000	Nil
£60,001 or more	1%	£150,001 or more	1%

Stamp duty

For contracts entered into, or varied, after 10 July 2003 and completed, or leases granted, on or after 1 December 2003, stamp duty is abolished for all transfers other than stocks and marketable securities, and interests in partnerships. Transfers of land are subject to stamp duty land tax (see above).

Transfers of stock and marketable securities 0·5%

Other transfers (including land and buildings)
Contracts entered into before 11 July 2003 or completed, or leases granted, before 1 December 2003.

	24.3.98–15.3.99	16.3.99–27.3.00	28.3.00–30.11.03
On transfer made pursuant to contract after	17.3.98	9.3.99	21.3.00
Conveyance or transfer on sale with certificate of value[1]			
Not exceeding £60,000	Nil	Nil	Nil
£60,001–£250,000	1%	1%	1%
£250,001–£500,000	2%	2·5%	3%
£500,001 or more	3%	3·5%	4%
Conveyance or transfer on sale without certificate of value	3%	3·5%	4%

Lease granted for a premium
The same duty is payable as above for a conveyance or transfer on sale. The nil rate, however, only applies where the rent under the lease does not exceed £600 p.a.

Lease rentals

Furnished residential accommodation for definite term of less than 1 year	£5 (£1 before 1.10.99)
Leases not exceeding 7 years, or for an indefinite term:	
—Up to £5,000 (£500 before 28.3.00) p.a.	Nil
—Over £5,000 (£500 before 28.3.00) p.a.	1% (50p per £50 or part before 1.10.99)
Leases over 7 years and up to 35 years	2%
Leases over 35 years and up to 100 years	12%
Leases over 100 years	24%

[1] These rates apply to the full consideration, not only to that in excess of the previous band.

Stamp duty — continued

Rounding

From 1 October 1999, the charging provisions provided for the rounding up to the next multiple of £5 in all cases (where duty was previously rounded up to multiples of between 50p and £12) other than for SDRT. (FA 1999 s 112, Sch 14). This does not apply for Stamp Duty Land Tax from 1 December 2003.

Before 1 October 1999 – Leases not exceeding 7 years

Rent	Over 7 years up to 35 years £	Over 35 years up to 100 years £	Over 100 years £
£5 or less	0·10	0·60	1·20
Over £5 up to £10	0·20	1·20	2·40
Over £10 up to £15	0·30	1·80	3·60
Over £15 up to £20	0·40	2·40	4·80
Over £20 up to £25	0·50	3·00	6·00
Over £25 up to £50	1·00	6·00	12·00
Over £50 up to £75	1·50	9·00	18·00
Over £75 up to £100	2·00	12·00	24·00
Over £100 up to £150	3·00	18·00	36·00
Over £150 up to £200	4·00	24·00	48·00
Over £200 up to £250	5·00	30·00	60·00
Over £250 up to £300	6·00	36·00	72·00
Over £300 up to £350	7·00	42·00	84·00
Over £350 up to £400	8·00	48·00	96·00
Over £400 up to £450	9·00	54·00	108·00
Over £450 up to £500	10·00	60·00	120·00
Over £500; for every £50 or fraction of £50	1·00	6·00	12·00

Fixed duties

(Stamp Act 1891 Sch 1; FA 1999 Sch 13; FA 2003 s 125, Sch 20)

The fixed stamp duties below are abolished for contracts entered into, or varied, after 10 July 2003 and completed, or leases granted, on or after 1 December 2003.

Leases other than above	£5 (£2 before 1.10.1999)
Declaration of trust; duplicate or counterpart; exchange or partition; release or renunciation; surrender	£5 (50p before 1.10.1999)

Exemptions and reliefs

(FA 2000 ss 129, 130; FA 2001 s 92; FA 2002 ss 110, 116; FA 2003 ss 57–75, 125–130, Schs 3, 6–8, 20)
(See stamp duty above regarding the general abolition for completions from 1 December 2003.)

(1) transfers to charities for use for charitable purposes
(2) transfers to bodies established for national purposes
(3) gifts inter vivos
(4) land transfers with groups of companies
(5) land transferred in exchange for shares on company reconstruction and acquisitions
(6) transfers of intellectual property (after 27.3.00)
(7) certain transfers to registered social landlords (after 28.7.00)
(8) certain leases granted by registered social landlords
(9) transfers of goodwill (after 21 April 2002)
(10) property transactions in disadvantaged parts of the UK designated for this purpose (see below)

Disadvantaged areas

(FA 2001 s 92, Sch 30; FA 2002 s 110; FA 2003 s 57, Sch 6; SI 2001/3746; SI 2001/3747; SI 2003/1056)

Areas designated as disadvantaged for the purpose of this exemption are set out in SI 2001/3747. Transfers of non-residential property are exempt from 10 April 2003. Transfers relating to lease rentals are also exempt from that date where the net present value of rent over term of lease is £150,000 or less. The exemption for transfers of residential properties, and non-residential property before that date, applies to transfers up to £150,000 and lease premiums up to £150,000 (unless annual rent exceeds £600).

Interest on unpaid tax

Stamp duty (Stamp Act 1891 ss 15, 15A; FA 1999 s 109)
For instruments executed from 1 October 1999: Interest runs from the end of 30 days after the date the instrument is executed until the tax is paid. Amounts less than £25 are not charged.

Stamp duty land tax (FA 2003 s 87)
For contracts completed after 30 November 2003: Interest runs from the end of 30 days after the effective date of transaction (normally completion), or the date of a disqualifying event, until the tax is paid. In the case of a deferred payment, interest runs from the date the payment is due until the tax is paid. A penalty carries interest from the date determined until the date of payment (FA 2003 s 88).

Rates: see page 13.

Repayment supplement

Stamp duty (FA 1999 s 110)
For instruments executed from 1 October 1999: Interest is added to repayments of overpaid stamp duty and runs from 30 days after the date the instrument is executed or the date of payment if later. Amounts less than £25 are not paid.

Stamp duty land tax (FA 2003 s 89)
Interest is added to repayments of overpaid stamp duty land tax and runs from the date tax was paid or an amount was lodged with the Inland Revenue, or the date a penalty was made, to the date the order for repayment is issued.

Rates: see page 15.

Penalties

Offence	Penalty
Stamp duty – for instruments executed from 1 October 1999:	
Failure to present instrument for stamping within 30 days after execution (or the day in which it is first received in the UK if executed outside the UK) (Stamp Act 1891 s 15B; SI 1999/2537). (Extended to instruments executed from 24 July 2002 for transfers of UK land and buildings, wherever executed (FA 2002 s 114)).	If presented within one year after the end of the 30 day period: the lower of £300 or the amount of the unpaid duty. If presented more than one year after the end of the 30 day period: the greater of £300 or the amount of unpaid duty.
Stamp duty land tax – contracts completed after 30 November 2003:	
Failure to deliver a land transaction return by the filing date (FA 2003 Sch 10 paras 3, 4).	£100 if return delivered within 3 months of filing date, otherwise £200. If not delivered within 12 months of the filing date, penalty not exceeding the amount of tax chargeable.
Failure to comply with notice to deliver return within specified period (FA 2003 Sch 10 para 5).	A penalty not exceeding £60 (on an order from the General or Special Commissioners) for each day on which the failure continues after notification.
Fraudulently or negligently delivering an incorrect return or failing to remedy an error without unreasonable delay (FA 2003 Sch 10 para 8).	A penalty not exceeding the difference between the amount payable in respect of the transaction and the amount that would have been chargeable on the basis of the return delivered.
Fraudulently or negligently giving a self-certificate for a chargeable transaction or failing to remedy an error in respect of such certificate without unreasonable delay (FA 2003 Sch 11 para 3).	A penalty not exceeding the amount of tax chargeable.
Failure to keep and preserve records under FA 2003 Sch 10 para 9 or Sch 11 para 4 (FA 2003 Sch 10 para 11, Sch 11 para 6).	A penalty not exceeding £3,000 unless the information is provided by other documentary evidence.
Failure to comply with notice to produce documents etc under FA 2003 Sch 10 para 14 or Sch 11 para 9 (FA 2003 Sch 10 para 16, Sch 11 para 11).	(a) Initial penalty of £50; (b) further penalty for each day the failure continues not exceeding £30 if penalty determined by an Officer of the Board, or £150 if determined by the court.

Value added tax

Annual accounting scheme

From 10 April 2003 a taxable person with a taxable turnover of up to £150,000 (£100,000 from 25 April 2002 to 9 April 2003) can join the scheme as soon as they register and will not have to wait for a qualifying period of one year. Taxable persons with a turnover above this limit (and before 25 April 2002 all taxable persons) must have been registered for at least one year at the date of application for authorisation (SI 1995/2518 Pt VII as amended).

	Can join if taxable supplies in next year not expected to exceed:	*Must leave at end of accounting year if taxable supplies exceed:*
1.4.01 onwards	£600,000	£750,000
9.4.91–31.3.01	£300,000	£375,000

Cash accounting scheme

A business may, subject to conditions, account for and pay VAT on the basis of cash paid and received. It can join the scheme at any time (SI 1995/2518, Regs 57, 59 as amended).

	Can join if taxable supplies in next year not expected to exceed:	*Must leave at end of accounting year if taxable supplies exceed:*	*Unless turnover for next year not expected to exceed:*
1.4.01 onwards	£600,000	£750,000	£600,000
3.1.94–31.3.01	£350,000	£437,500	£350,000

Registration limits

UK taxable supplies

	Past turnover[1]		**Future turnover**[1]
	1 year	*Unless turnover for next year not expected to exceed:*	*30 days*[2]
10.4.03 onwards	£56,000	£54,000	£56,000
25.4.02–9.4.03	£55,000	£53,000	£55,000
1.4.01–24.4.02	£54,000	£52,000	£54,000
1.4.00–31.3.01	£52,000	£50,000	£52,000
1.4.99–31.3.00	£51,000	£49,000	£51,000
1.4.98–31.3.99	£50,000	£48,000	£50,000
1.12.97–31.3.98	£49,000	£47,000	£49,000

[1] Value of taxable supplies (at zero and positive rates).
[2] Where there are reasonable grounds for believing that limit will be exceeded in this period.

Supplies from other EC countries

	Cumulative total[1] **from beginning of calendar year**
1.1.93 onwards	£70,000

[1] Value of supplies made by persons in other EC member states to non-taxable persons in the UK.

Acquisitions from other EC countries

VATA 1994 Sch 3

	Past acquisitions[1]	**Future acquisitions**[1]
	Cumulative total from 1 January	*30 days*[2]
10.4.03 onwards	£56,000	£56,000
25.4.02–9.4.03	£55,000	£55,000
1.4.01–24.4.02	£54,000	£54,000
1.4.00–31.3.01	£52,000	£52,000
1.4.99–31.3.00	£51,000	£51,000
1.4.98–31.3.99	£50,000	£50,000
1.1.98–31.3.98	£49,000	£49,000

[1] Value of acquisitions of taxable goods from suppliers in other EC member states.
[2] Where there are reasonable grounds for believing that limit will be exceeded in this period.

Deregistration limits

UK taxable supplies

Future turnover	Annual limit
10.4.03 onwards	£54,000
25.4.02–9.4.03	£53,000
1.4.01–24.4.02	£52,000
1.4.00–31.3.01	£50,000
1.4.99–31.3.00	£49,000
1.4.98–31.3.99	£48,000
1.12.97–31.3.98	£47,000
Unless during the year, the person will cease making taxable supplies (or suspend making taxable supplies for 30 days or more).	

Supplies from other EC countries

	Past supplies[1]	Future supplies[1]
	Supplies in preceding calendar year	*Supplies in following calendar year*[2]
1.1.93 onwards	£70,000	£70,000

[1] Value of supplies made by persons in other EC member states to non-taxable persons in the UK.
[2] Where C & E are satisfied that limit will not be exceeded in this period.

Acquisitions from other EC countries

VATA 1994 Sch 3

	Past acquisitions[1]	Future acquisitions[1]
	Acquisitions in preceding calendar year	*Acquisitions in following calendar year*[2]
10.4.03 onwards	£56,000	£56,000
25.4.02–9.4.03	£55,000	£55,000
1.4.01–24.4.02	£54,000	£54,000
1.4.00–31.3.01	£52,000	£52,000
1.4.99–31.3.00	£51,000	£51,000
1.4.98–31.3.99	£50,000	£50,000
1.1.98–31.3.98	£49,000	£49,000
1.1.97–31.12.97	£48,000	£48,000

[1] Value of acquisitions of taxable goods from suppliers in other EC member states.
[2] Where C & E are satisfied that limit will not be exceeded in this period.

Rate of tax

	Standard rate	VAT fraction	Reduced rate	VAT fraction
1.9.97 onwards	17.5%	7/47	5%	1/21
1.4.94–31.8.97	17.5%	7/47	8%	2/27

Flat rate scheme for farmers: 4% flat rate addition to sale price.

Optional flat rate scheme

Flat rate percentage (determined by trade sector of business) applied to tax-inclusive turnover (VATA s 26B; FA 2002 s 23; SI 1995/2518 Regs 55A–55V).

	Maximum annual taxable turnover[1]	*Maximum annual taxable turnover*[1] *plus exempt/non-taxable income*
10.4.03 onwards	£150,000	£187,500
25.4.02–9.4.03	£100,000	£125,000

[1] VAT-exclusive

Penalties and surcharges

Offence	*Penalty*
Failure to pay tax due under the payment on account scheme on time (VATA 1994 s 59A)	Default surcharge
Failure to submit return or pay tax due within time limit. (Where a return is late but the tax is paid on time or no tax is due, a default is recorded but no surcharge arises) (VATA 1994 s 59)	Default surcharge: the greater of £30 and a specified percentage of outstanding VAT for period, depending on number of defaults in surcharge period: 1st default in period 2%, 2nd default 5%, 3rd default 10%, 4th and further defaults 15% NB: Surcharge assessments are not issued for sums of less than £200 unless the rate of the surcharge is 10% or more
Evasion of VAT: conduct involving dishonesty (VATA 1994 s 60)	Amount of tax evaded or sought to be evaded (subject to mitigation)
Issuing incorrect certificate as to zero-rating (or, from 27 July 1999, as to eligibility to receive reduced-rate for fuel and power) (VATA 1994 s 62; FA 1999 s 17)	Difference between tax actually charged and tax which should have been charged
Misdeclaration or neglect (VATA 1994 s 63)	15% of VAT which would have been lost if inaccuracy had not been discovered
Repeated misdeclarations (VATA 1994 s 64)	15% of VAT which would have been lost if second and subsequent inaccuracies within penalty period had not been discovered
Material inaccuracy in EC sales statement (VATA 1994 s 65)	£100 for each material inaccuracy in 2-year penalty period (which commences following notice of second material inaccuracy)
Failure to submit an EC sales statement (VATA 1994 s 66)	Greater of £50 and a daily penalty (for no more than 100 days) depending on number of failures in default period: 1st failure £5, 2nd failure £10, 3rd and further failures £15
Failure to notify liability for registration or change in nature of supplies by person exempted from registration (VATA 1994 s 67). (From 10 April until 30 September 2003, failure to register for VAT, where businesses trade over the VAT threshold, within the statutory time limits will not give rise to a penalty provided any VAT arrears are paid in full and all returns and payments are made in time for 12 months after registration (Budget 2003).) Failure to notify liability for registration when business transferred as going concern (VATA 1994 Sch 1 para 7)	Greater of £50 and a specified percentage of the tax for which the person would have been liable, depending on the period of failure– 9 months or less: 5% Over 9, up to 18 months: 10% Over 18 months: 15%
Unauthorised issue of invoices (VATA 1994 s 67)	Greater of £50 and 15% of amount shown as or representing VAT
Breach of walking possession agreement (VATA 1994 s 68)	50% of VAT due and amount recoverable
Failure to preserve records for prescribed period (VATA 1994 s 69)	£500
Breaches of regulatory provisions, including failure to notify cessation of liability or entitlement to be registered, failure to keep records and non-compliance with any regulations made under VATA 1994 (VATA 1994 s 69)	Greater of £50 and a daily penalty (for no more than 100 days) of a specified amount depending on number of failures in preceding two years– No previous failures: £5 per day 1 previous failure: £10 per day 2 or more: £15 per day
Breaches of regulatory provisions involving failure to pay VAT or submit return by due date (VATA 1994 s 69)	Greater of £50 and a daily penalty (for no more than 100 days) of a specified amount depending on number of failures in preceding two years– No previous failures: greater of £5 and ⅙% of VAT due 1 previous failure: greater of £10 and ⅓% of VAT due 2 or more: greater of £15 and ½% of VAT due
Failure to comply with statutory responsibility to pay correct amount of tax on time (FA 1997 ss 51, 52)	(From 1 July 1997) Distress (diligence, ie poinding and sale and arrestment, in Scotland)
Failure to comply with VAT tribunal directions or summons (VATA 1994 Sch 12 para 10)	Up to £1,000
Failure by person to whom an attachment notice has been given and who is or becomes indebted to the defaulter to pay the required amount (FA 1997)	£250 plus £20 for each day failure continues after payment has become due
Failure to comply with the accounting, invoicing, record-keeping and notification requirements for supplies involving investment gold (FA 2000 s137).	(From 28 July 2000) 17·5% of the value of transactions concerned.
Import of goods from non-EU countries: – failures relating to non-compliance – evasion (FA 2003 ss 24–41)	 Maximum penalty of £2,500 Maximum penalty equal to VAT sought to be evaded (From date to be announced in Autumn 2003)

Default interest

The prescribed rate of interest for the purposes of VATA 1994 s 74 (the provisions of which were operative from 1 April 1990) has varied as follows:

	Rate
From 6 November 2001	6.5%
6 May 2001–5 November 2001	7.5%
6 February 2000–5 May 2001	8.5%
6 March 1999–5 February 2000	7.5%
6 January 1999–5 March 1999	8.5%
6 July 1998–5 January 1999	9.5%
6 February 1996–5 July 1998	6.25%
6 March 1995–5 February 1996	7%
6 October 1994–5 March 1995	6·25%
6 January 1994–5 October 1994	5.5%
6 March 1993–5 January 1994	6.25%
6 December 1992–5 March 1993	7%
6 November 1992–5 December 1992	7.75%
6 October 1991–5 November 1992	9.25%

Interest on VAT overpaid in cases of official error

(VATA 1994 s 78)

	Rate
From 6 November 2001	3%
6 May 2001–5 November 2001	4%
6 February 2000–5 May 2001	5%
6 March 1999–5 February 2000	4%
6 January 1999–5 March 1999	5%
1 April 1997–5 January 1999	6%
6 February–31 March 1997	8%
16 October 1991–5 February 1993	10.25%
1 April 1991–15 October 1991	12%
1 November 1989–31 March 1991	14.25%
1 January 1989–31 October 1989	13%
1 November 1988–31 December 1988	12.25%
1 August 1988–31 October 1988	11%
1 May 1988–31 July 1988	9.5%
1 December 1987–30 April 1988	11%
1 November 1987–30 November 1987	11.25%
1 April 1987–31 October 1987	11.75%
1 January 1987–31 March 1987	12.25%

Zero-rated supplies

A zero-rated supply is a taxable supply, but the rate of tax is nil.
(References are to VATA 1994 Sch 8)

Group 1—Food
Group 2—Sewerage services and water
Group 3—Books etc
Group 4—Talking books for the blind and handicapped and wireless sets for the blind
Group 5—Construction of buildings etc
Group 6—Protected buildings
Group 7—International services
Group 8—Transport
Group 9—Caravans and houseboats
Group 10—Gold
Group 11—Bank notes
Group 12—Drugs, medicines, aids for the handicapped etc
Group 13—Imports, exports etc
Group 15—Charities etc
Group 16—Clothing and footwear

Reduced rate supplies

(References are to VATA 1994 Sch 7A)

Group 1—Domestic fuel and power
Group 2—Installation of energy-saving materials
Group 3—Grant-funded installation of heating equipment or security goods or connection of a gas supply
Group 4—Women's sanitary products
Group 5—Children's car seats
Group 6—Residential conversions
Group 7—Residential renovations and alterations

Exempt supplies

No tax is chargeable on an exempt supply, and input tax cannot be recovered except as allowed under the partial exemption provisions (SI 1995/2518 Pt XIV; VAT Notice 706).
(References are to VATA 1994 Sch 9)

Group 1—Land
Group 2—Insurance
Group 3—Postal services
Group 4—Betting, gaming and lotteries
Group 5—Finance
Group 6—Education
Group 7—Health and welfare
Group 8—Burial and cremation
Group 9—Subscriptions to trade unions, professional and other public interest bodies
Group 10—Sport, sports competitions and physical education
Group 11—Works of art etc
Group 12—Fund-raising events by charities and other qualifying bodies
Group 13—Cultural services etc
Group 14—Supplies of goods where input tax cannot be recovered
Group 15—Investment gold

Partial exemption

De minimis limit for application of partial exemption rules
SI 1995/2518 reg 106

	Exempt input tax not exceeding
Tax years beginning after 30.11.94	(a) £625 per month on average; and (b) 50% of total input tax for prescribed accounting period
Periods beginning between 1.4.92 and 30.11.94	£600 per month on average

Capital goods scheme

Input tax adjustment following change in taxable use of capital goods
VATA 1994 s 34, SI 1995/2518 regs 112–116 (77/388/EEC art 20), SI 1999/599 reg 6.
From 1 April 1990

Item	*Value*	*Adjustment period*
Computer equipment	£50,000 or more	5 years
Land and buildings	£250,000 or more	10 years (5 years where interest had less than 10 years to run on acquisition)

Adjustment formula

$$\frac{\text{Total input tax on item}}{\text{Length of adjustment period}} \times \text{adjustment percentage}$$

The adjustment percentage is the percentage change in the extent to which the item is used (or treated as used) in making taxable supplies between the first interval in the adjustment period and a subsequent interval. (The first interval generally ends on the last day of the tax year in which the input tax was incurred.)

Car fuel

VAT-inclusive scale figures are used to assess VAT due on petrol provided at below cost price for private journeys by registered traders or their employees, where the petrol has been provided from business resources. The figures relate to return periods beginning on the dates shown.

	12 months	VAT due per car	3 months	VAT due per car	1 month	VAT due per car
From 1 May 2003						
Diesel engine						
Cylinder capacity: 2,000cc or less	£900	£134·04	£225	£33·51	£75	£11·17
Over 2,000cc	£1,135	£169·04	£283	£42·14	£94	£14·00
Any other type of engine						
Cylinder capacity: 1,400cc or less	£950	£141·48	£237	£35·29	£79	£11·76
Over 1,400cc up to 2,000cc	£1,200	£178·72	£300	£44·68	£100	£14·89
Over 2,000cc	£1,770	£263·61	£442	£65·82	£147	£21·89
1 May 2002–30 April 2003						
Diesel engine						
Cylinder capacity: 2,000cc or less	£850	£126·59	£212	£31·57	£70	£10·42
Over 2,000cc	£1,075	£160·10	£268	£39·91	£89	£13·25
Any other type of engine						
Cylinder capacity: 1,400cc or less	£905	£134·78	£226	£33·65	£75	£11·17
Over 1,400cc up to 2,000cc	£1,145	£170·53	£286	£42·59	£95	£14·14
Over 2,000cc	£1,690	£251·70	£422	£62·85	£140	£20·85
6 April 2001–30 April 2002						
Diesel engine						
Cylinder capacity: 2,000cc or less	£900	£134·04	£225	£33·51	£75	£11·17
Over 2,000cc	£1,145	£170·53	£286	£42·59	£95	£14·14
Any other type of engine						
Cylinder capacity: 1,400cc or less	£970	£144·46	£242	£36·04	£80	£11·91
Over 1,400cc up to 2,000cc	£1,230	£183·19	£307	£45·72	£102	£15·19
Over 2,000cc	£1,815	£270·31	£453	£67·46	£151	£22·48
6 April 2000–5 April 2001						
Diesel engine						
Cylinder capacity: 2,000cc or less	£930	£138·51	£232	£34·55	£77	£11·46
Over 2,000cc	£1,180	£175·74	£295	£43·93	£98	£14·59
Any other type of engine						
Cylinder capacity: 1,400cc or less	£1,025	£152·65	£256	£38·12	£85	£12·65
Over 1,400cc up to 2,000cc	£1,300	£193·61	£325	£48·40	£108	£16·08
Over 2,000cc	£1,915	£285·21	£478	£71·19	£159	£23·68

HM Customs and Excise: VAT notices

New notices no longer carry a designation of the year of issue or revision, but this is retained here as a guide to the year of publication of the latest version. Several leaflets and notices contain Update inserts, published from time to time. The notices can be obtained from the Customs and Excise website at www.hmce.gov.uk/forms/catalogue/catalogue.htm.

(Cancelled leaflets have been deleted from the list.)

Notice		*Date*	*Title*
48		2002	**Extra-statutory concessions** (with updates 1 to 3)
60		2002	**The Intrastat general guide**
101		2000	**Deferring duty, VAT and other charges**
400		2002	**HM Customs and Excise Charter**
431		1999	**Visiting forces**
700		2002†	**The VAT guide** (with update 1)
	700/1	2002	Should I be registered for VAT? (with supplement)
	700/2	2003	Group and divisional registration
	700/6	2003	Rulings
	700/7	2002	Business promotion schemes (with update 1)
	700/9	2002	Transfer of a business as a going concern
	700/11	2002	Cancelling your registration (with supplement and update 1)
	700/12*	2002	Filling in your VAT return
	700/14	1999	Video cassette films: rental and part-exchange
	700/15	2002	The ins and outs of VAT
	700/17	2002	Funded pension schemes
	700/18*	2002	Relief from VAT on bad debts
	700/21*	2002	Keeping records and accounts
	700/24	2003	Postage and delivery charges
	700/25	2002	Taxis and hire cars
	700/34	1994	Staff (with update 1)
	700/35	1997	Business gifts and samples
	700/41*	2002	Late registration penalty
	700/42*	2002	Misdeclaration penalty and repeated misdeclaration penalty
	700/43	2003	Default interest
	700/44	2002	Barristers and advocates
	700/45*	2002	How to correct VAT errors and make adjustments or claims
	700/46	2002	Agricultural flat rate scheme
	700/47	1993	Confidentiality in VAT matters (Tax advisers) – Statement of practice
	700/50*	2002	Default surcharge
	700/52*	2003	Notice of requirement to give security to Customs and Excise
	700/56	2002	Insolvency
	700/57	2002	Administrative agreements entered into with trade bodies
	700/58	2002	Treatment of VAT repayment returns and VAT repayment supplements (with update 1)
	700/60	1996	Payments on account
	700/64*	2002	Motoring expenses (with update 1)
	700/65	2002	Business entertainment
	700/67	2002	Registration scheme for racehorse owners
701	701/1	1995	Charities (with update 1)
	701/5	2002	Clubs and associations
	701/6	1997	Charity-funded equipment for medical, veterinary etc. uses
	701/7	2002	VAT reliefs for disabled people
	701/8	1997	Postage stamps and philatelic supplies
	701/9	2002	Derivatives and terminal markets
	701/10	1999	Printed and similar matter
	701/12*	2002	Disposals of antiques, works of art etc from historic houses
	701/13	1995	Gaming and amusement machines
	701/14	2002	Food
	701/15	2002	Animals and animal food
	701/16	2002	Water and sewage services
	701/18	2002	Women's sanitary protection products
	701/19*	2002	Fuel and power (with update 1)
	701/20	1996	Caravans and houseboats
	701/21	2002	Gold
	701/21A	2003	Investment gold coins
	701/22	2002	Tools for the manufacture of goods for export
	701/23	2002	Protective equipment
	701/26	1995	Betting and gaming
	701/27*	2002	Bingo
	701/28	1997	Lotteries
	701/30	2002	Education and vocational training (with update 1)
	701/31	2002	Health and care institutions
	701/32	2003	Burial, cremation and the commemoration of the dead
	701/35	1995	Youth clubs
	701/36	2002	Insurance
	701/38	1999	Seeds and plants
	701/39	2002	VAT liability law
	701/40	2002	Food processing services
	701/41*	2002	Sponsorship
	701/45	2002	Sport
	701/47	1996	Culture

	701/48	2002†	Corporate purchasing cards (with update 1)
	701/49	2002	Finance and securities
	701/57	2002	Health professionals
	701/58	2002	Charity advertising and goods connected with collecting donations
	701/59	2002	Motor vehicles for disabled people
702		1998	**Imports** (with update 1)
	702/4*	2002	Importing computer software
	702/6	1991	Import VAT certificates
	702/7	1993	Import VAT relief for goods supplied onward to another country in the EC
	702/9	1998	Warehousing and free zones
703		1996†	**Exports and removal of goods from the UK** (with updates 1 and 2)
	703/1	1995†	Supply of freight containers for export or removal from the UK
	703/2	2002†	Sailaway boats supplied for export outside the EC
704		2003†	**Retail exports**
	704/1	2003†	VAT refunds for travellers departing from the European Community
705		1995†	**Personal exports of new motor vehicles to destinations outside the European Community from 1 January 1993** (with update 1)
705A		1995†	**Supplies of vehicles under the personal export scheme for removal from the EC** (with update 1 and correction slip)
706		2002	**Partial exemption**
	706/1	1992	Self-supply of stationery
	706/2	2002	Capital goods scheme
708		2002†	**Buildings and construction**
	708/6	2002	Energy-saving materials
709	709/1	2002†	Catering and take-away food
	709/3	2002	Hotels and holiday accommodation
	709/5	1998†	Tour operators' margin scheme
	709/6	2002	Travel agents and tour operators
714		2002	**Zero rating young children's clothing and footwear**
718		2003†	**Margin schemes for secondhand goods, works of art, antiques and collectors' items**
719		2002	**VAT refunds for DIY builders and converters**
723		2003	**Refunds of VAT in the European Community for EC and non-EC businesses**
725		2002†	**The Single Market**
727		2002†	**Retail schemes**
	727/2	2002	Bespoke retail schemes
	727/3	2002†	How to work the point of sale scheme
	727/4	2002†	How to work the apportionment schemes
	727/5	2002†	How to work the direct calculation schemes
728		2003†	**New means of transport**
730		1994	**Civil evasion penalty investigations: Statement of practice**
731*		2002†	**Cash accounting**
732*		2003	**Annual accounting**
733*		2003	**VAT flat rate scheme for small businesses**
741		2002	**Place of supply of services**
742		2002†	**Land and property**
	742/3	2002	Scottish land law terms
742A		2002	**Opting to tax land and buildings** (with update 1)
744A		2002	**Passenger transport**
744B		2002	**Freight transport and associated services**
744C		1997	**Ships, aircraft and associated services**
744D		2002	**International services – zero rating**
747		2003	**VAT notices having the force of law**
749		2002	**Local authorities and similar bodies**
915*		2002	**Assessments and time limits: statement of practice**
920		1999	**The single currency**
930		2002	**What if I don't pay?**
950		2003	Open Government: Requesting access to information held by Customs and Excise
989*		2002	**Visits by Customs and Excise officers**
998		2003	**VAT refund scheme for national museums and galleries**
999		2002	**Catalogue of publications**
1000*		2002	**Complaints and putting things right**
CWL4		2001	Fund-raising events: exemption for charities and other qualifying bodies
MISC	02/CD/26	2003	The Joint Shadow Economy teams – tackling the shadow economy
MISC	02/CD/018	2003	Getting things VAT FREE if you have a disability
MSB2		2002	Anti money laundering guide
Explanatory leaflet:		1995	Appeals and applications to the tribunals

Information sheets: available also at http://www.hmce.gov.uk

4/93	Intra-EC processing of goods: simplification
5/95	VAT – changes to tour operators' margin scheme from 1 January 1996
6/95	VAT – NHS dispensing doctors
1/96	VAT – filling in your EC sales list (Form VAT 101)
3/96	Tour operators' margin scheme – practical implementation of the airline charter option following the changes which came into effect on 1 January 1996
4/96	Tour operators' margin scheme – practical implementation of the agency option following the changes which came into effect on 1 January 1996
1/97	Tour operators' margin scheme – practical implementation of the 'trader to trader (wholesale) option' following the changes which came into effect on 1 January 1996
6/97	Drugs, medicine and aids for the handicapped – liability with effect from 1 January 1998
2/98	Export house VAT provisions: withdrawal
3/98	Local authorities and NHS joint stores depots
5/98	Local authorities: supplies to new unitary authorities under local government reorganisation (transitional arrangements)
6/98	Local authority pension funds: VAT treatment and administrative concession
8/98	Charities – supply, repair and maintenance of relevant goods (including adapted motor vehicles)
2/99	Local Authorities: agreement of section 33 recovery methods
3/99	VAT: new deal programme
6/99	Charities: liabilities of routine domestic tasks
7/99	Construction services: new rule for accounting for VAT
8/99	Opticians: Apportionment of charges for supplies of spectacles and dispensing
9/99	Imported works of art, antiques and collectors' pieces: changes to the reduced rate of VAT
10/99	Financial exemptions: changes brought about by the 1999 Finance Order
12/99	VAT on business cars–changes to take effect on 1 December 1999
2/00	Exports and removals: Conditions for zero-rating
3/00	Supplies through undisclosed agents: revised VAT treatment
5/00	Construction and building materials
2/01	Single or multiple supplies – how to decide
3/01	VAT: Digitised publications
4/01	VAT Budget changes: VAT reduced rate – urban regeneration
5/01	VAT Budget changes: adjustments to the zero rate for sale of renovated properties
6/01	Changes to the VAT second-hand margin scheme
8/01	VAT: Speculative property developers: input tax
1/02	VAT civil evasion cases: a new approach to investigations – statement of practice
2/02	Budget 2002: a new optional flat rate scheme for small businesses
3/02	Budget 2002: VAT and construction
4/02	Budget 2002: partial exemption – standard method over-ride
1/03	Electronically supplied services and broadcasting services: new EU place of supply rules
2/03	Clarification of VAT treatment of services by financial advisers
3/03	Modernisation of face value vouchers
4/03	Electronically supplied services: a guide to interpretation
5/03	Electronically supplied services: evidence of customer location and status
6/03	Tribunal decision on VAT treatment of repossessed and voluntarily returned cars
7/03	Electronically supplied services: special scheme for non-EU businesses
8/03	Face value vouchers

† Publications having legal or quasi-legal force.
* Also published in a Welsh language edition.

Internal guidance manuals

1	User guide	18	Import reliefs
3	Supply and consideration	19	Warehousing and free zones
4	Place of supply	20	Exports and removals of goods from the UK
5	Taxable person	21	Personal exports (retail exports)
6	Business/non-business	22	Bad debt relief
7	VAT liability	23	Schemes
8	Land and property	24	Traders' records and Officers' information powers
8A	Construction	27	Civil penalties
9	Charities	28	Registration
10	Transfer of a going concern	28A	VAT trade classification
11	Time of supply	29	Reconsiderations and appeals
12	Valuation	30	Isle of Man
13	Input tax	31	Refunds to overseas business persons
14	Government and public bodies	32	Tax avoidance
15	Partial exemption	33	VAT refunds: unjust enrichment, statutory interest, ex gratia payments
16	Single market		

17.5% VAT (tax included in amount) – VAT fraction $^7/_{47}$

Am't	VAT incl. in Am't	**Am't**	VAT incl. in Am't	**Am't**	VAT incl. in Am't	**Am't**	VAT incl. in Am't	**Am't**	VAT incl. in Am't	**Am't**	VAT incl. in Am't
£ or p	£ or p	**£ or p**	£ or p	**£ or p**	£ or p	**£ or p**	£ or p	**£ or p**	£ or p	**£ or p**	£ or p
1	0·15	**71**	10·57	**141**	21·00	**211**	31·43	**281**	41·85	**810**	120·64
2	0·30	**72**	10·72	**142**	21·15	**212**	31·57	**282**	42·00	**820**	122·13
3	0·45	**73**	10·87	**143**	21·30	**213**	31·72	**283**	42·15	**830**	123·62
4	0·60	**74**	11·02	**144**	21·45	**214**	31·87	**284**	42·30	**840**	125·11
5	0·74	**75**	11·17	**145**	21·60	**215**	32·02	**285**	42·45	**850**	126·60
6	0·89	**76**	11·32	**146**	21·74	**216**	32·17	**286**	42·60	**860**	128·09
7	1·04	**77**	11·47	**147**	21·89	**217**	32·32	**287**	42·74	**870**	129·57
8	1·19	**78**	11·62	**148**	22·04	**218**	32·47	**288**	42·89	**880**	131·06
9	1·34	**79**	11·77	**149**	22·19	**219**	32·62	**289**	43·04	**890**	132·55
10	1·49	**80**	11·91	**150**	22·34	**220**	32·77	**290**	43·19	**900**	134·04
11	1·64	**81**	12·06	**151**	22·49	**221**	32·91	**291**	43·35	**910**	135·53
12	1·79	**82**	12·21	**152**	22·64	**222**	33·06	**292**	43·49	**920**	137·02
13	1·94	**83**	12·36	**153**	22·79	**223**	33·21	**293**	43·64	**930**	138·51
14	2·09	**84**	12·51	**154**	22·94	**224**	33·36	**294**	43·79	**940**	140·00
15	2·23	**85**	12·66	**155**	23·09	**225**	33·51	**295**	43·94	**950**	141·49
16	2·38	**86**	12·81	**156**	23·23	**226**	33·66	**296**	44·09	**960**	142·98
17	2·53	**87**	12·96	**157**	23·38	**227**	33·81	**297**	44·23	**970**	144·47
18	2·68	**88**	13·11	**158**	23·53	**228**	33·96	**298**	44·38	**980**	145·96
19	2·83	**89**	13·26	**159**	23·68	**229**	34·11	**299**	44·53	**990**	147·45
20	2·98	**90**	13·40	**160**	23·83	**230**	34·26	**300**	44·68	**1,000**	148·94
21	3·13	**91**	13·55	**161**	23·98	**231**	34·40	**310**	46·17	**1,100**	163·83
22	3·28	**92**	13·70	**162**	24·13	**232**	34·55	**320**	47·66	**1,200**	178·72
23	3·43	**93**	13·85	**163**	24·28	**233**	34·70	**330**	49·15	**1,300**	193·62
24	3·57	**94**	14·00	**164**	24·43	**234**	34·85	**340**	50·64	**1,400**	208·51
25	3·72	**95**	14·15	**165**	24·57	**235**	35·00	**350**	52·13	**1,500**	223·40
26	3·87	**96**	14·30	**166**	24·72	**236**	35·15	**360**	53·62	**1,600**	238·30
27	4·02	**97**	14·45	**167**	24·87	**237**	35·30	**370**	55·11	**1,700**	253·19
28	4·17	**98**	14·60	**168**	25·02	**238**	35·45	**380**	56·60	**1,800**	268·08
29	4·32	**99**	14·74	**169**	25·17	**239**	35·60	**390**	58·09	**1,900**	282·98
30	4·47	**100**	14·89	**170**	25·32	**240**	35·74	**400**	59·57	**2,000**	297·87
31	4·62	**101**	15·04	**171**	25·47	**241**	35·89	**410**	61·06	**2,100**	312·77
32	4·77	**102**	15·19	**172**	25·62	**242**	36·04	**420**	62·55	**2,200**	327·66
33	4·91	**103**	15·34	**173**	25·77	**243**	36·19	**430**	64·04	**2,300**	342·55
34	5·06	**104**	15·49	**174**	25·91	**244**	36·34	**440**	65·53	**2,400**	357·45
35	5·21	**105**	15·64	**175**	26·06	**245**	36·49	**450**	67·02	**2,500**	372·34
36	5·36	**106**	15·79	**176**	26·21	**246**	36·64	**460**	68·51	**2,600**	387·23
37	5·51	**107**	15·94	**177**	26·36	**247**	36·79	**470**	70·00	**2,700**	402·13
38	5·66	**108**	16·09	**178**	26·51	**248**	36·94	**480**	71·49	**2,800**	417·02
39	5·81	**109**	16·23	**179**	26·66	**249**	37·09	**490**	72·98	**2,900**	431·91
40	5·96	**110**	16·38	**180**	26·81	**250**	37·23	**500**	74·47	**3,000**	446·81
41	6·11	**111**	16·53	**181**	26·96	**251**	37·38	**510**	75·96	**3,100**	461·70
42	6·26	**112**	16·68	**182**	27·11	**252**	37·53	**520**	77·45	**3,200**	476·60
43	6·40	**113**	16·83	**183**	27·26	**253**	37·68	**530**	78·94	**3,300**	491·49
44	6·55	**114**	16·98	**184**	27·40	**254**	37·83	**540**	80·43	**3,400**	506·38
45	6·70	**115**	17·13	**185**	27·55	**255**	37·98	**550**	81·91	**3,500**	521·28
46	6·85	**116**	17·28	**186**	27·70	**256**	38·13	**560**	83·40	**3,600**	536·17
47	7·00	**117**	17·43	**187**	27·85	**257**	38·28	**570**	84·89	**3,700**	551·06
48	7·15	**118**	17·57	**188**	28·00	**258**	38·43	**580**	86·38	**3,800**	565·96
49	7·30	**119**	17·72	**189**	28·15	**259**	38·57	**590**	87·87	**3,900**	580·85
50	7·45	**120**	17·87	**190**	28·30	**260**	38·72	**600**	89·36	**4,000**	595·74
51	7·60	**121**	18·02	**191**	28·45	**261**	38·87	**610**	90·85	**4,100**	610·64
52	7·74	**122**	18·17	**192**	28·60	**262**	39·02	**620**	92·34	**4,200**	625·53
53	7·89	**123**	18·32	**193**	28·74	**263**	39·17	**630**	93·83	**4,300**	640·43
54	8·04	**124**	18·47	**194**	28·89	**264**	39·32	**640**	95·32	**4,400**	655·32
55	8·19	**125**	18·62	**195**	29·04	**265**	39·47	**650**	96·81	**4,500**	670·21
56	8·34	**126**	18·77	**196**	29·19	**266**	39·62	**660**	98·30	**4,600**	685·11
57	8·49	**127**	18·91	**197**	29·34	**267**	39·77	**670**	99·79	**4,700**	700·00
58	8·64	**128**	19·06	**198**	29·49	**268**	39·91	**680**	101·28	**4,800**	714·89
59	8·79	**129**	19·21	**199**	29·64	**269**	40·06	**690**	102·77	**4,900**	729·79
60	8·94	**130**	19·36	**200**	29·79	**270**	40·21	**700**	104·26	**5,000**	744·68
61	9·09	**131**	19·51	**201**	29·94	**271**	40·36	**710**	105·74	**6,000**	893·62
62	9·23	**132**	19·66	**202**	30·09	**272**	40·51	**720**	107·23	**7,000**	1,042·55
63	9·38	**133**	19·81	**203**	30·23	**273**	40·66	**730**	108·72	**8,000**	1,191·49
64	9·53	**134**	19·96	**204**	30·38	**274**	40·81	**740**	110·21	**9,000**	1,340·42
65	9·68	**135**	20·11	**205**	30·53	**275**	40·96	**750**	111·70	**10,000**	1,489·36
66	9·83	**136**	20·26	**206**	30·68	**276**	41·11	**760**	113·19	**11,000**	1,638·30
67	9·98	**137**	20·40	**207**	30·83	**277**	41·26	**770**	114·68	**12,000**	1,787·23
68	10·13	**138**	20·55	**208**	30·98	**278**	41·40	**780**	116·17	**13,000**	1,936·17
69	10·28	**139**	20·70	**209**	31·13	**279**	41·55	**790**	117·66	**14,000**	2,085·11
70	10·43	**140**	20·85	**210**	31·28	**280**	41·70	**800**	119·15	**15,000**	2,234·04

22% grossing-up table

Am't	Grossed at 22%	Am't	Grossed at 22%	Am't	Grossed at 22%	Am't	Grossed at 22%	Am't	Grossed at 22%	Am't	Grossed at 22%	Am't	Grossed at 22%	Am't	Grossed at 22%
£	£	**£**	£	**£**	£	**£**	£	**£**	£	**£**	£	**£**	£	**£**	£
1	1·28	**71**	91·03	**141**	180·77	**211**	270·51	**281**	360·26	**351**	450·00	**421**	539·74	**491**	629·49
2	2·56	**72**	92·31	**142**	182·05	**212**	271·79	**282**	361·54	**352**	451·28	**422**	541·03	**492**	630·77
3	3·85	**73**	93·59	**143**	183·33	**213**	273·08	**283**	362·82	**353**	452·56	**423**	542·31	**493**	632·05
4	5·13	**74**	94·87	**144**	184·62	**214**	274·36	**284**	364·10	**354**	453·85	**424**	543·59	**494**	633·33
5	6·41	**75**	96·15	**145**	185·90	**215**	275·64	**285**	365·38	**355**	455·13	**425**	544·87	**495**	634·62
6	7·69	**76**	97·44	**146**	187·18	**216**	276·92	**286**	366·67	**356**	456·41	**426**	546·15	**496**	635·90
7	8·97	**77**	98·72	**147**	188·46	**217**	278·21	**287**	367·95	**357**	457·69	**427**	547·44	**497**	637·18
8	10·26	**78**	100·00	**148**	189·74	**218**	279·49	**288**	369·23	**358**	458·97	**428**	548·72	**498**	638·46
9	11·54	**79**	101·28	**149**	191·03	**219**	280·77	**289**	370·51	**359**	460·26	**429**	550·00	**499**	639·74
10	12·82	**80**	102·56	**150**	192·31	**220**	282·05	**290**	371·79	**360**	461·54	**430**	551·28	**500**	641·03
11	14·10	**81**	103·85	**151**	193·59	**221**	283·33	**291**	373·08	**361**	462·82	**431**	552·56	**510**	653·85
12	15·38	**82**	105·13	**152**	194·87	**222**	284·62	**292**	374·36	**362**	464·10	**432**	553·85	**520**	666·67
13	16·67	**83**	106·41	**153**	196·15	**223**	285·90	**293**	375·64	**363**	465·38	**433**	555·13	**530**	679·49
14	17·95	**84**	107·69	**154**	197·44	**224**	287·18	**294**	376·92	**364**	466·67	**434**	556·41	**540**	692·31
15	19·23	**85**	108·97	**155**	198·72	**225**	288·46	**295**	378·21	**365**	467·95	**435**	557·69	**550**	705·13
16	20·51	**86**	110·26	**156**	200·00	**226**	289·74	**296**	379·49	**366**	469·23	**436**	558·97	**560**	717·95
17	21·79	**87**	111·54	**157**	201·28	**227**	291·03	**297**	380·77	**367**	470·51	**437**	560·26	**570**	730·77
18	23·08	**88**	112·82	**158**	202·56	**228**	292·31	**298**	382·05	**368**	471·79	**438**	561·54	**580**	743·59
19	24·36	**89**	114·10	**159**	203·85	**229**	293·59	**299**	383·33	**369**	473·08	**439**	562·82	**590**	756·41
20	25·64	**90**	115·38	**160**	205·13	**230**	294·87	**300**	384·62	**370**	474·36	**440**	564·10	**600**	769·23
21	26·92	**91**	116·67	**161**	206·41	**231**	296·15	**301**	385·90	**371**	475·64	**441**	565·38	**610**	782·05
22	28·21	**92**	117·95	**162**	207·69	**232**	297·44	**302**	387·18	**372**	476·92	**442**	566·67	**620**	794·87
23	29·49	**93**	119·23	**163**	208·97	**233**	298·72	**303**	388·46	**373**	478·21	**443**	567·95	**630**	807·69
24	30·77	**94**	120·51	**164**	210·26	**234**	300·00	**304**	389·74	**374**	479·49	**444**	569·23	**640**	820·51
25	32·05	**95**	121·79	**165**	211·54	**235**	301·28	**305**	391·03	**375**	480·77	**445**	570·51	**650**	833·33
26	33·33	**96**	123·08	**166**	212·82	**236**	302·56	**306**	392·31	**376**	482·05	**446**	571·79	**660**	846·15
27	34·62	**97**	124·36	**167**	214·10	**237**	303·85	**307**	393·59	**377**	483·33	**447**	573·08	**670**	858·97
28	35·90	**98**	125·64	**168**	215·38	**238**	305·13	**308**	394·87	**378**	484·62	**448**	574·36	**680**	871·79
29	37·18	**99**	126·92	**169**	216·67	**239**	306·41	**309**	396·15	**379**	485·90	**449**	575·64	**690**	884·62
30	38·46	**100**	128·21	**170**	217·95	**240**	307·69	**310**	397·44	**380**	487·18	**450**	576·92	**700**	897·44
31	39·74	**101**	129·49	**171**	219·23	**241**	308·97	**311**	398·72	**381**	488·46	**451**	578·21	**710**	910·26
32	41·03	**102**	130·77	**172**	220·51	**242**	310·26	**312**	400·00	**382**	489·74	**452**	579·49	**720**	923·08
33	42·31	**103**	132·05	**173**	221·79	**243**	311·54	**313**	401·28	**383**	491·03	**453**	580·77	**730**	935·90
34	43·59	**104**	133·33	**174**	223·08	**244**	312·82	**314**	402·56	**384**	492·31	**454**	582·05	**740**	948·72
35	44·87	**105**	134·62	**175**	224·36	**245**	314·10	**315**	403·85	**385**	493·59	**455**	583·33	**750**	961·54
36	46·15	**106**	135·90	**176**	225·64	**246**	315·38	**316**	405·13	**386**	494·87	**456**	584·62	**760**	974·36
37	47·44	**107**	137·18	**177**	226·92	**247**	316·67	**317**	406·41	**387**	496·15	**457**	585·90	**770**	987·18
38	48·72	**108**	138·46	**178**	228·21	**248**	317·95	**318**	407·69	**388**	497·44	**458**	587·18	**780**	1,000·00
39	50·00	**109**	139·74	**179**	229·49	**249**	319·23	**319**	408·97	**389**	498·72	**459**	588·46	**790**	1,012·82
40	51·28	**110**	141·03	**180**	230·77	**250**	320·51	**320**	410·26	**390**	500·00	**460**	589·74	**800**	1,025·64
41	52·56	**111**	142·31	**181**	232·05	**251**	321·79	**321**	411·54	**391**	501·28	**461**	591·03	**810**	1,038·46
42	53·85	**112**	143·59	**182**	233·33	**252**	323·08	**322**	412·82	**392**	502·56	**462**	592·31	**820**	1,051·28
43	55·13	**113**	144·87	**183**	234·62	**253**	324·36	**323**	414·10	**393**	503·85	**463**	593·59	**830**	1,064·10
44	56·41	**114**	146·15	**184**	235·90	**254**	325·64	**324**	415·38	**394**	505·13	**464**	594·87	**840**	1,076·92
45	57·69	**115**	147·44	**185**	237·18	**255**	326·92	**325**	416·67	**395**	506·41	**465**	596·15	**850**	1,089·74
46	58·97	**116**	148·72	**186**	238·46	**256**	328·21	**326**	417·95	**396**	507·69	**466**	597·44	**860**	1,102·56
47	60·26	**117**	150·00	**187**	239·74	**257**	329·49	**327**	419·23	**397**	508·97	**467**	598·72	**870**	1,115·38
48	61·54	**118**	151·28	**188**	241·03	**258**	330·77	**328**	420·51	**398**	510·26	**468**	600·00	**880**	1,128·21
49	62·82	**119**	152·56	**189**	242·31	**259**	332·05	**329**	421·79	**399**	511·54	**469**	601·28	**890**	1,141·03
50	64·10	**120**	153·85	**190**	243·59	**260**	333·33	**330**	423·08	**400**	512·82	**470**	602·56	**900**	1,153·85
51	65·38	**121**	155·13	**191**	244·87	**261**	334·62	**331**	424·36	**401**	514·10	**471**	603·85	**910**	1,166·67
52	66·67	**122**	156·41	**192**	246·15	**262**	335·90	**332**	425·64	**402**	515·38	**472**	605·13	**920**	1,179·49
53	67·95	**123**	157·69	**193**	247·44	**263**	337·18	**333**	426·92	**403**	516·67	**473**	606·41	**930**	1,192·31
54	69·23	**124**	158·97	**194**	248·72	**264**	338·46	**334**	428·21	**404**	517·95	**474**	607·69	**940**	1,205·13
55	70·51	**125**	160·26	**195**	250·00	**265**	339·74	**335**	429·49	**405**	519·23	**475**	608·97	**950**	1,217·95
56	71·79	**126**	161·54	**196**	251·28	**266**	341·03	**336**	430·77	**406**	520·51	**476**	610·26	**960**	1,230·77
57	73·08	**127**	162·82	**197**	252·56	**267**	342·31	**337**	432·05	**407**	521·79	**477**	611·54	**970**	1,243·59
58	74·36	**128**	164·10	**198**	253·85	**268**	343·59	**338**	433·33	**408**	523·08	**478**	612·82	**980**	1,256·41
59	75·64	**129**	165·38	**199**	255·13	**269**	344·87	**339**	434·62	**409**	524·36	**479**	614·10	**990**	1,269·23
60	76·92	**130**	166·67	**200**	256·41	**270**	346·15	**340**	435·90	**410**	525·64	**480**	615·38	**1,000**	1,282·05
61	78·21	**131**	167·95	**201**	257·69	**271**	347·44	**341**	437·18	**411**	526·92	**481**	616·67	**2,000**	2,564·10
62	79·49	**132**	169·23	**202**	258·97	**272**	348·72	**342**	438·46	**412**	528·21	**482**	617·95	**3,000**	3,846·15
63	80·77	**133**	170·51	**203**	260·26	**273**	350·00	**343**	439·74	**413**	529·49	**483**	619·23	**4,000**	5,128·20
64	82·05	**134**	171·79	**204**	261·54	**274**	351·28	**344**	441·03	**414**	530·77	**484**	620·51	**5,000**	6,410·26
65	83·33	**135**	173·08	**205**	262·82	**275**	352·56	**345**	442·31	**415**	532·05	**485**	621·79	**6,000**	7,692·31
66	84·62	**136**	174·36	**206**	264·10	**276**	353·85	**346**	443·59	**416**	533·33	**486**	623·08	**7,000**	8,974·36
67	85·90	**137**	175·64	**207**	265·38	**277**	355·13	**347**	444·87	**417**	534·62	**487**	624·36	**8,000**	10,256·41
68	87·18	**138**	176·92	**208**	266·67	**278**	356·41	**348**	446·15	**418**	535·90	**488**	625·64	**9,000**	11,538·46
69	88·46	**139**	178·21	**209**	267·95	**279**	357·69	**349**	447·44	**419**	537·18	**489**	626·92	**10,000**	12,820·51
70	89·74	**140**	179·49	**210**	269·23	**280**	358·97	**350**	448·72	**420**	538·46	**490**	688·21	**11,000**	14,102·56

INDEX